STALIN'S UNWANTED CHILD

Stalin's Unwanted Child

The Soviet Union, the German Question and the Founding of the GDR

Wilfried Loth
Professor of Modern History
University of Essen
Germany

Translated by
Robert F. Hogg

UNIVERSITY OF
LIVERPOOL
LIBRARY

First published in Great Britain 1998 by
MACMILLAN PRESS LTD
Houndmills, Basingstoke, Hampshire RG21 6XS and London
Companies and representatives throughout the world

A catalogue record for this book is available from the British Library.

ISBN 0–333–71657–4

First published in the United States of America 1998 by
ST. MARTIN'S PRESS, INC.,
Scholarly and Reference Division,
175 Fifth Avenue, New York, N.Y. 10010

ISBN 0–312–21028–0

Library of Congress Cataloging-in-Publication Data
Loth, Wilfried.
[Stalins ungeliebtes Kind. English]
Stalin's unwanted child : the Soviet Union, the German question,
and the founding of the GDR / Wilfried Loth ; translated Robert F.
Hogg.
p.   cm.
Includes bibliographical references and index.
ISBN 0–312–21028–0
1. Germany (East)—Foreign relations—Soviet Union.   2. Soviet
Union—Foreign relations—Germany (East)   3. Germany (East)–
–Politics and government.   4. Military government—Germany (East)
5. Military occupation.   I. Title.
DD286.5.L6713 1997
327.431047—dc21   97–38375
                                                                CIP

© Rowohlt Verlag GmbH 1998

Originally published in hardcover as *Stalins ungeliebtes Kind*
Rowohlt Verlag GmbH 1994
Paperback edition Deutscher Taschenbuch Verlag 1996

This book is printed on paper suitable for recycling and made from fully managed and
sustained forest sources.

10   9   8   7   6   5   4   3   2   1
07 06 05 04 03 02 01 00 99 98

Printed in Great Britain by
The Ipswich Book Company Ltd
Ipswich, Suffolk

Contents

List of Abbreviations

BA	Bundesarchiv Koblenz (Federal Archive at Koblenz)
BAP	Bundesarchiv Potsdam (Federal Archive at Potsdam)
BRD	Bundesrepublik Deutschland (Federal Republic of Germany)
CAB	Cabinet Papers
CDU	Christlich-Demokratische Union (Christian Democratic Union)
CPSU	Communist Party of the Soviet Union
CSU	Christlich-Soziale Union (Christian Social Union)
CWIHP	Cold War International History Project
DBD	Demokratische Bauernpartei Deutschlands (Democratic Peasants' Party of Germany)
DDR	Deutsche Demokratische Republik (German Democratic Republic)
DPD	Demokratische Partei Deutschlands (Democratic Party of Germany)
DWK	Deutsche Wirtschaftskommission (German Economic Commission)
EAC	European Advisory Commission
EDC	European Defence Community
FDGB	Freier Deutscher Gewerkschaftsbund (Free German Federation of Unions)
FDJ	Freie Deutsche Jugend (Free German Youth)
FO	Foreign Office
FRG	Federal Republic of Germany
FRUS	*Foreign Relations of the United States*
HICOG	High Commission for Germany
KPD	Kommunistische Partei Deutschlands (Communist Party of Germany)
LDPD	Liberal-Demokratische Partei Deutschlands (Liberal Democratic Party of Germany)
MfS	Ministerium für Staatssicherheit (Ministry for State Security)
MGB	Ministerstvo Gosudarstvennoi Bezopasnosti (Ministry of State Security)
NATO	North Atlantic Treaty Organization
NDPD	National-Demokratische Partei Deutschlands (National Democratic Party of Germany)

NKGB	Narodnii Kommissariat Gosudarstvennoi Bezopastnosti (People's Commissariat for State Security)
NKVD	Narodnii Kommissariat Vnutrennikh Del (People's Commissariat of Internal Affairs)
NL	Nachlaß (Personal Papers)
NS	National Socialist
PRO	Public Record Office
SAG	Sowjetische Aktiengesellschaft (Soviet Joint-Stock Corporation)
SBZ	Sowjetische Besatzungszone (Soviet Occupation Zone)
SED	Sozialistische Einheitspartei Deutschlands (Socialist Unity Party of Germany)
SCC	Soviet Control Commission
SMA	Soviet Military Administration
SOZ	Soviet Occupation Zone
SPD	Sozialdemokratische Partei Deutschlands (Social Democratic Party of Germany)
UN	United Nations
UNRRA	United Nations Relief and Rehabilitation Administration
USA	United States of America
USSR	Union of Soviet Socialist Republics
ZK	Zentralkomitee (Central Committee)
ZPA	Zentrales Parteiarchiv (Central Party Archive)

Introduction

The origins of the German Democratic Republic (GDR) are, by and large, regarded as well understood. The conventional version has it that the victorious Soviet Union utilized the presence of its troops on German soil at the end of the Second World War to export the Soviet societal model. The Soviet victors, and the German Communists aiding them, initially hid their true goals behind an "anti-fascist" façade but worked secretly to establish a Communist monopoly on power. Having achieved this, they then proclaimed the first "workers' and peasants' state" in German history. In this view, it remains uncertain as to whether the Soviet model was intended for all of Germany or whether Stalin, realistically assessing the overall situation, quickly set his sights on the separate organization of the Soviet Occupation Zone. Although opinions differ on that point, they all agree that the conflict between the systems of East and West was ultimately responsible for the division of Germany.

The historical literature in the GDR proclaimed a similar message but with a different evaluation: anti-fascist democratic transformation and the realization of the historical mission of the working class were, according to this literature, two sides of the very same coin. Consequently, the revolutionary vanguard of the German working class, supported by their Soviet "friends", brought together under its leadership a broad alliance of all anti-fascist and democratic forces. Together, these forces strove for a democratic republic and paved the way for socialism. The representatives of the German monopolistic bourgeoisie opposed these goals. Because these forces enjoyed the support of American imperialists in western Germany, the victory of the working class remained, for the time being, a limited one.

Admittedly, a few awkward facts always stood in the way of this straightforward view of the division of Germany as a consequence of the conflict between the East and West Blocs. Did Stalin not offer reunification on "bourgeois" terms in 1952, with the condition that the united Germany pledge itself to neutrality in the conflict between East and West? Were there also not reports that Moscow repeatedly considered such a solution and in the spring of 1953 even began to put it into effect? These reports fit so poorly with the general impression of Soviet policy that many in the West declared that the Soviet offer could not be taken seriously. Nevertheless, it proved difficult to verify this claim. Corresponding demonstrations were indeed always very well received; but a closer inspection always gave rise to doubts.

Disputes over the goals of Soviet policy on Germany provoked the comment that scholars would have something more specific to say only if, on some distant day, Eastern archives were to be made available for research, a development which hardly anyone could imagine. In the meantime, that has indeed come about: since the collapse of the GDR, the party archive of the Socialist Unity Party (SED) has been open to researchers, witnesses to Stalin's German policy have begun to speak out thanks to *Glasnost*, and, though hindered by many practical difficulties, the archives of the former Soviet Union are little by little becoming accessible. On the basis of this material, it is both possible and necessary to rewrite the history of the GDR's origins.

In this book, the new sources will be comprehensively analysed for the first time. The most important of these are notes made by Wilhelm Pieck. As chairman of the KPD and SED as well as the first President of the GDR, he made notes of conversations of the KPD/SED leadership with Stalin and with leading representatives of the Soviet Military Administration (SMA) and Soviet Control Commission (SCC). Although these notes only fragmentarily and unevenly recapitulate the course of discussion between the Soviet occupying power and the top functionaries of the SED, they do so without distortion and without interruption for almost eight years, from the beginning of the occupiers' rule in the early summer of 1945 to Stalin's death in the spring of 1953. These extraordinarily authentic and densely packed materials are supplemented by separate records of conversations written by other SED leaders, speech texts and minutes found in the SED Archive, files of the former Soviet Foreign Ministry, witnesses' reports and memoirs of Soviet and German functionaries, as well as source materials from Eastern European and Western archives.

The new sources shed new light on first-hand accounts which have long been available; and for this reason, these will be re-examined here. Especially informative was Erich W. Gniffke's report on his tenure with the SPD Central Committee and SED Central Secretariat. Although published in 1966, the many suggestive passages in Gniffke's book have been astonishingly little noticed.[1] It was also possible to gain new perspectives from Wolfgang Leonhard's well-known report on his activity as a Communist functionary.[2] This was also the case with many first-hand accounts concerning 17 June 1953. Finally, if one is familiar with these internal discussions, then the public statements of Soviet and German functionaries have much to offer that is new.

It is generally true that the various first-hand accounts of Soviet policy on Germany and of the GDR's origins become fully clear only when viewed in context. Individual quotations, which are frequently available to us only in fragmentary form, tell us little about the intentions of the actors and essentially nothing about the constancy or inconstancy of their views unless we know the context from which they stem. On the other hand, corroborative passages in parallel texts dispel doubts as to the meanings of individual statements. Many events and contexts are first illuminated only through comparing different sources. In this way, it first comes to light by such a comparison of internal discussions and public pronouncements that the Communist functionaries hardly thought any differently from how they spoke in public and that they were persuaded of the possibility of persuading others with their words. A study of the source materials covering a period of several years demonstrates above all that there was great consistency in Stalin's thinking. At the same time, it can be seen that other actors pursued thoroughly independent conceptions.

Overall, the comparative analysis of new sources leads to findings which will surprise many. Stalin wanted no GDR. He wanted neither a separate state in the Soviet Occupation Zone nor a socialist state in Germany at all. Instead, he sought a parliamentary democracy for all of Germany, one which would rob fascism of its social base and one which would allow the Soviet Union access to the resources of the Ruhr industrial area. This was to be achieved through the shared responsibility of the victorious powers. The separatist socialist GDR is above all a product of Walter Ulbricht's revolutionary zeal, which was able to unfold given the background of the Western walling-off policy.

These findings, which can be linked up with various differentiated though tentatively formulated analyses in the older historical literature, naturally do not fit at all with the GDR's self-conception. Its historical writing had to provide for a historical legitimation of SED rule within the framework of Soviet ideology rather than concern itself with the critical incorporation of past experience. More astonishing is that the results of this analysis of the sources also deviate markedly from the picture developed through free discussion in the West. Upon closer examination, this discrepancy is also understandable: until now, interpretations of Stalin's German policy could be derived only from a very narrow source base. Decision processes in the Soviet sphere of influence lay hidden behind a systemic veil of secrecy. It was easy for negative experiences with Communist class-struggle concepts and for subliminal fears of a Bolshevik revolution, which had a long tradition especially in Germany, to seep into the analysis in impermissible ways. Where exact information was lacking, generalizations came quickly to hand; and it was also here by no means rarely the case that political prejudice guided the pen.

Thus, it is no accident that the prevailing Western view of the origins of the GDR agrees in essentials with the official East German version, even if they differ fundamentally in regard to terminology and evaluation. Both interpretations reflect modern Germany's origins in the Cold War, in a time when people learned that East and West threatened one another's existence. That realities were more complex and that the conflict between East and West by no means had to lead to the intensification we in fact experienced will first become comprehensible when we free ourselves from this mindset.

The new sources are thoroughly quoted here, and it will be made clear in each instance how they contribute to the illumination of events. Where it is still only possible to make assumptions, this will be stated. The references indicate where the quoted text may be checked and which facts are verified in greater detail elsewhere. Wilhelm Pieck's notes, which are not easy to interpret owing to their fragmentary character, have been published in their complete form by Akademie Verlag in a scholarly edition. The interpretation offered here can be checked against that edition without much trouble.[3]

This account concentrates on bringing out major lines of development and on reconstructing central moments of decision. Operative details have been purposely neglected. Likewise, the Western role in the decision-making process which led to the permanent establishment of the GDR will be only cursorily mentioned so as not to disrupt the coherence of the presentation of Soviet and Soviet-Zone policy. Whoever becomes disoriented occasionally because of this can refer to the chronological table at the end of the book, which presents the structure of the process in a more taut form. Information on the role of persons treated is usually found at their first mention in the text, which can be easily located using the index. Likewise, detailed discussions of the historical literature will not be undertaken. Although this would not be difficult, the meagre source base on the one hand and the political implications of the East–West conflict on the other have given rise to an unusually large number of methodological errors. Even some of the most recent publications quoting from the first source materials to be gleaned from Eastern archives are not free of such errors.[4]

I would like first of all to thank Rolf Badstübner for his collegial cooperation in examining Pieck's notes. For their multi-faceted support,

I would like to thank those associated with my academic chair in Essen: Frank Bärenbrinker, Ralf Bettges, Claudia Hiepel, Dr Gerd Krüger, and Margret Löbbert-Urhahn. In Thomas Karlauf I have found an editor who has undertaken this project with great engagement as well as expertise and capacity for understanding. For that too I would like to express my sincere thanks.

Essen   WILFRIED LOTH

1 A Programme for Germany

What did the Soviet Union want for Germany in 1945? Neither the decisiveness with which the Soviet occupiers went to work beginning in the early summer of 1945 nor the opaqueness of Soviet decision-making for outside observers should be allowed to conceal the fact that Josef V. Stalin himself – after victory in "the Great Patriotic War", more than ever the final authority on decisions concerning German policy – for a time did not know exactly how he should deal with the defeated Reich. Those with influence over his decisions were often of diverse opinions. Decisions required time, and numerous essentially incompatible conceptions were frequently pursued parallel to one another, exactly as was the case with the Western occupying powers.

COMPLEX NECESSITIES

There were certainly some essentials which Soviet policy on Germany had to look at in any event. First of all was the goal of security against Germany. Actually a self-evident concern given that German aggression had been repulsed only with the greatest of efforts, this was often overlooked by those speculating over Soviet goals in Germany. Considering deeply-rooted fears of Bolshevism, abhorrence of a Stalinist repression so contemptuous of humanity, and the widespread tendency of the Germans to evade their own responsibility, it was possible to lose sight of the fact that the Soviet Union was the victim of a German war of aggression and that the Wehrmacht had conducted this war with the goal of completely exterminating its Bolshevik opponents.[1] According to the most recent estimates, at least 27 million Soviet citizens became victims of this conflict, a figure representing 14 per cent of the prewar population.[2] The Soviet state had been driven to the edge of collapse, Stalin's rule had been severely shaken, and the western Soviet regions which had fallen into German hands had been largely laid waste. In this situation, any Soviet government would have attempted to exploit military victory first of all to take preventative measures against further German aggression. Stalin received support in this goal from all those who speculated that Soviet victory would usher in a relaxation of the internal system of coercion.

1

For Stalin, it was beyond question that the German problem would not be resolved by military victory alone, regardless of its totality. His fundamental distrust of capitalist powers and his profound respect for industrial might led him to reckon with a renewed threat from the Germans. "The Germans will rise again," he said sometime in August 1944 to the Polish Prime Minister Mikolajczyk:

> They are a strong people. After Bismarck's triumph in 1871, forty years had to pass before they could undertake further aggression. When that failed, they needed a pause for recuperation of twenty or twenty-five years before they could try once again – this time, almost successfully. And who now knows if they won't be ready for battle again in twenty or twenty-five years? Yes, Germany is a strong land although Hilter is in the process of weakening it. We're convinced that a threat from the German side will repeat itself. It is for this reason, the talks on collective security currently being conducted in Washington are so urgent. I myself am for every possible and impossible measure to supress Germany.[3]

In a conversation with the Yugoslavian government delegation visiting in April 1945 for the signing of the Yugoslav–Soviet mutual-assistance pact, he estimated that a German resurgence would come even sooner: "They will recover and very quickly indeed. They are a highly-developed industrial nation with an extremely qualified and large working class as well as a technical intelligentsia. Give them twelve or fifteen years, and they'll be back on their feet."[4]

German reparations as a contribution to Soviet reconstruction were almost as important as measures to safeguard against renewed German aggression. According to initial estimates presented to Stalin by First Deputy Prime Minister N. A. Vosnessenskii at the end of 1945, war damage in the Soviet Union amounted to approximately 700 million roubles, some 30 per cent of national income.[5] Soviet representatives quoted a figure of $128 billion to the Western powers in 1947, representing approximately the same sum at the official exchange rate of 5.3 to 1, which, however, greatly undervalued the rouble. Later estimates by economic historians fall within the same range. The Soviet economist Michael Tamarchenko reported that the Second World War had cost the Soviet Union the equivalent of two Five-Year Plans.[6] The American historian Susan Linz came to the conclusion on the basis of her own calculations that with support from American Lend-Lease Deliveries, UNRRA assistance, and reparations already taken into account,

30 per cent of the capital stock and eight to ten annual incomes of the entire 1945 population had been lost. By including disruptions of production due to population loss, one arrives at a total cost of eighteen to twenty-five annual incomes.[7] The Soviet Union was thus far more dependent upon reparations from occupied Germany than were any of the other victorious powers. Measured against actual losses, the sum of $10 billion first claimed by Stalin for the Soviet Union at the Yalta Conference in February 1945 was indeed quite modest.

A third goal of Soviet policy on Germany was likewise obvious although hardly perceived by Western observers: the Soviet leadership had to prevent German potential from falling completely or largely into the hands of the Western powers. This danger loomed larger to the Soviets than can initially be assumed from a look at the military outcome of the war. Those in positions of responsibility knew from analyses prepared by economists of the Soviet Academy of Sciences under the direction of Evgenii Varga that the European nations would emerge impoverished from the war whereas the US was enjoying a massive expansion of production. Varga, whom Stalin consulted regularly, prophesied that overproduction would result from the transformation of the American war economy to a peacetime footing. As a consequence, there would be an American economic drive into the impoverished Europe, where new consumer and investment markets were to be won.[8] The political consequences of this American economic expansion were not easy to foresee. Given the great importance of economic factors in Marxist thinking and the profound distrust with which Stalin approached all capitalist powers, the obvious conclusion was that a new and dangerous opponent of the Soviet Union was manifesting itself. The idea of an alliance between American and German capital must have unleashed almost apocalyptic fear.

It is not possible to determine exactly how widespread such ideas were in Moscow. According to the report of Jean-Richard Bloch, who accompanied French Communist Party General Secretary Maurice Thorez in exile in Moscow, an influential segment of the Soviet leadership as early as 1944 regarded the "intensified subjugation" of France under its "Anglo-Saxon protectors" as unavoidable. Thorez won Stalin over to the idea "that even if Anglo-Saxon influence could not be averted, it could be restricted by aiding France in pursuing an independent policy".[9] Similar considerations may also have applied to the other western European nations in light of the loyal cooperation evinced by Communist parties in national reconstruction.[10]

Even in those lands within the Red Army's sphere of influence, it can be seen that Soviet leaders were by no means certain as to their possibilities. Before they left Moscow at the end of 1944, it was impressed upon Czech Communist Party leaders that "the question of Sovietization is not to raised. . . . That is not as simple an issue as many think".[11] The Bulgarian General Secretary Traitschko Kostoff announced to his Central Committee in March 1945 that an "attempt to establish Soviet-style rule" upon the arrival of the Red Army in Bulgaria in the autumn of 1944 "would have caused us and the Soviet Union great difficulties" and "would not have been approved by the commanders of the Red Army".[12] In any event, it is thus clear that military factors alone were not decisive in the Soviet view and that Soviet leaders felt themselves on the defensive in economic terms.

No clear plan of action emerged, however, from the three imperatives of the Soviets' German policy. Could the Western powers be trusted to the extent that a shared control of defeated Germany seemed possible? Was it prudent or dangerous to mobilize the Germans against the threat of American hegemony? What combination of coercion and concession was appropriate in order to prevent the Germans' following the imperialist course? How was the interest in reparations to be harmonized with the necessity of a permanent arrangement with the Germans? All these questions – which to an extent were posed by the Western powers in quite similar terms – could be answered in different ways, and we can be certain that Stalin did not find it easy to make these decisions.

UNCERTAIN SIZING-UP

As long as the Western Allies inclined toward resolving the German problem by dividing the Reich into several independent states, Stalin had signalled his readiness to assist in carrying out such a plan. For him, the dismemberment of Germany was certainly not an ideal solution. More important for him than the principle of division was that an agreement among the Big Three be reached on the future treatment of Germany. This is made clear when one considers that the initiative for the first dismemberment plan, discussed by Stalin and British Foreign Secretary Anthony Eden in December 1941, did not by any means originate from the Soviet side, as is usually claimed in the Western literature, but rather from Churchill. The British Prime Minister let it be known to Stalin just before Eden's visit that he deemed necessary the "complete disarmament of Germany for at least a full generation and the dismemberment of Germany into individual parts, above all the severing of Prussia from the other parts of Germany".[13]

Stalin reacted by suggesting that the Rhineland be separated off and that East Prussia as well as additional German territories be ceded to Poland. Beyond this, he proposed that an independent Bavaria be established "eventually".[14] He never attempted to make these dismemberment plans any more precise, however. In Teheran, he did accede to Roosevelt's extreme dismemberment plan on the spot but in the same breath warned the US President of an inevitable German struggle for reunification. When the British wanted to establish a Dismemberment Committee in January 1944 to implement the decisions of the Teheran discussions, the Soviet representative on the European Advisory Commission (EAC), Fedor Gusev, torpedoed every attempt to specify plans, arguing that the Soviet delegation did not possess sufficient information or experts to examine the subject matter.[15] At Yalta, Stalin did seek to have his allies pledge themselves to the principle of dismemberment, but added that a detailed determination was not necessary at the moment. In the draft of the instrument of surrender, he very quickly satisfied himself with a formulation at least allowing for doubt as to the Allies' actual intention of dismembering Germany.[16]

The Dismemberment Committee established at Yalta received from the British delegation a draft of guidelines in which dismemberment was cited as one possibility among others, one to be implemented "if necessary". After consultation with Moscow, Gusev agreed to this formulation on 28 March 1945. As the reason for this decision, he explained that "The Soviet government understands the Yalta Conference resolution not as an absolute commitment but rather as a possibility to put pressure on Germany in the event that other means do not prove effective enough in rendering that nation harmless."[17] In the West, this was regarded as a significant change in the Soviet position and led the British to shelve dismemberment plans, which they had long considered problematic. In truth, it had simply become clear how little Stalin had actually identified with dismemberment plans.

The British about-face on dismemberment sufficed to convince Stalin to stop pursuing the project further. In so doing, he was not driven by the hope of soon securing the entire Ruhr area owing to favourable developments in the war, although this was quickly suspected in the West. Rather, he was merely adapting his position to the state of the discussion among his allies. This adaptation demonstrates that he still concerned himself with fundamental consensus among the Big Three over the treatment of Germany but at the same time did not want to fall behind the Western Allies: if they were leaning away from the dismemberment principle, then in consideration of his own influence over the Germans, it seemed highly unwise to cling to the issue.

How pessimistic the responsible Soviet officials actually were in assessing their possibilities in Germany at the time of the Yalta Conference can be seen in a report presented to the West by Soviet Reparations Minister Vladimir Rudolph after his defection at the beginning of the 1950s. According to him, at the end of 1944 and the beginning of 1945,

> the Politburo had no confidence in the possibility of successfully Sovietizing even those parts of Germany occupied by Soviet troops. It was considered probable that the United States and Great Britain would insist on conditions of peace under which the Sovietization of Germany would be impossible. Some members of the Soviet government feared a repetition of the rapid German recovery after the First World War. Accordingly the idea was developed of the "economic disarmament of Germany", i.e., the dismantling of the German economy to a point where Germany would be unable for years, if not forever, to stage a comeback as a powerful state and a potential enemy.[18]

Rudolph's statements, whose precision and detail lend them thoroughgoing credibility in their basic lines, are confirmed by Soviet practice in regard to reparations. At Yalta, the Soviet Deputy Foreign Minister Maiskii presented a reparations plan envisioning an 80 per cent reduction in German heavy industry.[19] Moreover, in May 1945, the "Special Committee of the Council of People's Representatives" headed by Vice Premier Georgii M. Malenkov began requisitioning industrial goods and installations of all kinds in the Soviet Occupation Zone with the help of personnel who soon numbered seventy thousand. This was undertaken with great haste and more or less without planning.[20] It shows that Moscow actually regarded an economic disarmament of Germany as urgent and had little confidence in the stability of the alliance among the victorious powers. If it were to collapse, all that remained would be an opportunity for the quick exploitation of the vanquished opponent. The hiving off of industrial facilities had to continue as long as the presence of the Red Army made it possible. "Steal as much as you can" was the directive issued by Stalin in March 1945.[21]

UNITY AS THE GOAL

Undoubtedly, with the Red Army's advance into central Germany vanished the Soviet worry that it would not be possible to exercise any influence over the reorganization of Germany. In its place, the idea spread that there could in the future be two German states, a Western one and one under Soviet influence. Stalin's well-known statement, reported by Milovan Djilas at the reception of the Yugoslavian state and party delegation at the beginning of April 1945, pointed to this possibility: "This war is unlike those of the past; whoever occupies an area also imposes his own social system there. Everyone introduces his own system as far as his army can advance. There can't be any other way."[22] Warnings heard by German KPD-exiles in Moscow pointed in the same direction. KPD Chairman Wilhelm Pieck thus spoke in March 1945 of the danger that "in the British and American Zones, efforts will be encouraged to create a counterpoise to the growing influence of the Soviet Union and to give reformist leaders of the Social Democrats and labor unions an opportunity to establish their influence over the workers at the expense of the Communists". In general, he assumed that the regimes of the victorious powers "in the three Occupation Zones will be rather different from one another".[23] During schooling for the German émigrés, Wolfgang Leonhard was told that "the National Socialists [would] undoubtedly attempt to undermine the unity of the three victorious powers and to sow mistrust among them".[24] It was thus unambiguous what Pieck and presumably other top KPD functionaries were told when they spoke with Stalin, Molotov, and Zhdanov on 4 July about the future political conception of Germany: "Prospects – there will be two Germanies – despite the unity of the Allies."[25]

For the Soviet leadership, nevertheless, the prospect of two German states was disconcerting in a way similar to the dismal vision in the winter of 1944–5. Since the weight of German industry lay in the west, into which American troops and their allies were then marching, the danger of an alliance between American and German capital was undiminished and further, the situation regarding urgently needed reparations continued to look unfavourable. From their perspective, the East–West division of Germany was thus not something to be accepted easily, and certainly not a way station on the road to socialism. It was, rather, a danger to be confronted with all the means at their disposal. That follows from the logic of the situation and is strongly confirmed by the directives found in the source material. The Communists in Moscow exile were instructed, in cooperation with other "anti-fascist democratic forces, to support the activities of the occupying powers in the struggle to eradicate Nazism and militarism and for the reeducation of the German people and for the implementation of democratic reforms". Expected attempts to drive a wedge between the Anglo-Saxons and the Soviets "must be combatted ruthlessly".[26] The strategic goal decided upon in discussions on 4 June went still further: "Secure the unity of Germany."[27]

If Stalin actually had been working towards the establishment of a separate state on the territory of the Soviet Zone, then he certainly would have had to reconsider the westward shift of Poland to the Oder and Western Neisse, a plan pursued in its essentials since 1941 and sanctioned by the Western Allies. By consenting to Polish demands for the annexation of Silesia, he did indeed strengthen the position of the Polish "Provisional Government" he had installed and did compensate for the westward shift of the Polish–Soviet border. At the same time, he decisively weakened the chances of survival for a state in the Eastern Zone by transferring the Upper Silesian industrial area to Poland. The unrestrained plundering of the Zone, beginning soon after the end of hostilities, daily deprived such a state of further resources. As long as this continued, a minority in Moscow could regard a state in the Soviet Zone as at most a second-best solution. For the official policy, the Zone served only as a security, increasing the likelihood that the Soviet Union would have a say in the future organization of Germany. No separate concept was developed for the Zone as such.

After a putsch against Hitler failed to materialize, Stalin clearly focused his hopes fully on the alliance of the Big Three. Only if this alliance remained intact after the war's end could the spectre of an American–German pact be exorcised, only then could German society be transformed in such a way as to, pose no further threat, and only then was there a prospect of receiving reparations shipments from the Reich's heavy industrial centre along the Ruhr. First voiced at the Teheran Conference, Stalin's demand "to change the particular conditions in Germany with its Junkerdom and its large armaments firms"[28] met with a basically-positive response among the Western Allies, and "progressive" forces in the US developed wide-ranging plans for such a reorganization of Germany. This strengthened Stalin's hope for a common anti-fascist programme. To a certain extent, he allowed himself to be influenced by Varga's claim that the statist interventionism in economic life developed everywhere in Europe during the war would promote a transformation to "a democracy of a new kind". This would be characterized by social relations "in which the feudal remnants, large estates, would be liquidated; private property and private means of production would still exist but large industrial concerns, transportation systems, and finance would be nationalized; and neither the state itself nor its apparatus would any longer serve the interests of the monopolist bourgeoisie".[29] Clearly, Stalin was not fully certain, as can be gathered from his anxious warning about "two Germanies".

Exactly because the prospects for cooperation among the victorious powers in the reorganization of Germany were by no means heartening – and presumably even more sceptically assessed by the ever-mistrustful Stalin than by others – every effort had to be expended to improve those prospects. Hence the exhortation to do everything to support the joint work of the Allies. Hence too the admonition not to confuse anti-fascist reorganization of Germany with socialist revolution. Before their departure for Germany, KPD cadres in Moscow were told that

> the political goal does not consist in the realization of socialism in Germany or in the desire to bring about socialist development. On the contrary, these must be condemned and resisted as harmful tendencies. Germany is poised on the brink of a bourgeois-democratic reorganization, which in its content and essence will be the fulfilment of the bourgeois-democratic revolution of 1848. This fulfilment depends upon active support and upon resistance against any socialist solutions, as these would be nothing but pure demagogy under the current circumstances. The idea of socialism would only be discredited in such a situation.

Schooling in Moscow included special efforts to prepare KPD personnel for disputes in Germany with *Genossen* who wanted "to introduce socialism at last". Responsibility for the "bourgeois-democratic reorganization" lay unambiguously with the Allies:

> The occupying powers would come to Germany to eradicate fascism and militarism as well as to introduce the necessary measures for a democratic rebirth of the German people. The relevant measures are not yet known in detail; but it can be confidently assumed that besides the condemnation of war criminals, action against monopolist capitalism as well as action for land and school reform is being planned. It's a matter of actively cooperating in these reforms with meticulous attention to Allied instructions and of ensuring their strict implementation.[30]

The instructions issued in the spring were once again confirmed in top-level meetings with Stalin at the beginning of June. Under the rubric "Character of the anti-fascist struggle", Pieck noted: "Completion of the bourgeois-democratic revolution / bourgeois-democratic government / break the power of the estate-owning nobles / eliminate the remnants of feudalism."[31] This demonstrates that the corresponding passages in the KPD platform of 11 June, still being edited in Moscow by Anton Ackermann after having been worked out with Georgii Dimitrov,[32] were not a confidence game, but actually reflected what the Moscow leadership thought about Germany as a whole. Beyond that, it becomes clear that the Communists actually had a democracy of the Western type in view when they spoke of "setting up an anti-fascist, democratic regime, a parliamentary-democratic republic".[33] Contrary to the usual wholesale relegation of that 11 June platform to the category of People's Front rhetoric,[34] it must be emphasized that its authors definitely had the concrete situation of occupied Germany in mind and thus offered a programme which they hoped the Western powers would also help to implement. That could only be a programme for eliminating the authoritarian roots of National Socialism. In accordance with this – and in contrast to earlier discussions – a conception for the transition to socialism was lacking in all internal instructions and discussions. "The people must be told the truth," Ulbricht declared on 12 June. "The truth is that the anti-fascist Germany is still a capitalist nation."[35]

This, of course, did not mean that the Communist leaders had given up their revolutionary goals for Germany. It meant only that, just as in Western European nations,[36] these goals had to take second place to the strategic necessity of safeguarding Soviet power and, thus relegated, had to proceed into an uncertain future. Varga estimated that the postwar consolidation phase of capitalism would last ten years or more and then the universally-expected great crisis of overproduction would develop. He clearly did not want to venture more precise pronouncements as to its conditions or course of development.[37] Under the given circumstances, socialism in Germany was certainly a future concern. For the Soviet state – and, according to the understanding of the Communist leaders, for the Communist world movement – much had already been accomplished if the German danger were eliminated and at the same time the American danger were contained. Additionally, parliamentary democracy with its antimonopolist component was strategically (and not just tactically) welcome, even if it contributed nothing for the moment to the defeat of capitalism in Germany. If one were dependent on cooperation with the Western powers – and in the given

situation, that was the presupposition for a more or less tolerable peace
– then such a democracy was a good basis. Fairly sober considerations
of the situation in occupied Germany could lead to no other programme.

By no means was it the case that Stalin could have expected to have
a free hand in all of Germany after an early withdrawal of American
troops. In all analyses of the international situation, the presence of
the Western powers in Germany is considered a constant. Never is
there a reference to Roosevelt's comment at the Yalta Conference that
public opinion in the US would hardly allow him to keep US troops in
Europe for more than two years.[38] There is even a document from the
summer of 1949 indicating that the Soviet leadership definitely reckoned with a longer presence of the Western Allies: after a conversation with Vladimir Semyonov, since 1946 acting as Political Advisor
to the Chief of SMA, Pieck noted under the heading "Duration of the
occupation": "10 to 100 years". This was the American figure from 10
February 1945, i.e., from the closing stages of the Yalta Conference.
For 1946, statements by Dean Acheson ("at least 25 [years]") and
Eisenhower ("a long time") were cited.[39] Given Stalin's great respect
for the Western powers, he must have considered it completely unrealistic that Soviet troops could be maintained on German territory longer
than American troops could. He complained in 1947 that owing to the
delay in making a peace treaty, the Red Army had "to remain in Germany longer than we would like".[40] This demonstrates that he understood the presence of occupation forces to be of limited duration, justified
solely by the necessity of a democratic reorganization and limited to
the period of that reorganization.

Moreover, it can be seen that Stalin worried that a joint occupation
would not last long enough to complete the requisite reorganization of
Germany. At the first Foreign Ministers' Conference in London in
September 1945, American Secretary of State James F. Byrnes reminded
his colleague Molotov that Stalin had spoken at Yalta of the "danger
that, as after the last war, the United States might return home and
withdraw from European affairs, at which time the danger of a recru-
descence of German aggression might become real". Such a statement
is not to be found in the published Yalta protocols, but Molotov neither
contradicted it nor showed any surprise at it. Instead, he immediately
greeted the suggestion of a four-power pact for the disarmament of
Germany, with which Byrnes sought to respond to Stalin's worries, as
"a very interesting idea".[41] In Washington a year later, Soviet ambassador Nikolai Novikov wrote an analysis of the current situation in
which he warned his Moscow headquarters that the Americans were

considering "the possibility of terminating the Allied occupation of German territory before the main tasks of occupation – the demilitarization and democratization of Germany – have been implemented". He added in explanation that "this would create the prerequisites for the revival of an imperialist Germany, which the United States plans to use in a future war on its side. One cannot help seeing that such a policy [of prematurely ending the occupation] has a clearly outlined anti-Soviet edge and constitutes a serious danger to the cause of peace."[42]

Regardless of the role played by this document in the Soviets' internal decision-making process, its author must have assumed that Stalin would find plausible the argument that a premature end to the American occupation would endanger the peace. This indicates once again that the Soviet dictator definitely welcomed the American occupation forces as an instrument for reorganization. Given his respect for German capabilities and given his own weakness, it is even likely that he was convinced that elimination of the German threat was dependent on the support of the Western Allies.

FROM MILITARY REGIME TO MULTIPARTY STATE

Initially, Stalin thus set his hopes fully on cooperation among the Allies. The Germans were seen mainly as the objects of re-education, to whom political responsibility could be entrusted only after a rather long phase of reorganization. In March 1945, the German Communists in Moscow were told that "a long period of occupation would probably follow the victory. It may even be a matter of years before German political parties would be allowed. The task of the anti-fascist democratic forces is thus to cooperate actively in the local German administrations which would carry out their activities following the instructions of the Allies." According to this, a Communist Party was not initially envisioned. As soon as German organizations were allowed, the Communists should instead take part in creating a broad anti-fascist democratic mass organization under the name "Aggressive Democracy Bloc". To justify this limited form of German participation, explicit reference was made to the fact that Germany had given rise to no resistance movement worthy of mention, and the "unity of the anti-Hitler coalition" was thus the guarantee of victory.[43]

Such a conception was fully compatible with plans to divide Germany into several independent states, even if not a single word of such plans was mentioned to the German Communists. In any event,

Stalin no longer regarded division as very likely after the hesitancy of the Western Allies became known at Yalta; fundamentally, he was still prepared to follow the Western lead in this question. In practice, the Red Army initially did not at all hinder the various anti-fascist committees which formed in many places at the moment of collapse.[44] Their spontaneous and decentralized activity fitted very well with the idea that reorganization would primarily be carried out by the Allies working together.

After the German capitulation, however, this concept was modified in two stages. First, Stalin decided to offer the Germans national unity unambiguously. Without any longer showing consideration for divergent opinions among the Western Allies, he publicly declared in his victory speech of 9 May that the Soviet Union celebrated the victory "even if it was not preparing to dismember or destroy Germany".[45] With that pronouncement, the dismemberment concept was considered closed once and for all. In the moment of their defeat, the Germans were promised a much more attractive future than that sought by the Allies with their demand for "unconditional surrender" up until the last months of the war.

Barely four weeks later, Stalin also promised the Germans an early opportunity to participate in reorganizing their nation. At the beginning of June, Walter Ulbricht, Anton Ackermann, and Gustav Sobottka, who headed the three Initiative Groups supporting the Red Army in its administration of occupied areas, were summoned back to Moscow. Stretching the truth some little bit, Stalin initially presented himself once again as the advocate of national unity. Pieck noted: "Plan to dismember Germany existed on the Anglo-American side. . . . Stalin opposed it." Then they learned, per an order of 26 May, that parties and labour unions, which were not to be formed for a period of years, were now permitted. (Pieck added in explanation: "Thus SPD, Centre Party; not to be promoted by us.") It also followed from this: "Central Committee should work openly – toward the goal of forming a workers' party." This party was supposed to play a key role in the prevention of divisive tendencies between East and West: "Secure German unity through a unified KPD / unified Central Committee / unified workers' party / unified party as the centrepiece." The establishment of a "bourgeois democratic government" would be sought in the medium term.[46]

One can only speculate as to what induced Stalin to involve the Germans in the reorganization programme to a much greater extent than had initially been planned. It is possible that the wealth of Antifa activity corrected the pessimistic image of the Germans which Stalin had held since the failure of the conspiracy of 20 July 1944. It is also possible that he recognized the necessity of mobilizing the Germans for their national unity ever since the danger of the four-power administration's failure had grown following Roosevelt's death on 12 April and the consequent weakening of the "progressive" wing among American policy makers. Perhaps it was only that he saw that the partisans of dismemberment were losing ground in the American decision-making process.[47] If he were the first to adopt a solution that was already in the air, he could undoubtedly secure an impressive advantage in Germany. Not to be excluded is the possibility that efforts of German Communists played a role in making sure that the KPD would figure more actively in cooperation with Moscow. In any case, it was reported of Ulbricht that he had "already received the new directives from Moscow in the latter half of May to prepare for the refounding of the German Communist Party"; and he then rigorously pursued the dissolution of the Antifa committees.[48] To what extent he thus anticipated a decision from Stalin must remain open.

To launch the modified reorganization concept, Stalin skilfully made use of the circumstance that the Western Allies' troops had reached Saxony, Thuringia and Mecklenburg, but not Berlin. Before the Western Allies could take up the occupation of the western sectors of the capital at the beginning of July as had been planned, the authorization of "anti-fascist democratic parties" had been proclaimed on 10 June: the KPD, SPD, CDU, and finally the LDPD (on 5 July) established themselves. Moreover, the Social Democrats and the Communists had on 19 June agreed to work together in forming "Action Committees". This rapid advance without the consent of the Western Allies was clearly aiming toward an anti-fascist reorganization of the entire occupied area using the old capital of the Reich as a base. In the process, the politicians who had now become party founders were firmly assured that they would be needed for a new democratic beginning. Marshal Zhukov explained to the members of the SPD Central Committee: "Gentlemen, I have been sent to Berlin and to the Occupation Zone with the task – a task given by Moscow – to develop a democratic regime here. I am well aware that in accomplishing this task, I cannot primarily count on the Communist Party; but rather I am dependent on you, as I know that you have the masses behind you."[49] Ulbricht quickly let it be known at the first meeting of the KPD Central Committee that the socialist planks in the SPD platform of 15 June were not those currently held: "Democracy, not socialism, is the order of the day."[50]

In pushing through this concept among the Communists who had remained in Germany, the strategic necessities were to an extent quite openly addressed. Thus, according to notes for a speech, Leipzig KPD leader Fritz Selbmann explained in July 1945 that "Germany [is] now divided into zones of occupation, and the policy of the KPD must never be intended for only one of these zones." Moreover, he justified the deferment of all Sovietization plans as furthering "the strategic goal of democracy" by claiming that "upon the ruins of Germany . . . no socialism" could be built and that "the German people . . . [are] ideologically unready for Sovietization".[51]

Nevertheless, those returning from Moscow had great difficulty in explaining to their *Altgenossen* a party line implying the "completely unhindered development of free trade and of private entrepreneurial initiative on the basis of private property"[52] and leaving open the question of the future of the socialist programme. Not corresponding at all to the hopes most Communists had attached to the collapse of the National Socialist (NS) regime and the arrival of Soviet troops, this line inspired resistance which was only broken through the material support of the Central Committee by SMA and through the recruitment of many new party members.[53] This once again makes clear, indirectly, that this policy constituted not only a break with the binding party line up to 1933 but also a fundamental qualification of the party line of the Seventh World Congress of 1935.

DEMOCRATIC SOCIALISM

Socialism was first mentioned again when a common programmatic basis had to be negotiated with the Social Democrats during the campaign for the unification of both workers' parties. On 19 December 1945, the KPD Central Committee passed along a draft resolution on the unification question to the SPD Central Committee for the upcoming "Conference of Sixty". Following Lenin's Two-Revolutions Theory of 1905,[54] this draft referred to socialism as the more comprehensive political goal *after* the establishment of parliamentary democracy:

> The programme of this [unified] party should minimally call for the completion of Germany's democratic renewal in the sense of establishing an anti-fascist democratic republic of a parliamentary nature. Maximally, the programme should call for the realization of socialism through the exercise of political dominance by the working class in the sense of the teachings of strict Marxism.

Further, this formulation for the first time provided that the special conditions in Germany be considered not only in the current situation but also in the future transition to socialism:

> In the realization of the minimal programme, it [the Unity Party] should embark upon a special path given the specificity of our nation's development. The total suppression of the old state power apparatus and the decisive continuation of democratic renewal in Germany can also create special forms of transition to political dominance by the working class and to socialism.[55]

The prospects for socialism were, however, not made any more concrete in all this. Without giving up the immediate task at hand, social democratic questions concerning the path to socialism were taken into account through allusion to a connection between the current democratization programme and the future transition to socialism.

Stalin went a remarkable step further. When Ulbricht raised the programme question with him during their next meeting at the beginning of February 1946,[56] Stalin affirmed not only the differentiation between the minimal programme ("the unity of Germany") and the socialistic maximal programme but also unambiguously committed himself to the democratic path in the "transition question" as well. Directly after Ulbricht's return, Pieck noted: "Situation completely different / in Russia the shortest path / working-class dominance . . . / parl. traditions in the West / on the democratic path to workers' power / not dictatorship." Over and above that, he held to Stalin's pronouncements on elements of the democratic path: "purging of the state apparatus / communalizing [*sic*] of firms, dispossessing the large landowners / socialism".[57]

Relativizing the Soviet path in this manner was neither some programmatic subterfuge to lure the Social Democrats onto the course set by the Unity Party, nor only a momentary inspiration on the part of the Soviet dictator. In a conversation with Tito in April 1945, he had already spoken of the possibility of a parliamentary-democratic path to socialism: "Today, socialism is even possible under the British monarchy. A revolution is no longer necessary everywhere. A delegation of British Labourites was here just a little while ago, and we spoke about that."[58] In August 1946, as the "Labourites" had already been governing Great Britain on their own for over a year, he once again expressed himself in the same vein to a delegation of Labour leaders. As Harold Laski reported, he mentioned the possibility that Great Britain could become a socialist nation without having to undergo the stages of a dictatorship of the proletariat, violent revolution, or suppression of the bourgeois class. Stalin expressed the conviction that if the Labour Party realizes its programme of nationalizing industry, transport, finance, etc. and also implements a consistent foreign and domestic policy, it could reach the same level of socialist development as the Soviet Union, if not a higher one. Naturally, this would take longer and would demand a greater degree of patience toward the capitalist class; but it is nevertheless possible to achieve socialism through democratic-socialist methods.[59]

Stalin was again following Varga, who perceived a strengthening of the proletariat in the weakening of the monopoly bourgeoisie through the "democracy of a new kind" with its increasing state share in economic life. Implicit in this was the possibility of an evolutionary path to socialism. After the victory of the Labour Party in Britain and the formation of leftist coalition governments in France, Italy and Belgium, he drew the conclusion that the whole of Europe was on the road to socialism. "Today," he wrote in a reflection on the thirtieth anniversary of the October Revolution, "the struggle in Europe in its historical development is becoming more and more a struggle over the tempo and the forms of the transition from capitalism to socialism. Although the Russian path, the Soviet system, undoubtedly represents the best and most rapid method of transition from capitalism to socialism, historical development shows, as Lenin predicted, that there are also other paths by which this goal can be reached."[60]

Of course, one must ask how seriously Stalin regarded these speculations on a non-Soviet socialism in the West. In light of fears expressed elsewhere, he can at most have entertained vague hopes for the future. What he ultimately envisioned as "socialism" in this context is difficult to understand. The internal consistency of his remarks on the democratic path – made over a long period of time and made to very different listeners, among them Communist leaders such as Tito and Ulbricht – demonstrates that, despite his paranoia,[61] Stalin by no means confined himself to the Leninist model of revolution.[62] His concept of socialism was relatively open and was oriented toward what he regarded as required by the interests of the Soviet state. The *Realpolitik* necessities which he saw at war's end not only determined his programme but also encroached upon his thoughts as to the future of socialism. Democratic socialism became a possibility in his eyes; and in the German case, it even became the only conceivable option. If he actually meant "all Germany must become ours" when speaking to Yugoslav and Bulgarian party leaders in the spring of 1946 – Djilas reports somewhat imprecisely of statements by "Stalin and the Soviet leaders" and quotes only at second hand[63] – then he by no means had the Soviet model of socialism in mind.

The KPD leadership adopted Stalin's thesis of the democratic path in less than its full scope. In a subsequently oft-quoted article on the "special German path to socialism" written by Ackermann after Ulbricht's return from Moscow, autonomy from the Soviet model was even more clearly stressed than in the draft resolution of 19 December. But the pursuit of the democratic path was made forthrightly dependent upon the success of the democratic transformation in the meantime: "No one desires more ardently than we that new open struggles, new spilling of blood, be avoided"; the possibility was not to be excluded, however.[64] In accordance with this, the "principles and goals" of the Unity Party, discussed during this time, included the statement that "the SED seeks the democratic path to socialism; it will, however, resort to revolutionary means if the capitalist class abandons the foundation of democracy".[65] This limitation clearly resulted from a recourse to Marx and Lenin, indispensable for a theoretical justification of the special path, which Ackermann had to produce. As he wrote, one could gather from the classic works that, "under special circumstances, it [was] also possible to succeed without suppressing the bourgeois state's machinery", that is, "given the premise that the bourgeois-democratic regime cannot shore itself up by means of militarism or a reactionary bureaucracy". Consequently, the "completion of the bourgeois-democratic transformation" could be and had to be justified as the prerequisite for the democratic path to socialism. "If this task is accomplished," wrote Ulbricht in the second issue of *Einheit*, "then the democratic path is safeguarded."[66]

It is not possible to read substantial dissent against Stalin's ideas into the reference to the "revolutionary" alternative. Rather, that reference illustrates once again the difficulty which the German *Genossen* had in implementing a programme lacking a well-founded perspective on socialism. At the same time, it underscores once again the fact that the Communists did not seek to dupe gullible Social Democrats in the discussion of the programme. They insisted upon a successful bourgeois-democratic transformation as prerequisite for socialism and in connection with it, gave their assurance that the peaceful path was, of course, the preferred path. That the efforts of the German Communists were still concentrated on the democratic programme is indirectly demonstrated here: the transition to socialism was a theoretical problem for which convincing answers were hard to come by given the discrepancy between the Marxist-Leninist model of action and the current agenda.

INITIAL SUCCESSES

The Soviet leadership was quickly able to achieve some initial successes. With more or less clear intimations that cooperation among anti-fascist parties was the prerequisite for obtaining permission to undertake political activity, it was possible to convince the leaders of both "bourgeois" parties, the CDU and the LDPD, to agree to the formation of a "Bloc of Anti-Fascist Democratic Parties". This corresponded to the proposal included in the KPD platform of 11 June. The Social Democrats were immediately receptive to the idea of organized cooperation anyway, but insisted that decisions be reached only "by way of consensus". In this form, the "United Front" came into existence on 14 July, the name being a concession to the bourgeois parties. The United Front guaranteed to all the parties first of all that they could not be outvoted by coalitions formed against them. It also opened up the prospect of Communist participation in a future government – at least wherever it was possible to push through the party structure as stage managed from Berlin.[67]

This development was at the same time a step toward an "anti-fascist" party structure in all four occupation zones. At least this appeared to suggest itself at the next meeting of the Big Three beginning on 17 July in Potsdam. The Americans brought with them a draft of directives on the future treatment of Germany. These called for not only a thoroughgoing denazification and the gradual rebuilding of political life including democratic parties, but also the "elimination of the existing excessive concentration of the economy, especially as seen in cartels, syndicates, trusts, and other monopolistic combinations".[68] By way of supplement, Molotov needed only to propose the "organization of a Central German Administration", and then a common political programme essentially corresponding to Soviet ideas was complete. The final formulation of the Potsdam accord did not specify the shape of a future government for all of Germany as clearly as the Soviet proposal did, though. The Western Allies were only prepared to commit themselves to the formation of "some important centralized German administrative departments", not, however, to the coordination of the activity of the provincial administrations or the centralized oversight of "functions connected to resolving questions regarding Germany as a whole".[69] On this basis, a common Allied line on German policy could nevertheless be promulgated, a development which up to this time had been hoped for only on the Soviet side.

On the other hand, it was less important in the Soviet view that the Western powers at Potsdam suggested the Soviets content themselves initially with taking needed reparations from only their own zone. It was also less important that the Western Allies had earmarked for the Soviets some 25 per cent of the Western Zones' industrial facilities deemed "unnecessary for the German peacetime economy" without having determined the future level of peacetime production: 15 per cent was to be delivered in return for Soviet shipments of food and raw materials and the remaining 10 per cent without any shipments in return. Neither was it by any means perceived as a serious setback that the Soviet demand for a four-power administration of the Ruhr to assume possession of the regions' industrial products as reparations had been deferred. What had not yet been stipulated could well be secured in the future. Since Byrnes repeatedly assured Molotov that the two-stage handling of the reparations question did nothing to alter the American determination that all four zones be treated as a single economic unit,[70] the Soviets remained hopeful. At the close of the conference, Stalin explicitly praised Byrnes for his efforts to obtain productive results, and *Pravda* made reference to a "successful conclusion", which "has strengthened the bonds among the Allies".[71] According to Gregori Klimov, an SMA officer of the Allied Kommandatura in Berlin, the results of Potsdam were regarded in Moscow as "the greatest victory of Soviet diplomacy".[72]

Before the Potsdam Conference worked out a decision on the question of centralized administration on 30 and 31 July, the SMA had begun setting up "Central German Administrations" in its zone. Grotewohl was asked on 20 July to name Social Democratic candidates for the direction of these administrations. An official "order" went out on 27 July for them to be set up. As Arkadii A. Sobolev, political advisor to Marshal Zhukov, explained to his British colleague Christopher Steel at the beginning of September, this was first of all a measure for more effective control and coordination of state and provincial administration of the Soviet Zone by the SMA, but also a step in the direction of a single administration for Germany as a whole.[73] Lt General F. E. Bokov told Grotewohl that "it is possible for this group of economists to transform itself into a political authority at some later point. At the moment, however, it is merely a question of choosing experts who are highly qualified and at the same time are as popular as possible so that their names would be well known everywhere, including in western areas of the Reich, and who already have a particular programme to present".[74] The heads of the Central Administrations were then given to understand that if they proved themselves at this level, they could entertain hopes of receiving top positions in the German-wide administration.[75] After the programme for all of Germany had been sanctioned at the Potsdam Conference, it is clear that the Soviet leadership was determined to make swift progress in its implementation and, in so doing, utilize the human resources available in Berlin to their full extent.

2 First Setbacks

Why were these early successes followed only by setbacks? Why did Stalin end up with exactly what he had sought to avoid: the Western Zones' integration into an American-dominated power bloc, and linked with that, the establishment of a second German state, for which the only remaining practical option was organization along Soviet lines?

A principal reason for the failure of the democratic conception for all of Germany is certainly to be seen in the fact that it was hardly perceived on the Western side. From the very beginning, there were those among the Western Allies and among the Germans who considered the Soviet Occupation Zone lost and thus argued for organizing the Western Zones separately and linking them to western Europe. George F. Kennan, at that time still a staff member of the American embassy in Moscow, had committed himself to this course as early as the beginning of 1945, i.e., before any actual experience with Soviet occupation policy. From that summer on, Kurt Schumacher strove for a separate SPD organization in the Western Zones because he considered Social Democratic politics impossible under Soviet occupation and because he saw German-wide structures only as the tools of Soviet expansionism. For similar reasons, Konrad Adenauer likewise proposed all sorts of plans for the reorganization of western Germany into a state. Initially, such voices did run headlong into scepticism, but the sceptics did not succeed in eliminating a certain fundamental mistrust of Soviet intentions in Germany. In moments of decision, politicians found that "the shirt lay closer than the jacket", as the western German Social Democrats very frankly declared in their rejection of a nation-wide party organization.[1]

Certainly not to be underestimated was the strategic meaning of the French veto against setting up German Central Administrations as had been agreed upon at Potsdam. The French government rejected the Potsdam decision as early as 7 August 1945 in a letter to the Big Three, claiming that such a move would prejudice not only the borders of the future Germany but also the state-building process. Before an administrative arrangement for all of Germany came into effect, the French wanted to make certain that the Ruhr area and the Rhineland would be excluded from the association of German states. Further, Paris had in mind a larger degree of decentralization and direct control by the occupying powers than was consistent with the concept of German Central Administrations. The French representative on the Allied Control Council consequently delayed the establishment of such bodies. On 1 October 1945, Military Governor Koenig declared categorically that no decisions on Central Administrations could be made so long as the question of the Ruhr and Rhineland had not been settled.[2] The consequence of this French persistence was that the principal Potsdam decisions on reorganizing Germany were implemented separately in each zone. In that process, the different approaches of the occupying powers manifested themselves fully.

EVERYDAY STALINISM

At least as much a hindrance as the Western walling-off tendencies was the inability of the Soviet apparatus to put Stalin's conception consistently into practice. The army of occupation was certainly subject to strict discipline. For the task of organizing a new democratic beginning, however, it was extremely poorly prepared. Many of its members came from outside the realm of European civilization. After more than two decades of permanent mobilization and systematic terror, traditions of the rule of law were absolutely foreign to them. They lacked any experience with a pluralistic-democratic state. Likewise, they were completely ignorant of the land in which they now found themselves. There were almost no specialists on Germany among the fifty thousand people working for the SMA. Hardly anyone in the leadership ranks of the staff had been prepared for his tasks. The notorious reserve of Soviet representatives on the European Advisory Commission and in other Allied bodies betrayed not only uncertainty but also a lack of competence in planning, which was occasionally acknowledged by the Soviets themselves.[3] Systematic schooling organized by the SMA[4] for the leadership ranks in Berlin could only partially make up for the deficit of knowledge and experience.

This was all the more serious in that Communist ideology and Stalinist practice predestined the Soviets and their German co-workers to disregard continually the very democratic rules which they were supposed to introduce into Germany. Their perception of being leaders in the emancipation of the working class in a world-historical class struggle imbued them with suspicion towards anyone who was not prepared to subordinate himself or herself to the system of command in the regime of "democratic centralism". At the same time, this mindset justified without exception every means which could strengthen their position. Behind every objection made by German politicians to their ideas, the occupiers thus tended to see the class enemy, an enemy who had to be eliminated. Soviet personnel tended to rely on those German party members who were unconditionally submissive to the Moscow leadership. For the most part, these *Genossen* could imagine a democratization of Germany only as a democratization under their control. Given this mentality, it was completely natural that they fell back on such means as infiltration, conspiratorial intrigues, demagogic manipulation, and binding commitments – means which were known to them. Only a very few were aware that the new programme demanded not only a tactical adjustment but, further, a radical break with old methods. Still fewer were in a position to take consistently into account the requirements of a pluralistic order in political practice.

Clearly, not all Soviets and Germans in responsible positions remained prisoner to the old ways of thinking to the same degree. According to the impressions of Erich Gniffke, his colleague on the Party Executive, Anton Ackermann, had fully embraced the goal of "the political unity of Germany on the basis of parliamentary democracy".[5] Other accounts indicate that this was also true of Paul Merker, Wilhelm Zaisser, and Franz Dahlem. Even Pieck distanced himself from the Soviets to a certain extent.[6] In contrast, Walter Ulbricht always acted in strict accordance with the maxim he proclaimed in May 1945 at an action discussion of his "Initiative Group": "It must appear democratic, but we must have everything in our hands."[7] Vladimir Semyonov's confidential remarks to the Social Democrats in the SED leadership[8] and his various advances to bourgeois politicians demonstrate that he was much more clearly aware of the conditions necessary for a successful German-wide conception than was Sergei Tulpanov, the rigid and dogmatic chief of the Administration for Information and Head of the Party Work Team of the SMA. Nevertheless, even those who for reasons of common sense, anti-fascist solidarity, or national feeling earnestly concerned themselves with the realization of democratic principles often did not recognize what this process necessitated. Even those who were aware lacked opportunities to voice their misgivings, let alone supply remedies. In the system of "democratic centralism", important decisions could ultimately be made only by Stalin himself. He was, however, hopelessly overloaded with the diverse problems of running his imperium, often poorly informed, and lacking a feeling for the requirements of a democratization programme. The leeway for the momentum of the apparatus remained correspondingly large.

As early as the summer of 1945, tendencies became perceptible which ended in the exclusive control of the Soviet Zone by orthodox Communist functionaries. The dissolution of the anti-fascist committees was a first step in this direction. Another was the rejection of the first appeals for reconstituting the "organizational unity of the German working class",[9] which the SPD Central Committee directed to the Communist leaders in May and June 1945. Instead of giving anti-fascist impulses as much freedom of action as possible, those who had returned from Moscow sought to bring the remnants of the old KPD under their control with the help of the SMA. They then attempted to give organizational and ideological form to a party significantly expanded by the influx of new members. Parallel to this process, the SMA frequently gave key positions to the reconstituted KPD, certainly securing overproportional influence for the party, and supported it with diverse material and organizational privileges against the competing parties. A situation thus arose in the Soviet Zone which counteracted the pluralistic Germany-wide approach. Only in this zone did the occupying power rely chiefly on German auxiliaries of its own mould. Only in this zone was there a party which, with the assistance of the occupying power, was able to secure an advantageous position.

The unique development of the Soviet Zone was accentuated by the fundamental legal uncertainty which spread under the rule of the SMA. The looting, raping, and other violations perpetrated upon the civil population by soldiers of the Red Army upon their arrival in Germany could be stemmed only gradually despite protests to Zhukov lodged by the leadership of the KPD and the SPD.[10] For a long while, the order of the day remained the more or less capricious arrests by the NKGB/MGB, scorning all principles of the rule of law, as well as slavery and often death in the world of the camps for tens of thousands of innocent persons.[11] This gave rise to a climate of latent fear, which did make it easier for the SMA to impose its will on the Eastern Zone, but at the same time eroded the credibility of the democratic programme for all of Germany in the eyes of the West.

The first instances of discrimination against non-Communist elements came in the constitutive phase during the summer of 1945. The SMA and its German assistants did in many ways further the organizing of a pluralistic party spectrum. In some areas, things went so far as to witness the Soviet commandant's ordering Social Democrats who had joined the KPD to resign and to found an SPD organization. Such an incident was reported by Wolfgang Leonhard in a district of Brandenburg.[12] Frequently, though, Soviet commandants could not conceal their distrust of Social Democrats and "bourgeois" politicians. Leading Communists enjoyed exceptional privileges: they were given preference in the allocation of paper and printing presses, buildings, gasoline, and, not least of all, food supplies. In the filling of administrative posts, proven anti-fascists of Social Democratic or "bourgeois" origins were fairly often at a disadvantage. This held true even for those who, not without a dash of opportunism, had earlier found it within themselves to embrace the Communist cause.[13]

PUSHING THE SED THROUGH

The initial enthusiasm of many Social Democrats for the re-establishment of the "unity of the working class", leading to the first unification proposals from the Social Democratic side, soon gave way to growing "bitterness"[14] and disillusionment. At the same time, they were filled with satisfaction because, despite suffering discrimination, their party grew markedly stronger than the KPD and was also able to consolidate its position. This led the SPD Central Committee to lay claim to the leading role for the party in the reorganization of Germany. On 26 August 1945, Otto Grotewohl declared in a circle of Leipzig party functionaries that the SPD should establish itself nationwide as soon as possible, press for elections in the entire Reich in the near future, and see to it "that these elections are carried out with a sharp distinction made among the parties".[15] Consequently, the bonds of the Unity Front of Anti-Fascist Parties became looser and the project of unifying the two workers' parties was effectively shelved. Three weeks later, on 14 September, Grotewohl publicly announced the Social Democratic claim to the leading role. Before some four thousand SPD functionaries, he characterized the SPD as "first and foremost called to establish this new state". He declared the creation of a nationwide Social Democratic Party to be the order of the day and put off the unification of the two workers' parties to an undetermined point in the future when the existing rifts between them would have been overcome.[16]

Grotewohl's energetic move toward a German-wide pluralism alarmed the Communists. Instead of perceiving the chance for their own German-wide concept offered by Grotewohl's approach, they scented "betrayal" on the part of the "right-wing leader" of Social Democracy. Wilhelm Pieck, who participated in the 14 September SPD rally as a guest, responded to the proclamation by spontaneously crying out, "Create a unified party in order to complete the tasks already begun."[17] Hindered from speaking further by the ensuing tumult, he left the gathering "with a flushed face" and "shaking with rage".[18] Five days later, he spoke of the necessity of "unifying as soon as possible" the two workers' parties and of calling in "reliable" forces in place of the old leaders.[19] The KPD Central Committee immediately decided to prevent the publication of Grotewohl's speech. The brochure containing the text could in fact appear only in Leipzig.[20] For its publication in the SPD central organ, the passages on the expulsions from Eastern areas, the treatment of prisoners of war, and the future eastern border had to be struck out.[21]

This turning point in the Communist attitude toward the question of unifying the two workers' parties was thoroughly in line with Stalin's concept for Germany. As early as the talks in Moscow at the beginning of June, it was carefully noted that the "majority of [SPD] members [were] for unity" of the working class. In developing a strategy to secure the unity of Germany, the formation of a "unified workers' party" was envisaged. According to Pieck, this party was even to be at the centre of the unity strategy.[22] At their first meeting, General Bokov, chief of staff at the SMA, had told the SPD leadership: "This division must be overcome and a new one must be avoided."[23] The Communists had rejected the initial unification offers made by the Social Democrats only because the former wanted first to secure organizational and ideological control within their own party.

That consolidation within the KPD should no longer be taken into consideration resulted primarily from a fear of the fateful work of the Social Democratic "reformists". The Grotewohl strategy recognizably aimed at a rapid merger with the other Occupation Zones. There, however, democratization was not proceeding so "stringently", as was voiced at a meeting between Bokov and the KPD leaders on 25 September. As the complaints ran, "difficulties" were mounting up everywhere: "Opponents becoming mobile . . . increased attacks . . . danger of provocations". Social Democrats "sought to reduce authority of the C[ommunists]" and wanted to "prevent" the unity of the labour unions, considered at the time "the hottest question next to land reform".[24] To forestall supposedly-threatening treachery by the Social Democratic leaders, the unification of the two parties was to be completed soon. In so doing, the Soviets were clearly counting on the pro-unification mood of the Social Democratic base, which they still judged to be considerable: "Bourgeois understand / Hitler [came] to power due to division / Social D. / Guilt / Working class understands, Hitler [led] to catastrophe / but also that SU / strong growth and perspectives for G[ermany]."[25]

It seems that the turn to rapid unification was not undisputed among the Communist leaders. Concerning the decisive session of the Politburo at the "end of September – beginning of October", Anton Ackermann reports only that it was "taken into consideration" whether to propose a merger to the SPD Central Committee above and beyond that of the action units.[26] The KPD's systematic unity campaign began after 11 November, that is, after the SPD Central Committee had rejected a joint proclamation on the anniversary of the November Revolution and after Grotewohl at the SPD rally had spoken out against a merely "intrazonal union".[27] Until the beginning of November, Ulbricht avoided publicly committing himself to unification, and he declared at the beginning of December that "the unity of the working classes is only possible if the Communist Party conveys the Marxist–Leninist theory to the Social Democratic comrades and persuades them to accept it".[28] It is very clear that he was worried to a great extent about the internal coherence of the KPD and thus initially applied the brakes on the unity train.

The Soviet authorities certainly set different priorities. In the final analysis, they were concerned with creating not a flawless Marxist–Leninist party but rather an instrument for pushing through their nationwide democratization programme. Given this premise, Social Democratic reservations against a rapid unification seemed to be evidence that preparations for the Unity Party had been delayed too long and that too much consideration had been shown to the interests of the KPD leaders. This seemed all the more valid when Kurt Schumacher's course was confirmed at the party leaders' conference on 5 and 6 October, indicating that SPD leaders in the Western Zones were much less receptive to union than was the Central Committee. From the Soviet viewpoint, waiting must have seemed all the more a tactical error in light of the all-too-obvious election defeats suffered by the Communists in Hungary (4 November) and Austria (25 November). They demonstrated that, perhaps contrary to hopes, the Soviet victory had done nothing to improve upon the notorious weakness of Communist parties in Central Europe. These examples led to the expectation that the KPD would be marginalized in the upcoming German elections planned first for the zones and then for the national level. The SPD would then succeed in its claim to leadership.

If one understood the SPD's renunciation of the Unity Party project as a pact with the class enemy, then this was indeed an alarming prospect. As Ackermann wrote in his attempt at theoretically categorizing the situation, "the democratic republic" threatened to become "a new instrument of force in the hands of reactionary elements". This would have meant an across-the-board failure of Soviet policy on Germany. Ackermann characterized the situation as still open in his article written at the beginning of February 1946: "Everything in Germany at present is in the making, everything is fluid, only very little has been provisionally decided, and nothing has been definitively decided." He added in warning that "these conditions cannot and will not last long". He carefully noted signs which in his view suggested that the democratic reorganization was endangered: the "renewal of the administrative apparatus" left "something to be desired"; the "reactionary and imperialistic forces" had not everywhere been "deprived of their economic base"; the "workers' right to codetermination in firms and in the economy" still could not "be regarded as secured everywhere"; it was "nothing short of alarming", he continued, "that the forces of restoration of the reactionary and imperialistic Germany are already creeping out of their mouse holes again, are here and there daring a brazen attack, and are blatantly striving to re-establish legal instruments of their politics, above all a press and an organization for counterrevolution". Especially beseechingly, he pointed to a decision in the very near future: "The next weeks and months will decide whether, given the current point of departure, the working class can take possession of complete power in a peaceful process and through purely legal means," that is, through democratic reorganization.[29]

The real worries of the Communist leaders clearly peeped out from behind such constructs. Ackermann was concrete also in regard to the meaning of the union of the two workers' parties: "Along what path and at what tempo Germany will stride toward socialism in the future depends exclusively upon the tempo at which the Unity Party is realized!"[30] Thus, rapid unification was necessary not for building up socialism but rather for securing the democratic path. In the same context, Ackermann characterized the democratic reorganization of Germany as the "minimal programme" of the Unity Party. Aside from warding off the "Austrian danger" as formulated in a conversation among Ulbricht, Bokov, Tulpanov, and Volkov on 22 December,[31] nothing at all was left to do except force the unification process. Only then could the rug be pulled out from under the Social Democratic leaders' disruptive movement, only then could the looming catastrophe in the upcoming elections be avoided. If one equated the Social Democratic claim to leadership with betrayal of class interests, then this was also the only way to save the project of democratic reorganization.

In accordance with this, on 27 September, two days after the pessimistic analysis of the situation was made in the KPD leadership circle,

Bokov sought to persuade Gniffke of the necessity of parting company with the "right-wing" leaders of the SPD and of carrying out the unification of the workers' parties in spite of their opposition: "The right-wing Social Democrats are being towed along by the bourgeoisie. They ignore the advance made when classes and thus parties too disappear. This advance can only be accomplished through the unity of the working class in its struggle against the bourgeoisie." The fragmentation of the working class "bears the guilt for Hitler's coming to power. That must be made comprehensible to the workers, especially in the West."[32] On occasion, German Communists expressed themselves in the same vein to their Social Democratic *Genossen*.[33] Along a broad front, the campaign for unification thus opened in November. It was now obviously impermissible to give consideration to consolidation of the KPD. The needed process of clarification within its leadership ranks was brought to an end.

In the attempt to move the Social Democrats to unification, the Communists made remarkable ideological concessions which are usually overlooked. Instead of further persisting in the Leninist foundation as Ulbricht had demanded, texts from the likes of August Bebel, Wilhelm Liebknecht, Karl Kautsky, and Rudolf Hilferding were incorporated into ideological schooling. In place of the organizing principle of "democratic centralism", appeared the principle of "the members' right to democratic determination", first promulgated as a resolution at the two parties' "Conference of Sixty" on 20 and 21 December. The Communist claim to leadership vanished with the assurance of equal representation of Communists and Social Democrats in leadership bodies at all levels.[34] As with the thesis of "a special German path to socialism", these deviations from the previous course set by the KPD were not only tactical in nature. The Communist negotiators were just not prepared to make a binding commitment to the democratic path which would have been suitable for winning hesitant Social Democrats over to the unification project.[35] For the Soviets and for the German Communists, in so far as they were in a position to comprehend the Soviets' reflections, it was actually a matter of creating a "new" party whose first task was to be the "completion of Germany's democratic renewal", according to the formulation of the Communist draft resolution at the "Conference of Sixty". The realization of socialism would come much later, and the path leading to it had not as yet been determined.

During a one-to-one meeting at the end of January, Marshal Zhukov consequently had no difficulties in offering Grotewohl the removal of Ulbricht, who in the previous weeks had proved himself an especially stubborn champion of the Communist claim to leadership. The Soviet commander also promised Grotewohl the actual leadership of the Unity Party and assured him of support from the Soviet government in his candidacy for the position of first postwar chancellor.[36] Later, there was no question of such an offer, since Grotewohl had missed the right moment for a deal, that is, before his own party base had broken away. He had not acted very adroitly in other regards either.[37] This does not, however, prove that the offer was not seriously intended: it actually fitted well with the strategic objective of democratic reorganization for all of Germany.

When the Communists ran headlong into Social Democratic resistance to their desire for unification, they of course quickly fell back upon the instruments of power available to them in the Soviet Zone. It was not only the case that German Communists and Soviet commanders, acting in accordance with the "betrayal" thesis regarding the SPD leaders, sought to mobilize lower and mid-level SPD formations against the delaying tactics of the Central Committee. Diverse means of obstructing Social Democratic policy were also employed, such as interference in party life, bribery, as well as psychological and physical pressure on opponents of unification. A vicious circle of measures of force developed from December on: the more blatantly the Communists offended against democratic principles, the stronger grew the reservations in the ranks of the Social Democrats; and the stronger the resistance against unification grew, the stronger the pressure grew as well. At the beginning of February, Grotewohl complained to Christopher Steel, head of the political division of the British military government, that the Social Democrats were "being tickled by Russian bayonets", and "their organisation in the provinces had been completely undermined. Men who four days before had assured him of their determination to resist were now begging him to get the business over and have done with it."[38] In 1961, SPD Chairman Erich Ollenhauer reported that "according to very careful estimates, from December 1945 to April 1946, at least 20,000 Social Democrats were disciplined, imprisoned for short or very long periods, or indeed even killed".[39]

It is clear that initially the Soviets involved were not plagued by any considerations that such methods did not really ensure the unity of Germany but on the contrary furthered its division. Instead of perceiving the repulsive effects their actions had on the Social Democrats in the Western Zones, they counted on the signal to be provided by a unification resolution in the Soviet Zone. Social Democrats who warned of an East–West split in the workers' movement were met with references to the mood of the party base, which in all four zones wanted unity. As a secretary of the SPD Magdeburg District reported, "The Russians were possessed of an astonishing level of ignorance when one discussed with them conditions in the three Western Occupation Zones and the character of our party. . . . They simply were not at all familiar with [the situation] and believed that they could put through the unification in the Western Zones as well."[40]

Shortly before the end of the year, a directive came from Moscow to reduce the tempo of the unification campaign. Pieck noted: "In 4 months too early / not too much noise / on account of the Allies." At the same time, the KPD leaders were informed that the "Marshal wishes a visit."[41] Clearly, Stalin now was reconsidering whether the course he had embarked upon in September was correct. He had without a doubt approved it in its fundamentals but then had possibly not followed developments in any detail during his three-month cure in Sochi on the Black Sea.[42] Obviously, he now feared that all too drastic action against the Social Democratic leaders could occasion his Western allies' displeasure. Perhaps he was also entertaining doubts as to whether the German workers were really as ready for unification as had been claimed since the war's end. In any event, he wanted first of all to hear the report of his German *Genossen* before reaching a definitive decision on the unification question.

Without prior consultation with the KDP leaders, however, Stalin decided a month later to complete the unification as soon as possible. On 23 January, the German *Genossen* were informed that they should "hurry along with the unification of both workers' parties". This was to be accomplished "expediently before the elections at the end of May". As Bokov's report to the KPD leaders went on, such a deadline offered the additional advantage that in the future "the first of May [could be celebrated as] the day of unification".[43] Soviet commanders were instructed to exercise an influence "on the local-level unification" of both parties,[44] which they carried out virtually in the manner of a general staff. Not without a hint of pride, Tulpanov recounted that reports came in from the information departments of the komandanturas "every evening at 10 p.m. as to how the unification process stood, what difficulties the partisans of unity had, what resistance was to be noted, . . . which new arguments alongside the old ones . . . were adduced by the opponents of unity, which meaningful and significant facts were to be published in the newspaper, and more of that sort of thing".[45] When Ulbricht found himself sitting across from Stalin on 2 February in Moscow, it was essentially only a matter of determining the Unity Party's programme. As to the unification question itself, Stalin confirmed once again what he had already decided earlier: "Unification agreed – line correct." They set their sights on mergers at the provincial level for 21 and 22 April, the weekend of Easter. On the following weekend, the remaining steps to "unification on the first of May" would be taken.[46]

The factors which finally persuaded Stalin to hold fast to the forcible unification campaign, despite the obvious difficulties, can only be approximated, however. Was he banking on the appeal of the new party, which, according to his understanding, would not just represent a continuation of the KPD through other means? Poorly informed by compliant underlings, did he believe it was still possible to bring the Social Democrats of the Western Zones into line through energetic action? Did he seek refuge from the threat of the KPD's marginalization in the argument that a unification in the Soviet Zone would change the attitude of workers in the Western Zones? Did he hope to be able to hide the SMA's intervention from Western eyes? It is in any case certain that he suppressed the danger of an East–West division of Germany and continued to view the unification project as the central element of his policy for the country as a whole. During the same discussion with Ulbricht in which he affirmed the course of the unification question as "correct", he characterized the unity of Germany as the first goal of the Unity Party and once again presented himself as the advocate of this unity among the Allies. "Germany cannot survive without the Ruhr area"; for that reason, his approval was not given to the French demand for severing it from the future German state. Not one word was said on the subject of separate development of the Soviet Zone. Instead, Stalin held to the plan whereby the name of the KPD would be transformed into the Socialist Unity Party in the Western Zones. Further, land reform was to be advanced through petitions.[47]

In actual fact, unification of the two workers' parties made sense only within the framework of a strategy for all of Germany in which the Communists had to reckon with running in free elections. If unification were intended as preparation for an exclusive grab at their own occupation zone – as it is frequently interpreted – then such a measure would have been not only unnecessary but even counterproductive. Within the Soviet Zone, the occupiers could at will prevent free elections or limit the influence of elected bodies. In order to achieve hegemony over the party bloc in such a constellation, a powerful Communist cadre party was better suited than a mass party of the working class, which would initially have had considerable problems to solve regarding integration. To that extent, the decision against a consolidation of the KPD as favoured by Ulbricht served to strengthen rather than weaken pluralism among the parties. Pieck's assurance that the SED was by no means intended for the establishment of a one-party system[48] could be taken seriously in the spring of 1946. It was not without reason that the other two parties of the Unity Front followed the unification campaign with a good measure of composure. The circle around Jacob Kaiser even scented an opportunity for the CDU to inherit the role of main party of the little people from the SPD after such a unification.[49]

In practice, it quickly became clear that the unification would remain limited to the Soviet Zone. On 11 February, the SPD Central Committee voted by 8 votes to 3 to call a zone-level National Congress, which would decide on the fusion. This vote came only after nerve-racking debate and was influenced by pressure in the form of an ultimatum from pro-unification state chairmen as well as by vague hopes as to the strength of the Social Democrats in the united Germany of the future. With this move, the Social Democrats had succumbed to Soviet pressure, though only in the Eastern Zone. On 1 March, a Berlin conference of functionaries decided to carry out a ballot on the unification question on the last day of the month. The result was an overwhelming majority of 82 per cent in the Western Sectors of Berlin against an immediate unification. In the Soviet Sector, occupation forces had closed the polls immediately after they had opened. Action Committees of the KPD and SPD in the Western Zones rapidly lost all significance: fascination for the idea of workers' unity gave way to shock over Communist methods. Wilhelm Pieck's loudly proclaimed expectation that "this great deed [unification in the Soviet Zone] will spur on our friends in the West to unite soon as well"[50] lacked any foundation at all. With the unification at zone level officially carried out as planned on 21 and 22 April, not only did the responsible parties effectively seal the division of German Social Democracy; they also toppled an important pillar of integration and put wind in the sails of all those in the West who had always regarded cooperation with the Soviet Union as impossible.

TENDENCIES TOWARD SEPARATION

The counterproductive effect of Soviet pressure in the unification question was all the stronger when the SMA showed no compunction about also using its power to stack the democratic deck a bit during implementation of the anti-fascist reform programme. This could be seen in the question of land reform, which the Soviets viewed as the key to depriving the Junkers of power and thus completing the bourgeois revolution. When the leaders of both bourgeois parties took measures to oppose land reform or at least mitigate its impact on property relations, Zhukov intimated in early ·September 1945 that the occupying power could ban parties which it "did not like".[51] LDPD Chairman Waldemar Koch did not allow this threat to force him to give up his opposition to a dispossession of estate owners without compensation. He was then put under indirect pressure when in November his party friends were offered licences for numerous party newspapers in return for his removal. This contributed to Koch's decision to resign on 29 November after a final dispute in the Bloc Central Committee.[52] Like Koch, CDU Chairmen Andreas Hermes and Walther Schreiber also refused to approve, even after the fact, a dispossession without compensation. The SMA mobilized their party base against them. After this tactic had resulted in a call for the resignation of the Executive Committee, Tulpanov ordered the two politicians to resign during a meeting of the executive chaired by him on the evening of 19 December.[53] In both cases, Soviet "assistance" had strengthened the position of the pro-reform forces at the expense of democratic legitimacy.

Problematic too was the fact that the anti-fascist reorganization soon overstepped the boundaries of the "completion of the bourgeois revolution". Using the argument that the time had not yet come for the transition to socialism, the KPD and SMA explicitly opposed the demands made by many workers for the confiscation of their firms. Then, on 30 October, the SMA issued a confiscation order against "Nazi activists and war profiteers" which was so broadly written that it could be used numerous times in dispossessing employers who were hardly tainted by their past or were even completely untainted. By the war's end, moreover, many owners and directors of firms had fled to the West in anticipation of Soviet sanctions, their firms thus passing into public hands. When that fact was added to the effects of the loosely-written confiscation order, a powerful impulse toward nationalization arose embracing nearly all large enterprises and increasing the state's share of industrial production in the Soviet Zone to 40 per cent by the beginning of 1948.[54] Even though the initiators of this process by no means intended to lay the foundation for a socialist system of property – although this was claimed by Western observers and later GDR propagandists alike – it did lead to a transformation which was difficult to harmonize with sought-after unity. Those responsible did insist further that "all measures which we are presently carrying out for building up democracy and for the democratization of the economy must be so constituted that they can be realized in all parts of Germany", as Ulbricht stated in July 1946.[55] They had, however, lost the standard of measure by which to safeguard this principle.

In time, the anti-fascist slogan acquired at least a subliminal touch of anti-capitalism both in public phraseology and in many participants' minds. This resulted from the fact that Social Democrats and Communists frequently shared the leading positions in carrying out such measures and had to struggle against incessant resistance from bourgeois circles. The equating of anti-fascist and anti-capitalist was strengthened by the activation of class-struggle thought, which of necessity went along with the unification campaign and led to the SED programme's curious embracing of a nationalist and class-struggle formulation. Lastly, the sanctioning of expropriations through referenda led in the same direction: ordered by Stalin, beginning in February 1946, so as to raise the anti-fascist consciousness of the population,[56] they were in turn propagated mainly by the SED and thus appeared in fact as first and foremost an affair of the working class.

The drifting apart of the Occupation Zones resulting from these developments was accelerated because Soviet diplomacy did little to overcome France's efforts to block the establishment of a political organization reaching across zonal boundaries. Certainly, Marshal Zhukov and his deputy Vassilii D. Sokolovskii complained repeatedly in the Allied Control Council about the French blockade policy and issued increasingly indignant reminders on the realization of the Potsdam decisions as to Central Administrations and economic unity. At the end of March 1946, after the French representatives in the Control Council had also rejected the possibility of the parties' uniting to form German-wide organizations, Sokolovskii even spoke of the Soviet Union's "growing embitterment" over French resistance and darkly hinted at "unpleasant consequences" for the near future during a private conversation with his colleague Brian Robertson.[57] In general, the files of the Control Council also confirm the impressions of Lucius D. Clay, deputy American military governor of Berlin. In early April 1946, he told the State Department: "The Soviet representatives in Germany could not be accused of violating the Potsdam Agreement." Beyond this, they evinced "a sincere . . . desire to be friendly with us and also a certain respect for the US".[58]

Unnerved by French vetoes of almost all planning work in the Control Council, Clay suggested to his British and Soviet colleagues in the middle of October 1945 that common administrations be founded without France. He received only stalling answers at first. When he insisted on getting a definite answer during a session of the Coordinating Committee, Sokolovskii rejected such trizonal mergers by making reference to the rules agreed upon at Potsdam for all four zones.[59] This rejection betrayed first of all a lack of tactical skill characteristic of Soviet diplomacy, which was hampered by inexperience and an inflexible, hierarchical decision-making structure. It is also possible that a miscalculation was at the root of the Soviet rejection: on 22 October, the Soviet Komandantura informed the KPD leaders that suggestions were immediately to be prepared for filling posts in the "nationwide administration[s] for industry, finance, transport, communications, [and] foreign trade".[60] This implies that they were at this time expecting that the French veto would soon be overcome. Presumably, they were counting on a reorientation of French policy after the elections of 21 October, through which de Gaulle's position was considerably weakened and through which the Communists became the strongest party in the National Assembly. The roundabout route offered by Clay's trizonal project thus did not seem necessary. In light of perceptible British consideration for de Gaulle, it also did not seem likely to succeed.

The Soviet representatives admittedly stood by their rejection of three-zone administrations even when it became clear that neither the weakening of de Gaulle's position nor his resignation on 20 January 1946 would lead to a reorientation of French policy on Germany. No instructions were issued from Moscow for the French Communists to side with the Socialists against de Gaulle's course in order to attempt to override the veto. No proposal was developed for eliminating the veto in any way other than by temporarily excluding the French Zone. In the Administrative Committee of the Economic Directorate, the Soviet representative pleaded simply for a step-by-step transfer of competencies to a German-wide industrial administration. He did not want to commit himself to an exact date at which the zonal military governments would no longer have the right to object to the decrees of a Central Administration.[61]

This suggests that it was in the meantime no problem for the Soviets that the realization of Central Administrations would take somewhat longer. This meant that it was at least possible to prevent unwanted meddling by the Control Council in the reform project in the Soviet Zone, which even without such interference could only be carried out in the face of much resistance. Ulbricht at least indirectly indicated that such considerations were not foreign to him: in the extended Federal

Executive Committee of the Freier Deutscher Gewerksschaftsbund (FDGB), the Free German Confederation of Trade Unions, he urged that the forthcoming nationalizations be accomplished "as quickly as possible", that is, "before a German central administration can interfere in the affairs of our Zone".[62] It cannot be deduced from this, however, that the isolation of their own zone had in the meantime become the priority of Soviet policy on Germany, although such a deduction is often made in order to exonerate the French. There are grounds to assume, however, that interest in such an isolation and concentration on the reorganization process in the Soviet Zone did play a role in ensuring that there would be no Soviet initiatives to overcome the French veto.

At the end of April, Stalin then officially ordered a delay in establishing the Central Administrations. In a directive to "all important representatives in Germany and all Soviet agents within the KPD" it was stated that

> from the standpoint of the Soviet Union, it is not yet time to establish central authorities nor in general to continue with a policy of centralization in Germany. The first goal, organizing the Soviet Occupation Zone under effective Soviet control, has been more or less achieved. The moment has thus now come to reach into the Western Zones. The instrument is the united Socialist–Communist party. Some time will have to elapse before this party is organized in an orderly fashion in Greater Berlin itself, and this process will take even longer in the Western Zones. Only when the Soviet vision has been realized and the Unity Party has established itself in the Western Zones will the time have come to address once again the question of Central Administrations and of effective Soviet support for a policy of centralization in Germany.[63]

The motive for the conscious slowing down of Central Administrations can be discerned in light of the Soviet reaction to the draft of a treaty for the demilitarization of Germany presented by American Secretary of State Byrnes at the Paris meeting of the Foreign Ministers' Council which began on 25 April. To the Soviet mind, this initiative did not at all signal American readiness to participate permanently in the containment of the German threat this time around, as Byrnes had hoped it would. The draft addressed the period after the end of Allied occupation of Germany, and it proposed establishing an Allied Control Commission as the sole instrument for permanently assuring demilitarization.

These two features led the Soviets to suspect that American policy was aimed at a rapid end to the occupation regime without the realization of the guarantees agreed upon at Potsdam for preventing the re-emergence of an aggressive Germany. In a meeting with the SED leadership on 26 July, the Soviets spoke of the "possibility, that [the] period of occupation [could come] to a very rapid end" owing to "pressure from the Americans and British because of the financial burden". Pieck noted further that both "are taking the initiative on a new ordering of the state" – clearly without particularly concerning themselves with the Potsdam determinations on reorganization.[64] Nikolai Novikov, the Soviet ambassador in Washington, even interpreted the presumed abandonment of the occupation regime as part of a strategy "to prepare Germany and Japan to use those countries in a war against the USSR".[65]

Molotov then demanded in Paris that the demilitarization decisions made at Potsdam be implemented and that negotiations on measures for ensuring Germany's permanent demilitarization be conducted only thereafter.[66] In a declaration of principles at the beginning of the second round of talks on German policy, he clarified this position by stating that the Soviet Union regarded "the presence of occupation troops in Germany and the retention of occupation zones" as "absolutely necessary" until the determinations on democratization were implemented and reparations payments reliably organized. In a further declaration on 10 July, he added that a peace treaty with Germany could only be completed if a "single German government" were established, which would be

> sufficiently democratic in order to be able to extirpate all remnants of fascism in Germany and sufficiently responsible in order to be able to fulfil all its obligations towards the Allies including and more particularly those in respect of reparation deliveries to the Allies. . . . But even when a German government has been set up, it will take a number of years to check up on what this new German government represents and whether it is trustworthy.[67]

Far from rejecting the idea of a treaty or making demagogic advances to the Germans – two claims voiced repeatedly – Molotov was on the contrary issuing a reminder that the idea of a treaty must be given substance by the occupation regime.

Because the Soviet leadership could by no means be certain of winning approval for this demand, the Unity Party gained additional strategic weight for them: if the occupation troops were out of the picture, only the Unity Party remained as a relatively dependable instrument for guaranteeing the implementation of the determinations on democratization and reparations. At this juncture, it appeared all the more fatal that it had not been possible to establish the Unity Party in all four Occupation Zones at the first try. Only if the SED could attain a key political position in the Western Zones as well would German-wide structures further the implementation of the democratization programme rather than, conversely, bringing the already accomplished transformations in the Soviet Zone once again into question. After the close of the Paris meeting, it was for that reason impressed upon the SED leadership that everything now depended upon them. Pieck noted: "Perspective: SED large force, leading role, great responsibility / . . . strengthen the power of the party / must become state force." The agenda assigned to them was to win back the initiative in the struggle over the future state order in Germany. To this purpose, they were to "demand a unified German government [and] a national constitution to be established at an earlier date" and also to present "guidelines for [the] future state order [of a] democratic republic". In this way, a "corresponding government", meaning one which met Molotov's expressed standards, would in any case be available "for [the] peace conference", which sooner or later would become unavoidable.[68]

It may be the case that this tactically-determined Soviet reserve on the question of centralization made itself noticeable as early as the negotiations in the Allied Control Council over a law for parties. Taking the French into consideration, the British representative on the Coordinating Committee presented a compromise formulation in late April 1946 which on the subject of permitting of parties retained only the responsibility of the zone commander. The Soviet representative, Michail J. Dratvin, initially expressed approval of this formulation, and thus an agreement on a party law seemed within reach. The Soviet representative in the Legal Directorate immediately demanded clarification, however. Three days later, on 6 May, Dratvin asked for time to think. On 13 May, he insisted that the reference to zonal commanders be struckout. This, in turn, was unacceptable to the French representative, who for the time being wanted nothing of the merger of parties across zones. The negotiations thus came to a dead end.[69] Dratvin argued that the formulation could be interpreted in different ways and for that reason could lead to difficulties in fusing parties on the national level, a point which could not be completely denied. Fundamentally, it was the case that the whole project made no sense if it did not actually open up the possibility of party unifications across zones; that foundered repeatedly on French objections.[70]

In Paris, Molotov quite obviously practised the delaying tactic stemming from the April directive. It was not only the case that he made discussion of the American proposal for demilitarization dependent upon a review of the implementation of the Potsdam resolutions on demilitarization. He also rejected Byrnes's suggestion that deputies of the foreign ministers be set to the task of working up a proposal within six months for the peace agreement with Germany. He gave no reason initially but in the second round of negotiations made the revealing remark that one ought "to give more time to this question during the next year and to devote to German matters a special session of the Council of Foreign Ministers at a later date".[71] In the closing phases of the conference, the French Foreign Minister, Georges Bidault, finally came back to the question of Central Administrations. Having been jolted by the American offer of a zone fusion, he acceded on 12 July to the creation of "Allied Offices" at Four-Zone level as long as their authority did not extend to the Saarland. The Soviets then geared themselves for such a solution. The SED leadership was told to "sound the alarm" on the subject of the Ruhr area but "not to speak about [the] Saar".[72] At the conference table, however, Molotov initially only requested time "to study that big question".[73]

The Soviet leadership also did not make any particular haste to review the progress on demilitarization as Molotov had demanded. When a special commission of the Control Council was set up in late May for that purpose, Dratvin made no objection to its reviewing the dissolution of military organizations but refused to grant it the right to inspect the industrial facilities important for war production. In so doing, he touched off a conflict over the competencies of the commission. The fact that this considerably delayed the beginning of its work did not make him change his position at all.[74] Likewise, the Soviet representatives were now also quite openly playing for time in the planning for Central Administrations. Repeatedly, appointments for meetings were not observed, and compromise papers which had been announced failed to materialize on more than one occasion. When the American representative on the Economic Directorate pushed for adoption of the draft for a German-wide industrial administration, the Soviet representative termed its realization "premature" and made reference to the halt of reparations deliveries from the US Zone. When Clay, in the coordinating committee, nevertheless persisted in seeking an understanding on this question at least among the Americans, British, and Soviets, Dratvin's successor, Kurochkin, blocked this motion again with reference to the four powers' shared competence. As a result, Clay's efforts to forestall Washington's abandonment of the principle of Central Administrations failed.[75]

The Soviet leadership's hesitation on Central Administrations provoked de facto the pushing through of Bizonia. At the time of the Paris conference, neither Byrnes nor Bevin was convinced that the merger of the American and British Zones constituted a viable alternative to the principle of Central Administrations. At the close of the second round of negotiations, Byrnes forced upon Molotov the choice between a substantial contribution to unity in the question of Central Administrations and the formal fusion of individual zones. The American left no doubt as to his preference for the first option. Byrnes generously interpreted Bidault's acceptance of the creation of "Allied Offices" as evidence that the French had acceded to the principle of Central Administrations. Byrnes then invited his colleagues to adopt a resolution for the establishment of Central Administrations without delay.[76] By responding with a declaration of his need for clarity on the question of the Saar, Molotov spared Bidault a revelation of his actual intentions. In so doing, the Soviet Foreign Minister also let his chances of hindering the creation of Bizonia go by unused.[77]

It is possible that Molotov did not have a complete grasp of the situation at the conference. Perhaps, too, he was hindered from immediately demonstrating the necessary accommodation in the Saar question by the ponderous Soviet system of diplomacy. It is absolutely certain, however, that the strategic significance of the founding of Bizonia escaped the Soviet leadership: when the British representative on the Control Council announced his government's acceptance of the American fusion offer on 30 July, Marshal Sokolovskii contented himself with an expression of Soviet interest in Central Administrations.[78] On the Soviet side, substantial steps toward their realization, such as acceptance of the French demand for the Saar, still failed to materialize. Moscow obviously did not perceive that increasingly powerful forces in London and Washington approved of a separate organization of the three Western Zones. In the internal analyses of the situation, only the danger of the abandonment of the Potsdam reorganization programme was conjured up.[79] Also, the public propaganda busied itself solely with the deficit of democratization in the Western Zones.[80] Consequently, the Soviets underestimated the danger of a split emanating from the founding of Bizonia and unknowingly contributed decisively to the emergence of the two-state concept. After the insistence upon the Unity Party, this was the second fundamental strategic error of Soviet policy on Germany.

FORKS IN THE REPARATIONS ROAD

A third turning point in the division between East and West ensued more implicitly – from the logic of the situation and from the handicaps created by the Western powers in the question of German reparations. After the Potsdam compromise allowing substantial reparations deliveries from current German production, which revealed only too clearly the displeasure of the British and Americans, the Soviets initially continued with their dismantling. Given American pressure for a limit on German production, only the transfer of industrial facilities to the Soviet Union seemed a viable alternative. The partisans of an "economic disarmament" of Germany around Vice Premier Malenkov could consequently implement their ideas even after the decision for the democratization programme. This was the case despite the fact that reducing production capacity of course stood in latent contradiction to efforts aimed at securing the loyalty of the Germans. Influenced by such arguments from the KPD leadership, the SMA soon came out in favour of a restriction on dismantling.[81] In negotiations on the industrial plan for Germany, the Soviet representatives sought the lowest production level possible so as to receive as much dismantled hardware as possible from the Western Zones in accordance with the Potsdam settlement. Only little by little did they let themselves be won over to an annual steel-production quota of 5.8 million metric tons instead of the 4.6 million originally demanded, and to a determination on production capacity – that is, an upper limit on dismantling – of 7.5 million metric tons.[82]

Beyond that, the Soviet leadership drew from the Potsdam reparations agreements the lesson of making economic unity dependent upon Western pledges that reparations would be made from actual production and that until that time they would take goods from their own zone without concerning themselves about the effect upon the German-wide economic situation. They rejected the realization of the first-charge principle as propagated by the British and Americans, which referred to attaining an even German balance of trade before reparations were to be paid. The reasons for the rejection were that this concept made reparations payments from actual production completely subject to the will of the commericially-dominant Western powers and, moreover, because it threatened to eliminate access to resources in one's own zone as conceded at Potsdam. In light of the better food-supply situation in the Soviet Zone and the early successes of the SMA in reconstruction, it was anticipated that the Soviet reparations area would even need to subsidize the Western Zones temporarily. On the other hand, the representatives of the two Western powers insisted upon the first-charge principle, partly because they were not familiar with the distinction between products which were exportable and those which were appropriate for reparations and partly because they definitely did not want to allow any reparations from current production. Hence, negotiations on economic unity became blocked, leading to a situation in which the distinction between two separate reparations areas worked out at Potsdam increasingly took on the character of an intra-German economic boundary.[83]

Still more significant for the future development was the fact that Clay, in an attempt finally to achieve a breakthrough in the question of Central Administrations, announced on 3 May a temporary halt in shipments of dismantled facilities to the Soviets; and the British as well as the French also put a stop to their deliveries in accordance with the Potsdam agreements. These transfers had begun only shortly before, right after the signing of the industry plan on 28 March. In Moscow, the conclusion was drawn that shipments of dismantled facilities from the Western Zones were definitely not to be expected. In view of this, the Soviets decided it was better to seek a high production level, which would permit the taking of reparations from current production. It was to some extent possible to organize deliveries from production in the Soviet Zone; and in Soviet planning, these deliveries consequently took the place of hoped-for shipments of dismantled facilities from the West.

Such a reparations conception had had its advocates among the Soviet leadership for a long while: Minister of Foreign Trade Anastas Mikoyan, who regarded the practice of dismantling as economically ruinous; powerful Party Secretary Andrei Zhdanov, who did not share the scepticism of the supporters of "economic disarmament" regarding a rather long Soviet presence in Germany; and also the representatives of the SMA, who took seriously their commission to create a democratic Germany. Gosplan chief Nikolai Vosnessenskii, an old acquaintance of Zhdanov from Leningrad, had switched sides on this question in the late summer of 1945, thus significantly strengthening Mikoyan's position.[84] In January 1946, Stalin let the KPD leadership know that dismantling would cease "by the end of February".[85] In actuality, the process continued. The scope had been significantly reduced since the beginning of the year, but the threat of dismantling hung over all remaining facilities.

The opponents of "economic disarmament" made their breakthrough only after the shipments of dismantled facilities from the Western Zones had been halted. Through Zhdanov's influence, Malenkov lost his post as Central Committee Secretary;[86] and Sokolovskii publicly announced the suspension of dismantling. On 5 June, arrangements were made for the transformation of 213 confiscated German firms, representing between 20 and 30 per cent of remaining capacity and featuring a significant concentration in key sectors, into Sowjetische Aktiengesellschaften (SAGs), Soviet joint-stock companies. The Soviet Union held 51 per cent ownership of these firms, and their production was to a great extent handed over to the occupiers as reparations. Molotov completed this course change on 10 July at the Paris Foreign Ministers' Conference by advocating a rapid increase in the German production level:

> In order that the development of German peaceful industries may be of benefit to other peoples who need German coal, metal, and manufactured products, Germany should be granted the right of export and import and if this right of foreign trade is to be effectuated we should not put obstacles in the way of the increase in the output of steel, coal, and manufactured products of a peaceful nature in Germany, naturally within certain bounds and provided that an interallied control shall inevitably be established over German industry and over the Ruhr industries in particular.

Even when the production level set by the industry plan would not "by far" be met at present, "it should already now be admitted that peaceful industries in Germany must be given an opportunity to develop on a wider scale".[87]

The fact that dismantling had not provided even half of what had been estimated in the first Soviet reparations plan definitely played a role in the decision to extract reparations from actual production.[88] Likewise, it can be seen that after the founding of the SED, the possibility of a lasting influence over German affairs was no longer so pessimistically assessed as it had been a year before. To be sure, the decisive factor was the dwindling of hopes for dismantled facilities from the West, as the timing indicates. Indirectly, the reorientation of the Soviet reparations policy was thus also a consequence of the hesitation on the question of Central Administrations: because this drove Clay to halt deliveries, the reorientation became unavoidable. As the covetousness of some Soviet authorities was not to be completely suppressed, some further dismantling was conducted until the middle of 1948 despite Sokolovskii's announcement. Now, however, the emphasis lay quite unmistakably on reparations from current production and on increasing that production. From that point on, the members of the Dismantling Committee had to work under the supervision of the SMA.[89]

That the Soviet leadership fell back on the means of mixed ownership stemmed from the fear of a rapid end to the period of occupation. With the help of SAGs, they hoped to be able to secure a certain per centage of reparations deliveries even if a military presence were no longer a given and even if pressure for reparations agreements remained without result in Allied circles. Moreover, like the SED, the SAGs were intended to provide the Soviet Union a certain influence in a still-capitalist Germany. Mikoyan impressed upon the firm directors before their departure for Germany "that economics determines politics. Speaking metaphorically, you are Soviet colonists. If it should happen that our government decides to withdraw its troops from Germany, you will be left alone there to face a bitter struggle with capitalist competitors. Remember that the most important thing is the solvency of the enterprise, its profits!"[90]

The expectations of the Soviets were still directed at all of Germany. This is seen not only in the mission which was given to the SAGs but also in the intensity with which Molotov again demanded reparations deliveries amounting to ten billion dollars and addressed the issue of Four-Power control of Ruhr industry. None the less, the reorientation of reparations policy was linked to a further shift of emphasis in policy on Germany: much more strongly than at Potsdam, the Soviet Zone now gained a value of its own as a long-term source of reparations. The establishment of economic unity was thus to a much greater extent dependent upon substantial reparations pledges by the Western powers, and in the given situation, increasingly unlikely to occur. Separate organization of the Soviet Zone replaced "economic disarmament" as a second-best solution. Without commitments in the reparations question, the Soviet leadership could no longer give serious consideration to the American offer of a zone merger. This despite the fact that it was, however, fundamentally in line with their policy on Germany; and they had risked everything to hinder a separate organization of the Western Zones.

All in all, the Western refusal of reparations shipments touched off a conflict of goals between the interest in reparations payments and in a democratization of all four Occupation Zones. Because the Soviet leadership was not willing to give up its goals on reparations and was not even in a position to do so, its policy repertoire on Germany became increasingly restricted. The more unlikely became reparations from the Western Zones, the less attractive became the goal of shared control over a Four-Zone Germany. Admittedly, those responsible hardly perceived this conflict of goals and remained unaware of the implications of their decisions on reparations. On their own, they were by no means prepared to give up their maximal goals for all of Germany.

3 From Paris to London

Despite all the manipulation, political practice in the Soviet Zone remained fundamentally oriented toward a democratic, Four-Power Germany. Erich Gniffke reports that in the Central Secretariat of the newly-founded SED, "unanimity" initially existed on the issue

> that given the occupation, no situation of open class struggle requiring decisions for revolution would manifest itself in Germany for years. . . . Socialism can only be realized in a parliamentary, democratic way. The prerequisite for this can only be created by a working class which is organized and committed to the struggle in a social mass movement. The goal of the SED must therefore be to put political activity and initiative in motion. The immediate objective must be a reunited, parliamentary-democratic Germany."[1]

PLURALISTIC PRACTICE

That this programme required a fundamental revision of existing Communist policy was repeatedly made clear by Anton Ackermann in particular. "We Communists", he had declared as early as 2 March 1946, "have committed the error of simply copying the policies of the Bolsheviks under completely different conditions. In regard to overcoming dogmatism, sectarianism, and disregard for the national question, it is by no means a matter of a transitory, short-lived apparition but rather of a well-grounded inner transformation. We have become politically and ideologically more mature and have finally overcome the childhood disease of radicalism. The SED ought to overcome both the opportunistic politics of the old SPD as well as the dogmatism of the old KPD." In the Party Executive meeting of 17 July 1946, according to Gniffke, he went a decisive step further by acknowledging "the traditional democratic fundamentals of German Social Democracy as exemplary without encountering opposition from his colleagues" and reduced Marxism to one source of insight among others:

> We in Germany cannot talk of a "special German path to socialism" if we adopt and quote the sayings of Lenin and Stalin like parrots.

If need be, we must also have the courage to embrace new insights arising from the actualities of the German situation, insights which cannot be harmonized with a traditional theory ossified into a dogma – not even through quotes wrongly understood or introduced at the wrong point. We must return to original Marxism, which wanted to become no dogma, but rather only a set of instructions for action.[2]

Not only the former Social Democrats but also the majority of the Communists in the party leadership were convinced of the necessity of such a revision. "We know from Wolfgang Leonhard", reports the Social Democratic Central Committee Secretary S. F., "that he believed in this German path to socialism; and there were a few other people. Paul Merker believed in it . . ., also Wilhelm Zaisser, Franz Dahlem, Grotewohl, and others certainly believed in it." Pieck, who had taken a prominent stance in 1934 and 1935 during the carrying through of the People's Front concept in the KPD, seems to have been persuaded as well:

In my opinion and after my experiences and observations, Pieck definitely had reservations against the Russians, he certainly had them, and I am persuaded, though it has never clearly come out, but at that time I believed anyway, that he supported Anton Ackermann in his efforts to formulate and organizationally prepare for the "German path to socialism," because in this way he probably entertained hopes of getting away from the Soviets' making decisions for us and to achieve an independent position.

On this issue, Pieck and Grotewohl understood one another "splendidly", likewise Dahlem and Gniffke.[3] Ulbricht, who continually presented himself as the top appeaser of the Moscow party leadership, "was avoided by everyone".[4]

That thoughts frequently ran along similar lines at the party base can be gathered from a report in which Gniffke mentions that "letters of complaint from our [i.e., former Social Democratic] functionaries" were becoming "fewer from month to month".[5] This is partially explained by the fact that the most intensively engaged champions of Social Democratic autonomy had in the meantime been silenced and had resigned whereas those who in the end had helped bring about the party unification were now under pressure for it to succeed. Arrests and other encroachments did also affect Communists who had pragmatically concerned themselves with improving conditions where they happened to be and in the process had run afoul of the occupation forces. And the willingness to embrace the new programme, at its core no longer Leninist, was also to be found in their ranks. This was even more markedly the case among the great number of new members who had streamed into the party after unification: Among the more than 700,000 new members up to the middle of 1948 joining some 600,000 former Communists and 680,000 former Social Democrats,[6] there were probably some opportunists who saw party membership as primarily a means of social advancement under the banner of anti-fascist transformation. There can, however, be no doubt that the overwhelming majority took the party programme seriously. Not a few were genuinely enthusiastic about the goal of an anti-fascist "new Germany", to which the title of the party newspaper appealed daily.

The élan growing out of the will to a new order made itself apparent in the cultural realm as well. The SMA had cultural and educational officers familiar with German intellectual history. They saw to it that not only the Marxist classics were made accessible to a wide audience but also literary classics and the works of many authors who had gone into exile. Scholars, intellectuals, and artists of standing took advantage of the new opportunities to work. Not a few engaged themselves in the "Kulturbund zur demokratischen Erneuerung Deutschlands", the Cultural Confederation for the Democratic Renewal of Germany, with which Johannes R. Becher sought to incorporate the "creators of culture" into the anti-fascist transformation. Members of the younger generation eagerly welcomed this stimulus, as they did the possibilities which grew out of the democratization of the school system and higher education. In Berlin, Leipzig, and Dresden, intellectual and artistic circles developed whose excellence shone far and wide. Very diverse voices were heard in the debate on the origins of fascism, and highly controversial discussions over artistic and politico-cultural concepts ensued.

Pluralistic too, although at the mercy of pressure for standardization, was the workers' council movement which had developed in the "masterless" period after many employers and factory managers had fled in the summer of 1945. Guided by pragmatic survival strategies and socialistic hopes for reorganization, these councils frequently brought about dispossessions even before the passage of relevant SMA decrees or German laws. After the Allied Control Commission had passed the law on workers' councils in April 1946, these organizations compelled agreements for about 70 per cent of industrial workers and white-collar employees in the Soviet Zone. The agreements guaranteed wide-ranging rights of codetermination in the planning of firms as well as in pricing and personnel policy.[7] Under pressure from the movement, the Central Committee of the SED embraced demands for "equal codetermination for the workforce in all questions relating to the firm and to production" as well as codetermination above firm-level by industry-wide workers' council members and workforce representatives on the overseers' board. These demands, incorporated into the SED's "Socio-Political Guidelines" of 30 December 1946, had originally been part of the Social Democratic programme for "economic democracy".[8]

With reference to the mood of the people, the Social Democratic leaders of the SED were even able to ensure that the party openly opposed the Soviet occupiers on the question of Germany's eastern frontier. These demands on the part of the Social Democrats were initially rejected during negotiations over unification. The KPD had, in contrast, pushed for acceptance of the loss of the eastern territories: "Germany will lose considerable territory in the east – we must reconcile ourselves to that fact."[9] When the results of the communal elections in Saxony-Anhalt and Thuringia on 8 September 1946 proved less favourable than had been expected, the Social Democratic members of the executive could openly declare their claims for revision with an eye to future elections. On the eve of communal elections in Mecklenburg, where the border problem was especially acute owing to the large number of refugees from the east who had settled there, *Neues Deutschland* published with great fanfare a declaration by Max Fechner "that the SED will oppose any reduction of German territory". Such specificity was too much for the Communist members of the executive. After some debate, a resolution was passed in the executive meeting of 19 September ensuring that the SED would "do everything so that in questions regarding the future borders of the new Germany the voice of the German people would be heard at the peace conference".[10]

The parties actually found themselves, incidentally, in a relatively open competition over the shape of the future social order. In the re-forming of education, the CDU demanded confessional church schools and ended up completely isolated because the Liberal Democrats came out in favour of the separation of church and state at least as vehemently as did the Communists and Social Democrats. On the other hand, both middle-class parties sought to apply the brakes in the question of dispossessions. From the beginning, the CDU steered a middle course while the tendencies toward fundamental opposition in the LDPD did not find the required internal majority. The two parties' stance contributed to the return of about two thousand commercial enterprises to their owners before the referendum in Saxony.[11] It also played a role in delaying the nationalization of the mining and mineral industries in Thuringia and Saxony-Anhalt, which was put through only in 1947–8. On the other hand, strikes and protests against owners who had been reinstalled resulted at times in their removal once again.

The first elections to communal parliaments, district parliaments, and provincial parliaments in the autumn of 1946 were carried out largely in accordance with democratic principles. The SMA did, to be sure, take pains to promote "its" party discretely: The middle-class parties were discriminated against in the distribution of paper, space for assemblies, motor vehicles, and so on. Applications for registration of their local organizations were often improperly delayed. Also, a double standard was employed when investigating candidates for a possible National Socialist past. When it came to setting dates for the elections, it was carefully determined that the earliest was to be in the workers' stronghold of Saxony (communal elections 1 September) and the latest in Berlin (20 October, together with the district and provincial elections); in the capital, competition from the SPD in the Western Sectors had to be reckoned with. When Ulbricht suggested putting up representatives of "mass organizations" as candidates, he met with opposition even in the Central Committee of the SED, so that alongside the parties only the Vereinigung der gegenseitigen Bauernhilfe, the Organization for Peasants' Mutual Assistance, was in the end permitted in the elections. In Saxony, the Kulturbund and the Frauenausschuß, the Womens' Committee, were permitted as well. Strong protests by Jacob Kaiser against discrimination led to a simplification of the process for turning in election lists, both on time and late.[12] The elections themselves were held without hindrance, and their results were not falsified either.

The outcome of this test of strength – overall in the Landtag elections, the SED won 47.5 per cent, the CDU 27.4 per cent, and the LDPD 21.6 per cent – increased the already quite pronounced self-assurance in the leadership bodies of both the non-socialist parties. In light of their success, both Jacob Kaiser and Wilhelm Külz intensified their efforts to establish a nationwide organization for their parties, which would simultaneously secure them greater autonomy in the Soviet Zone as well. Unchecked by the occupying power, the LDPD leadership was able to persuade the reluctant liberal parties in the Western Zones to form the "Demokratische Partei Deutschlands" (DPD), the Democratic Party of Germany, which was constituted on 17 March 1947 in Rothenburg with Theodor Heuss and Wilhelm Külz as chairmen of equal status. Owing to much greater resistance on the part of

Konrad Adenauer, Kaiser was able to achieve only an "association" of zone and state CDU/CSU organizations. Constituted on 5 and 6 February 1947 in Königstein im Taunus, its executive nevertheless embraced the demand for a "national representation" of the Germans.[13]

The SED leadership, secretly fearing that it would be held responsible to a still greater extent for the supply bottlenecks and for the encroachments by the occupation forces,[14] now concentrated on better schooling for its members[15] and intensified propaganda for the democratic, united Germany without fundamentally correcting the party.'s course. Based on the catalogue of "basic rights of the German people" which it had presented during the election campaign, the SED issued a draft constitution of the "German Democratic Republic" on 15 November 1946. Both documents had been worked out in direct connection with the strategy meeting after the Paris foreign ministers' gathering[16] and were intended not only to define the SED as a national and democratic party but also to spark a broad discussion on a nationwide level through which the Soviet side hoped to regain the initiative. In the Party Executive, Grotewohl justified the necessity of quickly approving the draft constitution with the prospect that it could possibly serve as the "basis for discussion among the four foreign ministers".[17]

The contents of the draft constitution tied onto the Weimar Constitution, in accordance with the suggestion of Semyonov and the other SMA representatives.[18] In line with contemporary Marxist thought, however, it did away with the principle of the separation of powers. As key elements of the Soviet democratization programme, it imbued land reform, dispossession of Nazis, and a ban on monopolies, with the status of constitutional commandments.[19] It is clear that neither the SED leadership nor the SMA authorities who had collaborated on the draft gave any thought to the question of whether these provisions would hamper the constitution's chances of finding a consensus. Not being very familiar with issues of constitutional law, they relied on the power of their arguments to persuade. The relied too on the impression to be made on the Western Allies when large segments of the German public were mobilized. "A great congress in Berlin of all parties from the four zones"[20] would be the climax of the discussion inspired by the draft, according to Grotewohl in the October session of the Party Executive. When the Bloc Central Committee, in May 1947, discussed preparations for a "national representation", Grotewohl explicitly characterized the SED's draft as "a basis for discussion", and he went on to state that a counter proposal from the other parties should definitely be put up against it. "As far as we are concerned", Pieck added, one could also "take the Weimar Constitution as the basis for discussion".[21] During talks on the state constitutions in the winter of 1946–7, the CDU and LDP deputies were able to put through a whole series of fundamental constitutional provisions against the SED.

Beyond mobilization for the anti-fascist ideal, the SED and SMA also engaged themselves in promoting the economic attractiveness of their zone once the Soviet leadership had changed its stance on production policy. Grotewohl perceived that "Germany [is] . . . already divided into a Western and an Eastern part," attributing this – not completely without foundation – to the Western Allies' fear of the "growing influence . . . of our movement in the Soviet Zone". In the meeting of the Party Executive on 18 June, he voiced the expectation that "the West will become subject to political as well as economic pressure and tension stemming from us". Not least of all, the better food-supply situation in the Eastern Zone would have its effect. "Political and economic development in the Eastern Zone will one day exercise an influence on the other German states as well."[22] The SED leadership assumed that tendencies toward separation in the West lay behind the various federalistic projects as well as the Bizonia project, which they regarded as doomed to failure for economic reasons. Pieck persisted that "Two-Zonism is nonsense" during a discussion in Karlshorst on 23 December 1946: "Conditions do not allow for it to be put through."[23]

THE SECOND TRY

The Soviet authorities only gradually became aware that the drumbeat of the anti-fascist ideal alone would not suffice to banish the danger of the looming East–West division. In October 1946, they finally committed themselves once again to actively promoting economic and political unity without waiting for the SED to establish itself in the Western Zones. By announcing "wide-ranging concessions", the Soviets set bilateral negotiations with the Americans in motion on the sidelines of the Control Council. In return for reparations deliveries from current production, the Soviets offered not only to supply the Western Zones with raw materials and a balanced import–export plan based on a doubling of production quotas, but also the immediate economic unification of the four zones and the establishment of administrative authorities for all of Germany. With their help, a currency reform was to be introduced straightaway and the issue of shared usage of the available raw materials and financial resources was to be tackled. In order to save the unity of Germany, Clay was prepared to make concessions in the reparations question in connection with raising the production level. By the month's end, it was thus possible to work out the draft of a compromise agreement through which the realization of the Potsdam determinations on unity for once came within reach.[24]

At the New York meeting of the foreign ministers, taking place between early November and the middle of December with the purpose of working out peace treaties with the former allies of the Reich, Byrnes suggested gathering again for the planned special session of the council for the German question. Molotov immediately agreed. Likewise, he now accepted the suggestion that deputies of the foreign ministers be given the task of preparing for the conference. He was further amenable to the suggestion that the Control Council present the ministers with a report as to the status of the implementation of the Potsdam determinations.[25]

From December 1946 on, the Soviet leaders additionally considered allowing the SPD in their Occupation Zone once again. On the one hand, this was intended to get around Kurt Schumacher's resistance to all forms of German-wide representations. The Western powers, on the other hand, were to be convinced that the SED should be allowed as an additional party in their zones. If it were not possible to bring about a unification of the workers' parties in the Western Zones, this would at least cause a split in the Schumacher party and eliminate the worst hindrance on the road to an understanding encompassing Germany as a whole. First mentioned on 23 December at a discussion in Karlshorst,[26] this plan did not meet with enthusiasm from the SED leadership since for lack of support in all four zones it threatened to bring about the reversion of the SED into the KPD.[27] Stalin was clearly convinced that with "leftist elements in the SPD" it would be possible to create so-called "unity-front committees" and "committees against reaction in the West". Consequently, he directed the SED leaders during their first working visit to Moscow on 31 January 1947 to bring the KPD in the Western Zones into line with the SED programme ("In the West, KPD burdened by the old programme of the KPD: Fear of dictatorship – revolution"). Further, they were to set themselves for competition with the SPD in the Eastern Zone ("Whether SED has fear of SPD – it must be politically beaten").[28]

After their return from Moscow, the top comrades established a "Socialist Work Group" on 14 February. This they did despite continuing uneasiness in the Party Executive.[29] Through the work group, they arranged for the KPD state organizations to adopt the programme and statutes of the SED during a series of party conferences from early March to early June. Concurrently, at the Moscow meeting of the foreign ministers, Molotov pushed for passage of a law on parties which would allow all parties "to unite within the bounds of Germany as a whole".[30] At the beginning of April, Tulpanov disclosed to Gniffke that the task of implementing the re-admission of the SPD "could fall upon" him: "The unification of the KPD and SPD was perhaps premature, or perhaps it was wholly an error for the Soviet Occupation Zone. Errors made should be corrected."[31] After this, the Party Executive assumed that it would have to reckon with Social Democratic competition in the Soviet Zone once the Allies issued a law on parties.[32] As a precaution, there was detailed discussion with the state executive committees about what would have to happen "if the SPD . . . is allowed or a free press appears".[33] In order to prevent accusations that the parity principle was not being adequately respected, Sokolovskii even ordered that the people's education minister in Thuringia, Walter Wolf, a Communist of outstanding merit, give way to a former Social Democrat.[34]

With the re-admission of the SPD, Stalin probably also hoped to win the parties' agreement in all four zones to hold a "referendum on the establishment of the united state with democratic self-administration by the provinces and local communities". This had been propagated by the SED since 1 March 1947.[35] Grotewohl gave the introductory report at the Moscow discussions on Stalin's wish ("one wants to become more familiar with it"[36]). Grotewohl estimated that in such a referendum, "thirty to fifty million" eligible Germans would support the concept of an anti-fascist united state. Stalin expected a "still larger majority".[37] In any event, it was believed that in this way the danger of a division could be banished.

Further measures for supporting the unity project were discussed in Moscow but not finally decided upon: bringing together the "sincere patriotic elements" among the "Nazi forces" into a party of their own which would "belong to the bloc" (Stalin's idea), the release of prisoners of war from Soviet camps, as well as a temporary suspension of reparations deliveries: "If reparations hinder the advance, then they can be postponed." Grotewohl also raised the question of the German eastern territories, and Stalin replied by showing the limits of his obligingness: "To bring the eastern border [into question] means also to bring other borders [into question] – means war."[38] From then on, the SED leadership guarded against nurturing any hopes for a revision of the Potsdam decisions on borders. On 2 April 1947, Franz Dahlem declared at their behest in *Neues Deutschland* that "loss of the eastern territories" strikes "the German people hard. But life must go on."[39]

It was especially the course change on the politics of production in the spring of 1946 which allowed Stalin to continue backing the Germans in the struggle against the tendencies in Western policy which in his view were destructive. He declared to the SED leadership that the Soviet Union was in favour of Germany's rise because American monopolistic aspirations could be confronted in that way ("thus prices lower and goods better – it is advantageous for humankind"). He also declared that German revanchism must be prevented: "Seventy million Germans cannot continually live in a state of impoverishment, as beggars. . . . Subjugation and suppression nourish revanchist thoughts, i.e. another war." In contrast, the Western powers aimed to keep Germany down because they feared German competition in international markets. As he continued, "America wants the world market under its domination, wants monopolistic prices." With their federalistic proposals for a new order, the Americans were in reality working for a weakening of Germany. Conversely, it was true that "the faster unity of Germany and German government [can be achieved], the more we ease the rise".[40]

Against all warnings from Zhdanov and others "that dollar imperialism was in the process of endangering the victory over German fascism and Japanese imperialism",[41] Stalin behaved as if convinced that the correspondence of German and Soviet interests would in the end come to fruition: the Americans lived under "the illusion that alone [they] can dominate [the] world market"; "70 mill. Germans" cannot, however, "be erased from world history".[42] It was only to be conceded that the struggle for a democratic Germany would be more difficult and would require more time than had originally been hoped: "In the question of the unity of Germany, we must advance little by little. We must advance despite all opposition. Only we must not give in to the illusion that the struggle to be waged for this unity will be won quickly. It could last five, six, or even seven years."[43]

Worries about an over-hasty end to the period of occupation clearly plagued him no more. Nor, however, did he any longer count on rapid success in establishing a German government: "Given American resistance, it will be difficult for a German government to come into existence." In his view, it seemed more straightforward to set up a "German Central Administration", which, going beyond the Potsdam decisions, would be responsible "for all areas" except defence and national security: "Will be somewhat easier." The setting up of such a central administration as a step toward government was sought as the immediate operational objective.[44]

Stalin possibly expected a breakthrough on this question as early as the upcoming Moscow meeting of the Foreign Ministers' Council. At any rate, he initially deferred the creation of a German Bureau for Economic Planning for the coordination of the Central Administrations in the Soviet Zone, a move which had been discussed as early as October 1946. The zonal organ, according to SMA economic chief Koval, "itself [a] kind of government",[45] should only be established "if [a] Central Administration does not [come] into existence".[46] In an interview with Elliot Roosevelt published in *Pravda* on 23 January, Stalin not only characterized the "danger of a new war" as "not real" but also said that the deficit in Western denazification policy, which had been the target of Soviet propaganda for months, gave "no cause for serious concern".[47]

THE MOSCOW MEETING OF THE FOREIGN MINISTERS' COUNCIL

From the outset of the Moscow council gathering, which began on 10 March 1947, the Soviet leadership demonstrated great interest in a successful conclusion. The new American ambassador, Walter Bedell Smith, appreciatively noted the Soviets' efforts to enable their guests to enjoy a comfortable stay.[48] Truman's speech to Congress on 12 March, in which he called for supporting the freedom of peoples against the danger of totalitarian repression – the so-called "Truman Doctrine" – was demonstratively ignored on the Soviet side. In a carefully prepared interview with the Republican Presidential aspirant Harold Stassen, Stalin avoided addressing the accusations contained in Truman's speech. He did, though, once again characterize cooperation between the Soviet Union and the USA as possible and "desirable" despite their differing social systems. He simply insisted that each side "respect the system approved by the people".[49]

In the negotiations, Molotov single-mindedly worked for the setting up of Central Administrations. In his first important programematic speech on 17 March, he characterized these as the first step on the road to Germany's economic unity. In a discussion two days later over the different statements of principle, he insisted that Central Administrations be taken up without further delay. During discussion of constitutional concepts on 22 March, he clarified his position by stating that political unity should be secured before economic unity. At the beginning of detailed negotiations over the political structure of the future Germany, he presented the demand for setting up Central Administrations in the form of a motion on principles.[50]

The new American Secretary of State George C. Marshall and his British colleague Bevin quickly agreed to this principle.[51] On the other hand, French Foreign Minister Bidault continued to avoid committing himself on the issue of the area over which the Central Administrations would exercise authority. Further, he demanded that the administrations be headed by executive committees composed of representatives from the seventeen states and that decisions be made by majority vote. This would make for an extremely weak central authority and one in which the states of the Eastern Zone would continually risk being outvoted. When Bevin agreed to this model and also conceded the French desire for exclusion of the Saarland from the Central Administrations' area of authority; the unity which had almost been achieved retreated into the distance. Bevin had in the meantime become convinced of the necessity of not allowing any weakening of Bizonia through further concessions to Soviet desires.[52] Marshall took up the British position. Having been isolated, Molotov persisted, after some hesitation, in the appointment of state secretaries as heads of the bureaus as had been agreed upon at Potsdam. Nevertheless, he assured the others of his willingness to review the question of the Saar. Bevin, however, saw to it that the Soviets' willingness to make concessions on this point was not further tested.[53]

In that the question of Central Administrations was again deferred, a hindrance created by the Soviets themselves remained: in the conference's Coordinating Committee, which was supposed to assist the foreign ministers, Molotov's deputy Wyschinski had insisted that zone commanders should have the right to prevent the Central Administrations from applying guidelines which stood in contradiction to their own directives.[54] This demand clearly sprang from the fear of being outvoted by the Western powers and the consequent fear of possible revisions of the transformations which had already occurred in the Soviet Zone. This was difficult to harmonize with the goal of a unified administration of Germany, above all when such an administration was regarded as a preliminary step towards a government for the nation as a whole.

It cannot be claimed, however, that the Soviet representatives would have persisted in this demand if through some other means they had been guaranteed that they did not need to fear losing their say in German affairs. In regard to the constitutional law principles for the future German state, Molotov accommodated the Western powers to a remarkable extent at the Moscow conference: first, with his orientation toward the Weimar Constitution (with limitations on the institution of the presidency), he spoke out in favour of a constitutional model which largely corresponded to British conceptions and, with some deletions, could also be harmonized with American conceptions. Further, he declared himself ready to accept a still more marked decentralization if it was to be approved by the German people in a referendum, which was, however, unlikely. He also pushed for efforts finally to clarify the relationship between the Reich and the states. When it turned out that the Western Allies would entrust the working up of a constitution not to the Control Council, as he had suggested, but rather to a German consultative council, he accepted this as well. Finally, he refrained from requiring that the commitment to carry out demilitarization, denazification, and reparations decisions be explicitly incorporated into the constitution.[55] During a reception in the Kremlin on 24 March, Stalin once again explained Soviet conceptions of a constitution and expressed confidence that it would be possible to overcome the differences which still existed.[56] On this point as well, Bevin succeeded with Bidault's help in preventing any substantial discussion.

Even in the reparations question, the Soviet side made significant concessions to Western misgivings. Beyond the guarantee of a balanced import–export plan, conceded to Clay by Sokolovskii in October 1946, Molotov now offered to have reparations payments stretched out over twenty years rather than ten, consequently halving the actual burden on the German economy. Beyond that, he announced an end to unilateral extractions from current production in the Soviet Zone. By way of introduction, Molotov presented the results of Soviet calculations of the war damage inflicted upon his country, which ran to many times the amount demanded as reparations. He then proceeded to reckon goods seized from current production up to that point as initial reparations instalments. He wanted to grant the Western powers another year of separate seizures from production. Molotov incidentally assured his listeners that he was willing to deduct the value of all that was seized from production "down to the last kopek".[57]

Molotov's soliciting of support, which reminded one British conference participant of a "cooing dove",[58] did not lead to the hoped-for success. Not only did Bevin reject all seizures of goods as reparations from production as long as a deficit existed in a zone, he also demanded that the existing deficit in the British Zone be eliminated through transfer of Soviet seizures and that the Soviet Joint-Stock Companies be dissolved. After some hesitation, Marshall was in principle willing to take reparations from production into consideration, though only in place of dismantling within the bounds of the Potsdam agreements and only when an equal trade balance existed. But after President Truman in a telegram expressed his objection to this idea (it was nothing more than an idea), Marshall declared that raising the amount of reparations conceded at Potsdam was out of the question. In the American conference delegation, Clay had fought in vain for substantial accommodation of the Soviets on the reparations issue. At the beginning of April, he returned to Berlin in a spirit of resignation. His reports on the compromise he had achieved with Sokolovskii remained unanswered by Washington.[59]

On 2 April, Bevin succeeded in arranging for possible determinations on the realization of political unity to be made dependent upon a prior understanding on economic unity. This clamped down further on the danger of an understanding on the basis of a too far-reaching willingness to compromise on the part of the Soviets. The subsequent detailed negotiations on questions of political structure initially had only a theoretical character. Molotov put up no great resistance to the British package deal combining economic and political unity because for him the clarification of economic questions in view of sought-after reparations was likewise important. He thus in effect offered up the goal of political unity once again to the interest in reparations, which could still be satisfied from what was available in the Eastern Zone even if nothing more could be achieved on the issue. On the other hand, Molotov had to take as a premise that political unity without any prospect of reparations was not acceptable to the Soviet Union. He could further tell himself that an understanding on the political structure of the future German state would further the compromise still to be reached in the reparations question.

In the meantime, however, his efforts for a clarification of the political questions all came to nothing. Even while he was making up his mind on 15 April about whether to acknowledge Byrnes's draft of a demilitarization treaty explicitly as a basis for negotiation of the peace treaty,[60] he did not even succeed in achieving discussion of his supplemental demands by a special committee. At the close of the conference, the deputy foreign ministers were merely given the general task of taking up the clarification of procedural questions in the preparation of a peace treaty. Bevin prevented them from concerning themselves with economic questions as well, questions whose clarification was now the premise for the political arrangement's coming into effect.[61]

Greater flexibility and more adroit manoeuvring on Molotov's part might possibly have been able to advance the efforts on the issue of unity. In Moscow, Marshall was still obviously concerned with achieving a precise orientation; and public opinion in western Europe at the time of the conference was by an overwhelming majority still by no means ready to accept a break with the Soviet Union. A temporary deferral of Soviet reparations claims would certainly have forced Bevin to give in against his will, above all if it were to be coupled with a presentation of agreements on political questions which would appeal to the public. Bidault himself could not have escaped from accepting a Soviet offer to join Bizonia, given certain guarantees in view of the future peace treaty.

Admittedly, it appeared in the Soviet view that half a success had been achieved, whereas Bevin and Bidault regarded the outcome as a successful failure and then presented it to the public as a break, which is how it is characterized in most Western accounts. For the Soviets, the danger of a premature end to the occupation regime was finally off the agenda; and in questions of the future political order, the sides had come fairly close to one another, when one disregarded the trouble-maker France. In a closing conversation with Marshall on 15 April, Stalin once again expressed himself on this optimistically: "Differences had occurred before on other questions, and as a rule after people had exhausted themselves in dispute they then recognized the necessity of compromise."[62] It was believed internally, as Pieck reported to his Party Executive at the end of May, that there would be "a kind of transitional period until the November conference of the foreign ministers. It can be assumed that it will bring about the economic and political unity of Germany."[63]

FAST FAILURE

The situation began moving in the opposite direction very quickly, however, and without the authorities in Moscow or East Berlin really comprehending the implications of decisions. The referendum project ran into staunch resistance among the Western Allies. Making reference to the recent past, Bevin declared that he was "unwilling to expose the security of the country I represent to a referendum carried out by the Germans".[64] The "Socialist Work Group" of the KPD and

SED was permitted in neither the British nor the French Zone. When the KPD's state party conference reacted by deciding to adopt the programme and statutes of the SED, the American occupation forces also stepped in: the KPD was banned from joining the SED using the argument that this would constitute a false fusion of the KPD and SPD, a fusion which had actually not occurred in the Western Zones.[65] In accordance with a secret arrangement between Bevin and Marshall made on the sidelines of the Moscow council meeting, the British and American military governors agreed to set up an "economic council" for Bizonia. With its legislative and executive functions, this body featured the essential characteristics of a parliamentary regime for western Germany.

Attempts to mobilize the Germans' desire for unity against the by this point hardly disguised British and American orientation toward a western German state foundered quickly owing to the rigorism of Kurt Schumacher. He made the SPD's participation in a "national representation" of the German parties, as pushed by Jakob Kaiser in particular, contingent not only upon the re-admission of the SPD to the Eastern Zone but also upon de facto elimination of the bloc principle. When Bavarian Prime Minister Hans Ehard on 7 May invited all German state prime ministers to a conference in Munich, the SPD Chairman insisted the prime ministers from his party give their Eastern Zone colleagues no opportunity to express their concepts regarding policy on Germany.

The SMA leadership had initially signalled its fundamental agreement to the holding of the conference despite worries that federalistic tendencies would possibly be strengthened thereby. Sokolovskii had told the Eastern prime ministers on 10 May that "it is in any event important that you present your point of view".[66] In light of the planned muzzling of the Eastern prime ministers, however, the SMA began working to derail the conference. Ulbricht agitated in the SED Central Secretariat for a refusal of the invitation, making reference to "advice" given by "Soviet friends".[67] On 2 June, Sokolovskii declared to the prime minister of Saxony-Anhalt, Erhard Hübener, that he "would view participation in the conference at Munich as an action lying in American interest". The other four prime ministers in the Eastern Zone who belonged to the SED would "not go to Munich".[68]

With that, however, the break was still not complete. On 3 June, the majority of the SED Central Secretariat decided against Ulbricht, with Anton Ackermann, Paul Merker, and Elli Schmidt emphatically joining Gniffke and Fechner in supporting participation in the conference at Munich.[69] When this was added to Hübener's threats to resign his post as Prime Minister, the SMA at the last minute (the evening of 4 June) approved the trip of the prime ministers from its zone to Munich. The SED prime ministers simply went with instructions from the Central Secretariat which stemmed from a suggestion made by Ulbricht: "To put forward a proposal for broadening the agenda if it does not sufficiently take our standpoint on the issue of the re-establishment of German unity into account."[70]

During a preliminary meeting on the evening of 5 June, the Western prime ministers refused to include as the first point "Formation of a German Central Administration by means of an agreement between the democratic parties and trade unions." Only then did the attempt to demonstrate in this way the existence of common ground among Germans definitively fail. The Thuringian Prime Minister, Rudolf Paul, who had spoken out in the Central Secretariat in favour of participation, did succeed in convincing his colleagues they should remain in the event that they were given an opportunity to read out a declaration "corresponding to the proposal". When this too was denied them, the Prime Minister of Mecklenburg, Wilhelm Höcker, and the deputy Prime Minister of Saxony, Kurt Fischer, an intimate of Ulbricht's, left immediately. Paul, Hübener, and their Brandenburger colleague Karl Steinhoff stayed until the middle of the day on 6 June. When no movement was to be seen on the Western side, they too saw no alternative other than to leave.[71]

After the débâcle in Munich, termed "not successful" by Tulpanov in a report over the internal situation of the party on 11 July,[72] those on the Soviet side began to consider "whether federalism [were] better than division into two parts".[73] That is, whether they should save the unity of the country by becoming more accommodating to the American conception of a gradual building up of the new Germany in a process beginning at the level of the provinces. During the twelfth session of the SED Party Executive from 1 to 3 July, Max Fechner acted on this by formulating a concession which went significantly beyond the position represented by Molotov in Moscow: "We must now set everything on bringing together for a German-wide discussion at one table the representatives of the large parties, the unions, the other mass organizations, and, I would like to add, if it must be so, also the prime ministers and the presidents of the parliaments from all German provinces."[74] In the request for approval of such a meeting, which the prime ministers of the Eastern Zone sent to the Allied Control Council on 4 July, "the representatives of the large cities, as well as presidents of the parliaments and prime ministers of the provinces", with no limitations, were named as participants in the meeting.[75]

The willingness demonstrated here to give more consideration to federalistic elements could certainly not change the direction of developments. In the meantime, decisions had been made through which the problem of Germany slid into the vortex of the clash between East and West: the Americans had decided to offer an integrated rebuilding programme for Europe, announced in a speech by Marshall on 5 June; and the Soviets had made clear their refusal to participate in this "Marshall Plan" on 2 July. The newfound willingness to make concessions on the part of the SED and the Soviet leadership could make no headway against this current – their willingness was not significant enough to do so.

Stalin had clearly made heavy weather of the rejection of the Marshall Plan. Documents from the Soviet Foreign Ministry now confirm what could hitherto only be ascertained from the participation of a large delegation of Soviet experts at the British–French–Soviet preliminary conference from 25 June to 2 July in Paris: that Soviet participation in the rebuilding programme had been seriously considered and that Soviet diplomacy had been prepared in detail for the negotiations over the modalities of the plan. With time, however, negative assessments accumulated: experts pointed out "that the adoption of the plan contained the danger of the Eastern European nations' becoming separated from the Soviet Union". Others argued "that the economy of the US is on the brink of the next crisis and Soviet participation in the plan would create new consumer markets for the Americans and thus aid them in overcoming the manifestations of a crisis".[76]

The decisive factor in Stalin's decision against the Marshall Plan was certainly the behaviour of Bevin and Bidault. As the British Foreign Minister subsequently reported to his cabinet not without a bit of pride, he and his French colleague had "aimed from the outset" of the Paris Conference "on thrashing out the differences of principle between us, making that the breaking point".[77] After both Western diplomats had blown up minimal differences of opinion into fundamental ones, Molotov received a telegram from Stalin on 1 July "after the reading of which he said not a word for the rest of the day". On the following day, he rejected the Anglo-French proposals as "incompatible with the preservation of national sovereignty", and left the conference.[78]

What the refusal of the Marshall Plan meant for the ordering of the German question became clear to those in Moscow and East Berlin only gradually. At the end of July, the control officers of the SMA noted "that the preparations in the organizations [of the SED] for the Second Party Congress are going poorly. In the discussions at the members' meetings, the resolution of the party executive [which placed the bringing about of a German-wide discussion at the centre point] is still not being dealt with. Or, insofar as this is occurring, discussion does not revolve around the political problems raised by the resolution but rather continues to focus mainly on questions of food, living conditions, and so on."[79] Party meetings were poorly attended, "30 to 50 per cent, in many places even lower", and little understanding was in evidence for the party leadership's course emphasizing all of Germany, but all the more displeasure over the practices of the Soviet occupiers.[80]

In many locations, "a lack of understanding for bloc politics" ("One is forced to grant the bourgeois parties many concessions which go against the principles of our party") as well as an "anti-peasant mood" manifested themselves. "There was much talk to the effect that it now made sense to transform the Soviet Occupation Zone into a Soviet Republic, as a consequence of which a rise in the standard of living would be achieved." Among the complaints from other speakers in the discussions were "that the KPD and SPD united too early and can exercise no influence over the Western Zones". There were also calls to oppose further reparations deliveries from out of the Soviet Zone and even that the party must "declare its independence from the occupying powers". As was noted in an analysis of the district party conference of 16 and 17 August, there was "no sharp criticism of the Schumacher ideology". But above all "an atmosphere of irreconcilability with the Marshall Plan was lacking".[81]

The prospects of the Western Zones' participation in the Marshall Plan made the reparations payments from the Soviet Zone seem increasingly unbearable and beyond that, raised immense new hindrances against the realization of the SED's mission for all of Germany. This was formulated in a letter to Stalin prepared by the party leadership in the wake of the Party Executive session of 20 August:

> The promised dollar-aid has a very strong effect among the working masses and is linked to the hope of finding a way to end the everyday want suffered by the masses. On the other hand, the reaction tries everything to stir up the masses with the claim made against the Soviet Union and the Soviet occupation forces that the taking of reparations from production as well as the dismantling of facilities contribute to the continual worsening of conditions for the people.

As a consequence, the SED leaders perceived that the situation of the party was "extremely serious". They wrote that "the worst thing is that the Socialist Unity Party does not yet exist in the Western Occupation

Zones, and the Communist Party is still too weak to exercise a broad influence over the masses".[82]

The situation appeared so desperate and so lacking in prospects that they decided to send Stalin an out-and-out call for help. They also added the minutes of the most recent session of the executive, in which Anton Ackermann summarized a host of depressing reports by speaking of the "dangerous developmental tendency of deficient and dwindling confidence in the SED".[83] The SED leaders hoped in general that a course correction would take place, one which would either bring the tasks of the party into better harmony with realities or, conversely, improve the conditions for achieving the current tasks. They especially pushed for an accommodation in the economic realm – in other words, for a halt to dismantling, which was still going on despite repeated announcements from Sokolovskii. They perhaps also sought some kind of economic aid which could be put up against the promises offered by the Marshall Plan:

> We would like to have had a discussion with you on the most important questions, especially on economic questions, on supply of raw materials, improving the economic plan, and creation of a distribution plan for the civil sector. Due to the shortage of time, such a discussion cannot take place. It is therefore our request that you send us one or two comrades with whom we can discuss these questions before the party congress.[84]

Admittedly, the "advice and assistance" which the SED leaders urgently hoped for failed to appear. It has still not been documented whether they were able to send this letter at all, the text of which they discussed with Sokolovskii, Makarov, and Tulpanov.[85] By way of reply, they in any event had to listen to a longwinded lecture by Tulpanov to the effect that "the fulfilment of reparations deliveries is the most important prerequisite for the democratization of Germany" and that, incidentally, the Marshall Plan would fail on its own: "Plans such as Marshall's have often been proposed, and the fuss about the USA also occurred after the First World War. All these plans failed. They will fail this time as well." As the justification for this thoughtless prognosis, he quoted from Lenin's last words to Stalin in 1923: "They [the imperialist powers] are avaricious and deeply hate one another. They will defeat one another. We ourselves need not hurry."[86]

With such ideologically grounded optimism, displayed to Jakob Kaiser too in hopeful tones ("The louder the cries, the nearer the agreement"),[87] no course correction of Soviet policy was needed in order to over-come the current difficulties in Germany. As was clearly believed in Moscow, it was sufficient to explain the present course better; and then all the difficulties about which the German comrades were complaining would evaporate. "The policy of the Soviet Union in Germany", as Tulpanov argued *ex cathedra*,

> orients itself in general toward representing the interests of the German working class. We want no division of Germany, no weakening of Germany as an economic power in Europe. We are basically interested in an actual democratization of this country and are helping the working class carry on its struggle with reaction. . . . The English and the Americans, however, are attempting to enslave Germany, to split it, to take from it free trade on the world market, and to liquidate the German state. They support the reaction and are against the interests of Germany's working class. We are not explaining this clearly enough and persuasively enough to our comrades in the ranks of the anti-fascists. If we were to do this properly, it would certainly have an effect on the general political situation in the Zone.[88]

The leaders of the SED, closer to realities in this case and at the same time more materialistically minded, had argued against such idealistic voluntarism in their letter to Stalin by asserting that "political progress" in the Eastern Zone would not "compensate for the growing destitution of the masses".[89] It in fact could have come as no surprise to them that they advanced not an inch in their main strategic goal of breaking the resistance offered by Schumacher, their "main opponent",[90] to a German-wide discussion and to the fusion of the workers' parties in the West. The chairman of the western SPD could now go so far in his tactic of isolating the SED that he was able to exclude Paul Löbe, the former President of the Reichstag, from the foreign policy committee of the SPD. His justification was Löbe's participation in a "private" German-wide meeting of personalities "without a commission from a party" organized by the Berlin Mayor Ferdinand Friedensburg, a member of the CDU, on 9 November; two SED members, the Brandenburg Prime Minister Steinhoff and Cultural Association president Johannes R. Becher, had also participated in the meeting. Friedensburg's initiative was denounced by the SPD executive as a manoeuvre directed by the Soviets.[91]

Already in July, the SED had therefore pushed, in the bloc committee, to issue a joint declaration of the bloc inviting the western German parties to German-wide discussions. Owing to the foreseeable negative reaction of Schumacher, such a plan would amount to German-wide discussions without the participation of the SPD; at the very most it would result in a split within western German Social Democracy. The SED attempted to enlist support in the West with the assurance that their suggestions to the Control Council had been intended as a basis for discussion and were in all points negotiable. Further, every "usable suggestion" for creating a representation for all of Germany would be supported.[92] In the middle of November, Grotewohl declared that he was also prepared to participate in a "nonpartisan meeting" if the invitation were to come "from the West".[93]

Such an invitation failed to materialize, however, not least of all because on the same occasion, Grotewohl pointed out that a manifestation of the Germans' desire for unity would cause the Marshall Plan to fail. "Adhering to the demand for German unity", he declared with great openness, with a remarkable misreading of the popular mood in the Western Zones, "makes implementation of the Marshall Plan impossible."[94] Against a joint manifestation of will by the bloc parties of the Eastern Zone alone as a first step, Jakob Kaiser asserted that such a move would only make the present "image of German disunity stand out all the more clearly".[95] It was indeed the case that a positive response from the Western parties to such a manifestation was not to be expected. Rather, Kaiser's efforts to inspire a German-wide orientation within the western German CDU were threatened with another setback. Kaiser thus stuck by his negative attitude when on 19 November Tulpanov put severe pressure on him.[96]

After the route via a declaration by the bloc parties had been closed off, definitively after the session of the Bloc Central Committee on 24 November, invitations to a German-wide manifestation went out from the SED per force alone. In a hastily called extraordinary session of the Party Executive on 26 November, Grotewohl dubbed the event a "German People's Congress for Unity and a Just Peace". This initiative arose as an improvisation under pressure from the SMA, which still absolutely wanted to bring about a manifestation of German will to unity for the Foreign Ministers' Council meeting about to begin in London. Pieck, who according to Kaiser's impression "was not completely comfortable with the whole matter",[97] expressed himself to Otto Nuschke, a member of the CDU executive: "The Russians did demand it of me. They gave us the task of implementation only because we have the large apparatus."[98] He himself did not really believe in genuine success in the matter. Meanwhile, in light of the Soviet expectation and after all other possibilities had failed, no other option remained to him but to plunge into the agitation for a direct mobilization of societal forces with the courage born of desperation.

The campaign's success was nevertheless more than a modest one. At the "People's Congress" which met in the German State Opera House in Berlin on 6 and 7 December, just over a third of the 2,215 delegates did come from the Western Zones. These were, however, very predominantly from the KPD and from the KPD strongholds in the Ruhr area. The SPD was represented by only a minority and the middle-class parties of the West were virtually unrepresented.[99] Although the Eastern CDU did not officially take part, it respected the fact that members of the party did attend, be it out of concern for their position in the zone or in the hope of the enterprise's having an above-the-parties character and thereby a transzonal character. Wilhelm Külz got the LDPD to agree to official participation but paid for it with the breakup of the transzonal DPD and the withdrawal of its Berlin state organization. Under these circumstances, the British government found it easy to deny entry into the country to the eighteen-member delegation which sought to deliver the "message" of the People's Congress to the foreign ministers assembled in London. When Molotov proposed that the conference receive the delegation of the People's Congress, he was turned down with the argument that this body was not representative of political opinion in Germany.[100]

After all this, there was no longer any chance at all for agreement in London. "Almost desperate", as Marshall said to his deputy Lovett,[101] Molotov sought to bring about a resolution on the rapid establishment of a German central government. The Western foreign ministers, who in the meantime were negotiating over the terms by which the Western Zones would participate in the Marshall Plan and who had already in principle reached agreement over the French Zone's joining Bizonia, saw Molotov's action only as an attempt to impose the Soviet model on the whole of Germany. Consequently, they caused all the attempts of their Soviet colleague to fail by making reference to the agenda or to the required "comprehensive solution" to all disputes. Molotov made new concessions in the reparations question: a reparations arrangement no longer had to be a precondition for establishing economic unity, the first-charge clause had to be acknowledged. In so doing, he prevented the Western diplomats from finding a point "about which we were so right and the Russians are so wrong that a break can be clearly justified in the eyes of the world".[102] When on 15 December Marshall brought about an adjournment of the conference for an indefinite period by his demand for a comprehensive solution, Molotov was once and for all manoeuvred out of the way.

For the Soviet leadership, the conference ended, as they themselves admitted, "with a fiasco".[103] "That Germany will be torn into two zones can no longer be doubted," as Grotewohl said in the Party Executive session of 14 and 15 January 1948.[104] For representatives of the Yugoslavian and Bulgarian party leaders in February 1948, Stalin conjured up the dismal vision which threatened to emerge: "The west will adopt West Germany, and we will create our own state in East Germany."[105] His great plan from the spring of 1945, which was supposed to have prevented this very development, had obviously failed.

4 The Cominform Line

The Soviet side was not completely innocent of the catastrophic result of the London Foreign Ministers' Conference. It was not only the case that Stalin's decision against the Marshall Plan brought him into conflict with American policy on Germany, a conflict which could only be overcome with difficulty. Also, Soviet administrators reacted to the increasing difficulties in realizing their political project for Germany with the means of class struggle, means which were in fundamental opposition to that project. Instead of courageously persevering along the path of compromise – for example, by making an unmistakable offer of free elections or by publicly offering to re-admit the SPD into the Soviet Zone even without a corresponding request from Schumacher – they became set on a struggle against actual and supposed opponents of their unity project. This struggle made them seem more and more like conquerors demanding submission as the price of unity.

FIGHTING SPIRIT AND UNITY

From the summer of 1947, the SED was to demonstrate more "fighting spirit", ideological unity, and a more distinct commitment to the Soviet Union according to Tulpanov.[1] At the First Federal Conference of the Cultural Association on 21 May 1947, Johannes R. Becher had warned against "imposing the forms of government and modes of living of other peoples, be they Russian, American, English, or French, onto the German context, which is historically completely different".[2] Internally, this statement was suspected of being "bourgeois nationalism".[3] Offensive professions of belief in the democratic path – in the terms of the party officers, "denial of the historical meaning of the experiences in building socialism in the Soviet Union" or "orientation on Western democracy" or "rebirth of nationalism" – were criticized as expressions of "Schumacher ideology".[4] "In the innermost circle," Tulpanov stated, "one should soon put an end to the theory of a special German path." Markus Wolf, at the time a 25-year-old radio inspector with good connections to the "Administration for Propaganda", reported this statement to Wolfgang Leonhard and gave him confidential advice that he should "no longer say or write too much about that. The future adjustment will then be easier for you."[5]

Following this, complaints about Communist surprise moves and other negative aspects of Soviet policy, voiced in astounding scope at the party meetings in preparation for the Second Party Congress, were regarded as a product of a hostile "Schumacher agency within the party".[6] Not only were the resolutions of the painstakingly-observed district party conferences "correspondingly improved with the assistance of the information officers" so as to ensure that these manoeuvres would come to nothing;[7] there were also increased cases of arrest, defamation of character, and intimidation against critical Social Democrats and independent Communists. "In a whole series of cases, leading functionaries from the former ranks of Social Democracy" lost the elections to the district executives, in so far as these were conducted as secret elections.[8] In reviewing the list of delegates to the Second Party Congress, meeting from 20 to 24 September 1947 in Berlin, Gniffke despondently noted that "many names of former Social Democrats [are] no longer there".[9]

Demands for more fighting strength and unity showed other results as well. The SED leaders now sought to incorporate the "mass organizations" into the party bloc and identified their engagement for a democratic Germany increasingly with a struggle for "progress" and against "reaction". In this struggle, the unified workers' party naturally stood at the vanguard of progress whereas its opponents by definition harboured reactionary intentions. The boundary between the democratic agenda at hand and the socialistic project of the future was thereby blurred. The beginnings of the old hegemonic claim of the party of class conflict manifested themselves again behind the key role which the SED was supposed to play in the realization of unity. In the official "basis for discussion in preparation for the Second Party Congress", the "unified working class" was aggressively termed "the decisive power centre" of the "anti-fascist democratic bloc". Further, it was announced that a "consequence" of bloc politics "will be that the progressive elements within the bourgeois parties will be strengthened and the reactionary wing will be driven back".[10]

The international situation too was viewed by the SED leaders ever more exclusively under the rubric of a world divided in two. At the Party Congress, Grotewohl stood out favourably against Jakob Kaiser's programme of a German "bridge" between East and West by arguing that the Soviet Union stood "on the side of all who defend their freedom and independence from international monopolistic capital". He thereupon emphasized, continuing in a line of argument pursued since January 1947,[11] what the Soviet Occupation Zone and the Eastern

European nations had in common as well as the significance of the Soviet Union for the transformations which were occurring in both areas: "The strength of the new democratic order which has arisen in Eastern and South-eastern Europe rests upon the fact that it enjoys the support of the Soviet Union."[12] In the resolution of the Party Congress on the political situation, the "fundamental difference" between anti-fascist, democratic order in the Soviet Union and the old social relations in the West was emphasized accordingly.[13]

Wilhelm Pieck even adopted internally, at the Party Executive meeting of 16 and 17 October 1947, the pessimistic interpretation of Western policy which was meanwhile making the rounds in Moscow:

> Developments in the three Western Occupation Zones hold great dangers for the peace and are suitable to encourage the efforts which increasingly openly aim to organize a new war. These efforts are directed against the Soviet Union and against those measures which the Soviet occupation forces have employed in Germany in order to implement the Potsdam decisions. Naturally, these efforts are also intended to reverse those measures which the democratic organs of the German people in the Soviet Occupation Zone have taken to deprive the reaction of power as well to allow democracy and the democratic building up of the economy to unfold.

Almost imploringly, he added that "the situation is especially serious for Germany because a new war would be waged mainly on its soil and would destroy the rest of what Hitler's war has left intact."[14]

After that, it was only consistent that Jakob Kaiser came into conflict with the SED leadership as well as the Soviet occupation forces given that he supported the Marshall Plan, strictly rejected the SED claim to leadership of the bloc, and at the CDU party conference in early September 1947 also came out demonstratively in favour of a revision of the eastern border. That the SMA leadership this time once again employed the method of intimidation was consistent with the siege mentality which had in the meantime developed. At a session of the CDU executive on 2 December, Kaiser succeeded in ensuring that the party would not officially participate in the People's Congress; and he was then asked twice to resign the party chairmanship because he had lost the confidence of the occupying power. When he refused, Tulpanov explained to the state chairmen of the CDU, who had been summoned to him, that they would do well to part company with Kaiser. Without being convinced of the necessity of the party's participating in the People's Congress movement, the chairmen gave in to the pressure anyway. Thus, in effect, Kaiser lost his position. On the next day, the SMA withdrew the licence of Wilhelm Gries, a party supporter of Kaiser's, as editor-in-chief of the party newspaper *Neue Zeit*. The People's Congress participants Nuschke and Dertinger were informed that until further notice, the state chairmen and the third and fourth vice-chairmen should take over direction of the party.[15]

Contrary to appearances, all this signified no conscious abandonment of the goal of completing the bourgeois revolution together with the Western occupying powers. In his criticism of the lack of ideological unity in the SED, Tulpanov explicitly addressed the "complete" lack of any engagement with the "earlier errors in the policy of the KPD". Among these errors in the Weimar period, he continued, were the "undervaluing of democratic parliamentarianism at a time when [the] revolutionary situation [was] over" as well as "mechanical enthusiasm for old revolutionary solutions".[16] In a conversation with Jakob Kaiser during the second half of August 1947, he declared, with the German-wide perspective in mind, "We know that the CDU is the strongest party and will probably also have a very strong influence in a future German government, stronger than that of the SED. We really want to work with the CDU, not merely play around."[17] With the LDPD chairman Wilhelm Külz, as late as the end of November 1947, Tulpanov discussed the question of participation in a government for all of Germany. "He repeated several times", Külz noted in his diary, "that he believes that I am also thoroughly acceptable to the other occupying powers."[18] Again and again, Semyonov insisted to Grotewohl that there must be a German-wide representation: "Firstly, in order to counter the planned intertwining of two of the Western Zones, and secondly, in order to establish economic unity as a preliminary step toward a government for all of Germany."[19]

In accordance with this, the SED did not participate in the founding of the Cominform. Having been entrusted with securing German unity, the party was in Soviet eyes not Communist and thus had nothing to do with the conference on coordinating the activities of the Communist parties, which met from 22 to 27 September in the Silesian town of Szklarska Poreba (Schreiberhau). The leaders of the SED did not know that this conference had taken place. When on 5 October the founding of the "Information Bureau of the Communist Workers' Parties" was declared, they were completely surprised: "No indication," according to Gniffke, "no hint had prepared us for this event."[20] Confronted by journalists with the Cominform agenda of working out a "joint-action programme against the main forces of the imperial camp",[21] the leadership issued a declaration prepared by Ackermann. In the vaguest of terms, it assured the public that "up to now, the SED has not been engaged in the various efforts to found new international organizations. It will, however, give every development which serves the strengthening of the peace its approval and cooperation."[22]

The increasing friend–foe mindset, however, hindered the Soviet administrators, and the SED leaders who let themselves be influenced by them, from recognizing in its full scope the necessity of compromising with the West and at the same time gave rise to exaggerated perceptions of threats. This led them once again to employ repressive measures against democratic politicians who did not willingly bow to Soviet conceptions of the realization of the "democratic" task. At the same time, it tempted them to make cheap appeals to imaginary "masses" below the democratically legitimated representatives. With both of these actions, they drove developments within the Eastern Zone in a direction which became ever more difficult to harmonize with the sought-after democratic ideal. Simultaneously, they also undermined to an ever greater extent the credibility of their German-wide programme.

Because they did not know and moreover hardly could know what they were doing, they could also perceive the resistance offered by the democratic forces against their supposed hegemonic claims as nothing other than an attack on the democratic order itself. Consequently, the compulsion for a return to repression and agitation was felt ever more strongly, and the praxis stemming from it aggravated the democrats' fear still further. At the same time, the influence grew of those who – consciously or not – were actually out after hegemony. In this way, a vicious circle arose out of which there would be no very quick exit.

Gniffke, who immediately recognized the strategic meaning of Jakob Kaiser's having been booted out, sought in the last moment to save what still could be saved. "It's to be prevented," he advised Grotewohl in a one-to-one conversation on the fourth Sunday in Advent, "that either Nuschke or Steidle [the two main advocates of CDU participation in the People's Congress] become CDU chairman. The CDU chairman should only be a personality who will be acknowledged as a discussion partner in western Germany and despite some differences with the western German politicians would remain in dialogue with them." This was all the more important, as he argued to Ernst Lemmer on 26 December, because the SED with its "overemphasized, one-sided orientation toward the East" had already lost its chance to negotiate as a credible advocate of German unity with the politicians of the Western

Zones. Accordingly, he attempted to convince Lemmer that he should concern himself with the succession to Kaiser. He wrung a commitment from Grotewohl to stand up for such a solution to the leadership crisis in the Eastern CDU when dealing with the occupying power.[23] Meanwhile, it was soon to be seen that the advocates of a "comfortable" solution with Otto Nuschke as new CDU chairman were quicker in solving the problem.

A NEW COURSE?

The strengthening of class-conflict attitudes in East Berlin went along with an increasingly pessimistic assessment of the international situation in Moscow. As early as his election speech of 6 February 1946, Molotov had warned of imperialists in the capitalist nations who were speaking of a "third world war". After his frustrating experiences with the Western powers at the Paris meeting of the foreign ministers in the spring and summer of 1946, he ordered a specialist report from the Soviet Ambassador to the US, Nikolai Novikov. Completed on 27 September 1946 after having been discussed with Molotov, it insinuated that the USA was "striving for world domination" and described the unleashing of a war against the Soviet Union as the logical conclusion of this policy. The report further asserted that the US had given up on democratizing Germany and was striving to penetrate the Eastern European nations. The Americans were putting pressure on the Soviet Union and sought to secure a high level of armaments by provoking a war psychosis. "All of these measures for maintaining a high military potential are not goals in themselves. They are only intended to prepare the conditions for winning world supremacy in a new war, the date for which, to be sure, cannot be determined now by anyone, but which is contemplated by the most bellicose circles of American imperialism."[24]

It appears that this interpretation of the world situation was not uncontested within the various levels of the Moscow leadership, finding resonance only gradually. In contrast to Molotov as well as Malenkov, Zhdanov still spoke in his February election address explicitly of the beginnings of a "period of peaceful development" and in accordance with this, came out in favour of the expansion of the production of consumer goods.[25] On 6 November 1946, in his main address on the 29th anniversary of the October Revolution, which he was allowed to deliver in the presence of Stalin, Zhdanov pointed to the atomic danger and the war threats made by imperialistic politicians.[26] At Stalin's reception of the SED delegation in late January 1947, he warned that "dollar-imperialism is in the process of endangering the victory over German fascism and Japanese imperialism".[27]

In May 1947, Evgenii Varga came under fire. In three joint sessions of the Institute for Economy and the Political-Economy Department of the Moscow State University, dogmatic Leninist academics criticized his book on the *Changes in the Capitalist Economy in the Wake of the Second World War* for attributing to the Western governments planning capacities largely independent of monopolistic capital. This equalled the assumption of, as it were, a "state-capitalistic" and thus non-revolutionary transition of the previously capitalist nations to socialism. In the debates and in the subsequent public exchange of blows, Varga was able to acquit himself quite well.[28] In a contribution to the thirtieth anniversary of the October Revolution in the autumn of 1947, he even went over to the offensive by characterizing the elements of nationalization and centralized planning in the Western states as indications of "other paths" to socialism.[29]

Initially, Stalin wanted to give no credence to the warnings of a breakthrough of imperialistic tendencies among his main allies. In no fewer than four detailed interviews with Western conversation partners from September 1946 to April 1947, he emphasized in direct contradiction to Novikov's analyses that there was no danger of war and that the extension of cooperation with the Western powers was not only desirable but also possible.[30] In conversations with Bevin and Marshall on the sidelines of the Moscow foreign ministers' meeting, Stalin spoke with similar optimism in regard to the future of the anti-Hitler coalition. At the meetings with the SED leadership in late January 1947, he radiated a confidence almost unshakeable in its core.[31]

At the same time, he quite obviously was seeking arguments with which the Cassandra calls of his diplomatic apparatus could be disproved. At the visit of the SED delegation in January 1947, Grotewohl had first of all to present a thorough explanation of the situation in Germany, then he was questioned for "positive" answers. After Stalin had "listened attentively" for a long time and then had "paced back and forth for a while", he ended the session with an assessment drawing together the "difficulties" addressed by Zhdanov and others into a confident overall perspective.[32] When Harold Stassen sought him out for an interview in early April, Stalin asked insistently if the US were in a position to regulate its economy and thus avoid a crisis of overproduction, as Varga had asserted: "What about the businessmen? Will they be prepared to be regulated and restrained?" When Stassen answered that it would depend upon whether the government would act intelligently and quickly, Stalin agreed with him unconditionally: "That is true."[33]

First concerns that East–West cooperation had indeed after all been brought into question seem to have come to Stalin after the exclusion of the Communist ministers from the French government in early May 1947. *Pravda*, at any rate, published the Stassen interview on 8 May only in paraphrased form, which was not its custom. At the same time, the Soviet organ took issue with the English-language version published by Stassen four days earlier in the *New York Times*, claiming that it contained a series of "capricious alterations and imprecisions". An English-language programme from Radio Moscow insisted that Stalin had spoken not of "regulation" of the American economy but rather of "control".[34] Given that Varga exactly a day before had had to lay himself open to "academic" criticism of his book for the first time, it may well be that in the same context a distancing from his theses was beginning. In a Soviet government decree of 26 May abolishing the death penalty, the Soviet leadership once again officially assured "that the cause of peace can be regarded as secure for a long time".[35] After this, public evaluations of the world situation were not to be heard for several months.

An official assessment of the situation was first made again in late September at the conference for the founding of the Cominform. Presented to a small circle of Communist leaders under conspiratorial circumstances, the assessment was made public after the conference only little by little and in edited form. Not only did Zhdanov, as leader of the Soviet delegation, give a report in Szklarska Poreba on the international situation but also, within the framework of a political overview, Malenkov did so as well, Zhdanov's rival in the power struggle to succeed Stalin. Owing to the later publication of the proceedings, this fact was always overlooked. Both expositions were completely identical in form and matched each other in content as well. Many passages correspond word for word. It was only that Zhdanov presented the analyses and the conclusions in much greater detail.[36] A comparison can only lead to the conclusion that both versions derived from a common draft, which had been approved by Stalin, and that they consequently reflect authentically what the General Secretary of the CPSU, who at the time of the conference was taking a cure in the Crimea, sought to communicate after the discussion over the Marshall Plan.

This conclusion is supported by documents in Soviet archives which show that Zhdanov had his report approved by Stalin beforehand, and during the conference asked for confirmation of the planned course of events.[37] It is also supported by information from the Polish party functionary Ostap Dluski, who reported from Belgrade that Stalin had concerned himself personally with editing the first issue of the Cominform newspaper *For Lasting Peace, for People's Democracy*, which contained the text of Zhdanov's report.[38] According to a processing note in the Archive of the Polish Workers' Party, the text which was publicly attributed to Malenkov had in actuality been delivered by Zhdanov.[39] This is unlikely because the report made from memory by the Italian conference participant Eugenio Reale features the same ordering of the texts as that which was the basis of successive publications.[40] That the texts at least reflect the personal views of the presenters is also evident, however.

What is above all remarkable about the situation analysis which Stalin had the rivals present is that even at that point it did not embrace the pessimistic warnings of the Molotov apparatus in their full scope. It certainly did concede that the imperialistic forces in the US had clearly succeeded in taking the helm: "With the prerequisite of eliminating the main competitors of the US, Germany and Japan, along with the weakening of England and France," according to Malenkov, "the US went over to a new, openly expansionistic policy which aims at the establishment of world domination." The "ruling clique of American imperialists" has "gone down the path of open expansion, the path of subjugating the weakened capitalistic nations of Europe, of subjugating the colonial and dependent lands, the path to preparation of new war plans against the USSR and the lands of the new democracy under the banner of the struggle against the 'Communist threat'". The move away from the commitments of the Potsdam agreement, the search for "new allies among the classes hostile to democracy in Germany and Japan, anti-democratic Turkey, and monarchic–fascistic Greece" as well as the support of "anti-democratic, anti-state elements" in the "genuinely democratic states" all play a central role in the text's argumentation.[41] Clearly, they were proof enough for Stalin to regard this interpretation of the Truman Doctrine and the Marshall Plan as accurate.

According to the Zhdanov text, Stalin was especially concerned that "the majority of the leaders of the Socialist Parties are acting as agents of imperialist circles of the USA".[42] In all this, it is obvious that he had not reckoned with the situation in Germany, where despite all expectations Schumacher was able to strengthen his position more and more, or with that in Great Britain, whose Labourite foreign minister very actively participated in the consolidation of the Western camp, or with that in France, whose government under the leadership of the Socialist Ramadier had parted company with the Communists and supported the Marshall Plan. The prominent place accorded the "rightwing-oriented Socialists" in Zhdanov's description of the situation and then also in the "declaration" issued by the conference at Szklarska Poreba[43] suggest once again that it was probably the exclusion of the Communists from the French government in early May 1947 that first gave Stalin the impetus to rethink his heretofore positive assessment of the situation.

Varga, who had for a long while supported hopes of an evolution of the Western states in the opposite direction, toward socialism, lost some of his influence at exactly this point, which was probably not coincidental. After an article of 15 September in *Bolshevik* had for the first time reported the attacks on his book, his institute was merged with the Institute for World Economy in early October; and Gosplan was made subordinate to Nikolai Vosnessenskii. The journal of the institute was replaced with a new organ. Vosnessenskii's book on the war economy of the Soviet Union appeared in December. In it, he dismissed Varga's ideas on the growing importance of the state in the capitalist economies as "sheer nonsense". Whereas the Soviet press praised this new work as an authoritative publication, Varga was now openly accused of having represented "clearly non-Marxist ideas".[44]

After he had denounced the supposed US plans for world domination, Malenkov, by way of qualification, spoke immediately of the "danger of this reorientation which is now coming from the side of some former wartime allies of the USSR".[45] Just so, he spoke as if it were still by no means certain if this reorientation would actually occur. And then, like Zhdanov, he emphasized "that between the imperialists' desire to unleash a new war and the possibility of organizing such a war, there is a very big gap". As he continued, "The peoples of the world do not want war. Those forces that stand up for peace are so considerable, so large, that if these forces are steadfast and firm in defence of peace, if they show stamina and firmness, the plans of the aggressors will fail utterly."[46]

Stalin thus held to the belief that no cause for panic existed. Still more: he criticized the defeatism he detected in the warnings of the Molotov apparatus: "The main danger for the working class today lies in underestimating its own strength and overestimating that of the enemy," according to Zhdanov's formulation, which was also quickly adopted in the first published text of the conference, the "declaration" of 5 October.[47] This is all the more remarkable because a new document from the embassy in Washington reached the Moscow centrale at this time; the text criticized Novikov for having placed the accent of his analysis of American politics too strongly on mere intimidation of the Soviet Union. According to this new warning, whose author has still not been identified, the USA was in actuality transforming western Germany and Japan "into a staging ground for military aggression against the USSR" and was preparing such a war immediately.[48] It is very clear that Stalin remained far behind this intensified interpretation. That he consciously wanted to steer against alarmism is perhaps one reason that he let the main texts of the Cominform conference reach the public only little by little: the Zhdanov report appeared on 22 October, the Malenkov text on 9 December. In an interview with the leftist Labour deputy Konni Zilliacus on 14 October, he challenged the belief that the Cominform meeting signified a change in Soviet policy and promoted once again an improvement in the political and economic relations between the Soviet Union and "all nations, beginning with Great Britain and the USA".[49]

Stalin's continuing confidence (or was it only a last desperate hope, which he presented with composure so as not to demoralize his troops?) rested above all, according to the Zhdanov text, on the conviction that the "peoples of Europe" would in the end not be pleased with "exploitation by American capital": "If in its time the plan to 'Dawesise' Europe was doomed to failure when the forces of resistance to the Dawes Plan were so much weaker than now, today in postwar Europe, there are fully sufficient forces not to mention the Soviet Union, which given the will and resolution can disrupt this slave plan." The Europeans' resistance had to receive an additional impetus from the fact that "the prospect of restoring German imperialism cannot tempt either Britain or France". Moreover, when one added to this the fact that the USA, as Zhdanov further set out, "itself is threatened with an economic crisis" in the event that the Europeans did not buy enough of its goods, one could indeed expect that American imperialism soon would be "forced to retreat".[50]

The prerequisite for this, however, was that "the European countries show themselves sufficiently steadfast and prepared to resist America's enslaving conditions for credit".[51] Stalin therefore once again wanted intensified political education. Because the Social Democratic leaders were overwhelmingly acting "as loyal accomplices of the imperialists",[52] the Communists were to put themselves at the forefront of resistance. In the process, they were not to limit themselves to the use of parliamentary means: "Strikes, demonstrations, political strike, mass mobilization", noted the Yugoslavian delegates in Szklarska Poreba regarding Zhdanov's elucidation of the means to be implemented.[53] The goal, however, remained a defensive one: "To fight against the threat of new wars and imperialist expansion, to consolidate democracy, and to uproot what remains of fascism."[54]

The programme of the conference founding the Cominform was thus aimed primarily at western Europe. Unlike the way it was gradually perceived in the West, however, it was no programme for unleashing revolutionary putsches, but rather one for mobilizing all "democratic and patriotic forces"[55] far beyond the ranks of the workers' movement. Stalin obviously was counting on this mobilization being possible on a short-term basis: "If only two million people bellow," as Zhdanov said according to notes made by the Yugoslavian delegation, "they [the French] would chase out the Americans and the English." Thereafter, one would once again be able to proceed as before: "Later, we will see if any coalitions are possible."[56]

The presumed breakthrough of the imperialistic forces in the US led Stalin to make no fundamentally new assessments of the situation or any new strategy. As Zhdanov and Malenkov assessed the situation in agreement with one another, "Soviet foreign policy proceeds from the fact of the coexistence, over a lengthy period, of two systems – capitalism and socialism. From this it follows that cooperation between the USSR and the countries of other systems is possible provided that the principle of reciprocity and fulfilment of obligations undertaken is observed."[57] Malenkov presented this passage in the past tense and then immediately added: "The USSR insists upon this policy."[58] In order not to let any misunderstandings arise, however, these sentences were likewise put into the present tense for the publication of the text.

The political education and mobilization of the European peoples were supposed to put the Soviets in a position to hold "to the course of maintaining loyal good-neighbourly relations with all states which show a desire for cooperation".[59] In the negotiations at Szklarska Poreba, there was still no talk of socialism, in regard neither to western Europe nor to the nations of the "new democracy", as the eastern European regimes were termed following Varga's phraseology. Zhdanov justified the Soviet Union's engagement on behalf of a "lasting democratic peace" exclusively in terms of domestic policy: it was an essential "condition" for the "construction of Communist society" in the Soviet Union itself.[60]

Similarly, there was no discussion at Szklarska Poreba of a division of the European continent into eastern and western halves. The "two camps" of which Zhdanov spoke at the beginning ("On the one hand the imperialist and antidemocratic camp and, on the other, the anti-imperialist and democratic camp") were not meant geographically, as it was immediately interpreted under the rubric of bloc thinking. Rather, it was meant politically as the term for "the two tendencies in present-day international politics", as it was more clearly formulated by Malenkov.[61] If the democratic and patriotic forces could succeed thanks to mobilization by the Communists, then the formation of blocs in Europe could be avoided.

The absurdity of the imagined threats, and the aggressiveness with which American "imperialism" and its Social Democratic "accomplices" were associated with fascism of the Hitler variety at the conference in Szklarska Poreba, had as a consequence the fact that the West did not at all perceive the cooperative fundamental line of the Cominform programme. Since Moscow was, however, demonstrably convinced of the danger of imperialistic expansion on the part of the US, there is no reason not to take Zhdanov and Malenkov at their word in regard to their explanations over the future course of the Communist movement. This is all the more the case given that it is by no means certain that the analyses and the directives presented by the two candidates for Stalin's succession to a circle of hand-picked Communist Party leaders were from the outset intended for publication. Moreover, the other statements of the Soviet delegation, as related by various participants, in no regard stray from the line of the published texts.

BERLIN AS A MEANS OF PRESSURE

The still principally optimistic assessment of the situation which lay at the base of the Cominform programme included the point that there need not be any new goals for Germany. "As is well known, the USSR stands for the creation of a united, peace-loving, demilitarized, democratic Germany," Zhdanov explained in Szklarska Poreba.[62] The Soviets would not need to go beyond this determination of goals, assuming that the mobilization of the democratic and patriotic forces in western Europe and also in the western part of Germany would soon exorcise the spectre of the Marshall Plan.

Since no progress was being achieved at the level of the Allies, it was not possible to avoid taking steps for an at least temporarily separate organization of the Soviet Occupation Zone. After Bizonia had received a parliament with the establishment of an "Economic Council"

in late May 1947 and its administration had been concentrated in Frankfurt, the SMA carried out the creation of the "Deutsche Wirtschafts-
kommission" (DWK), the German Economic Commission, on 14 June
1947. This was intended to coordinate Eastern-Zone Central Administrations, a step which had up to this time been deferred, and to strengthen
their position over against the state governments. In the middle of
September, Tulpanov explained to the LDPD chairman Külz that he
"had to keep himself available in case an independent Eastern state
became necessary".[63] He hinted rather bluntly about the position of
head of state. In late November, Tulpanov scouted out once again the
readiness of the LDPD leader to take over responsibility for the government. According to the impression received by Külz, it was in this
context a matter both of preparations for a "government for all of
Germany" and also "in the other case" about the organization of an
"East-Zone government".[64]

After the fiasco of the London foreign ministers' meeting and the
Frankfurt resolutions of the Western military governors of 7 January
1948, by which the organs of Bizonia were expanded into governmental institutions, so to speak, Stalin fell into resignation for a certain
period. What the SED leaders had warned of since May 1947 in the
event of a failure of the London Conference now became all too clear:
"The formation of power blocs," according to Ackermann, "of a bloc
in the West and of another in the East" – with the consequence that
the Elbe became the "boundary between two Germanies".[65] In talks
conducted between Stalin and Communists from Bulgaria and Yugoslavia in February 1948, the German question was treated exclusively
from this perspective.[66]

"New resolutions on the basis of the new situation", as Pieck had
announced in May 1947, in the event of a failure of the next foreign
ministers' meeting,[67] failed to materialize, however. Without changing
anything in regard to formulation or objectives for all of Germany, the
standing committee of the People's Congress movement decided on 15
January 1948 at the request of the SED to call a second "German
People's Congress" to Berlin. The meeting was set for 17 and 18 March
1948, symbolically on the one hundredth anniversary of the March
Revolution of 1848. With the announcement of the formation of a
permanent "German Peoples' Council" through this second congress
on 21 February, the campaign to mobilize all Germans was even further intensified. When on 7 February Külz sought support from
Sokolovskii against critics within his party, it was given to him in
such a way that holding firm to the goal of the "unity of Germany on

a democratic basis" (according to a resolution of the SED executive on 15 January)[68] was made to stand out more clearly: "He professed his support for a professional civil service and for the free initiative of entrepreneurs, declared himself ready to receive a delegation from the middle class of trade and industry, and assured us he would issue a decree which would halt sequestering, and another decree which would foresee the conclusion of the denazification comedy by the middle of June of this year." For Külz, these were "concessions . . . in a scope which I never would have held to be possible".[69] Both decrees did indeed appear soon thereafter.

Above all however, Stalin took courage when the London discussions, begun on 23 February among the three Western occupying powers and the Benelux nations over the form of the founding of the western German state, were surprisingly interrupted on 6 March. The communiqué released by the six nations at the close of that round of negotiations let it clearly be known that the French government was not prepared to concede more than a confederation of western German states and, for its part, persisted in the internationalization of Ruhr industry, which was not acceptable to the other nations. Following the elimination of democratic forces in Czechoslovakia on 25 February, the British and French pushed additionally for direct US military assistance, from which the Truman administration in turn shrank back. These were sufficient indications of conflicts within the Western camp for a person to grasp on to.

As rotating chairman of the Allied Control Council, Sokolovskii sought on 20 March to bring up the joint protest of the governments of Poland, Yugoslavia, and Czechoslovakia against the Frankfurt resolutions. He then demanded information about the six-power discussions in London. After both ventures foundered on the categorical refusal of the Western military governors, as was to be anticipated, he read a declaration prepared beforehand. Not wrong factually, it established "that the Control Council virtually no longer exists as the supreme body of authority in Germany exercising quadripartite administration of that country". He then added that he saw "no sense in continuing this meeting", declared it "adjourned", and left the conference room with his staff.[70] Two days later, the Soviet military government announced it would not attend any sessions of the Coordinating Committee, the directorates, or the Control Council committees.

The purpose of the manoeuvre was initially to demonstrate to world public opinion where the incorporation of the three Western Zones into the Marshall Plan threatened to lead, and thus to strengthen further the resistance to a division of Germany, a movement which had already made itself apparent. Stalin presumably had above all the Germans in mind, who up to this point had in his view accepted with astounding indifference the preparations for the founding of a western state. Perhaps he also presumed, however, that behind the difficulties which had arisen in the London negotiations lay an aversion in wide circles within the US and above all within the western European nations to letting themselves be drawn onto an adventurous confrontational course by the American leadership.

The operation, then, also served as preparation for a threat: the SMA organ *Tägliche Rundschau* as early as 19 December had declared that Berlin could only "preserve" its Four-Power status "to the extent" that the Four-Power administration of Germany was carried forward. On 25 March, the *Berliner Zeitung* then wrote that the day was "no longer far off" on which American, British, and French occupation forces would have to leave Berlin. That this was no empty threat was demonstrated by the SMA with a sudden obstruction of access to Berlin: on 27 March, a French train en route from western Germany to Berlin was painstakingly inspected. As of 31 March, no Allied trains at all could pass without all on board being checked. On 2 April, the navigable waterways leading to Berlin were blocked.

After this "mini-blockade" had sufficiently demonstrated the power of the Soviets to obstruct the Western powers' access to Berlin and thereby to undermine their presence in the city, it was lifted on 5 April. Waterways could once again be used, and Allied trains were once again allowed to pass uncontrolled. Selective measures such as the supervision of all telephone connections between Berlin and the Zones on 15 April, or the limitation on the import of newspapers and magazines from the Western Zones on 20 April, ensured that authorities in Washington, London, and Paris were constantly reminded how precarious their position in Berlin was. At the same time, Molotov and Stalin repeatedly suggested to the American leadership that the contentious problems be negotiated in top-level discussions.

The whole business was therefore only a warning. Stalin signalled to the Western powers that the establishment of a western German state would in his view mean a break with four-power responsibility for Germany, that the Western Allies would thereby also forfeit their right to be in Berlin, and that he possessed the means to put into effect the Soviet claim to all of Berlin which would result in such a situation. In other words, he threatened to throw the Western powers out of Berlin if they actually established such a state.

There can be no doubt that he made this threat in earnest and that he believed that he was able to carry it out if it should become necessary. When France gave in on the main issue during the second phase of the six-power discussions in London from 20 April to 7 June, and the Western powers then actually began their plans for founding a state by introducing the currency reform in the Western Zones on 18 June, Stalin wagered everything to bring the Western Sectors of Berlin under his power. If information from British intelligence is to be believed, he let his eastern European allies know that as of 7 July, the Soviet Union alone would exercise supreme authority in Berlin.[71] If the eastern state had already been thrust upon him, then its viability, questionable in any case, should not be further impaired by the fact that a large portion of the capital was in the hands of "imperialist" powers.

Meanwhile, the fact alone that at a point when the project for a western state had clearly run into difficulties, Stalin initially only threatened rather than taking action, amply demonstrates that the incorporation of Berlin into the eastern state was not his actual goal. He presumed that the threatened blocking of access to Berlin would significantly strengthen the demonstrative effect of having terminated the work of the Control Council. In that he gave the Western powers the opportunity to avert the whole affair, he speculated that they would shy away from both a conflict over Berlin as well as the loss of face resulting from a retreat out of the capital.

However Stalin may have calculated the details, his hopes were bolstered by information he received from the SED leadership. Pieck and Grotewohl, summoned not coincidentally to report in Moscow at exactly this time, described the situation in Germany. Their presentation had to have strengthened the impression that the western state project was in trouble and that in the event of a conflict, the German people would stand on the side of the Soviet Union. In the situation report he delivered on the evening of 26 March, Pieck granted that "certain successes" had been achieved by the "constant rabble-rousing" of the "Western powers and their satellites" and also acknowledged the existence of "confusion among the masses". With notable openness, he pointed out that this "rabble-rousing" had been "aided" by the "infringements by the troops" and by the determination regarding the German–Polish border, likewise by the "anxiety" of the bourgeoisie in the wake of dispossessions and the "measures against reactionary activities in the bourgeois parties" and "among the Social Democrats". He thereupon claimed, however, that the SED was gaining more "political confidence [among the people] . . . anyway". As he said, "Broad circles of the bourgeoisie are being successfully incorporated into the [People's Congress] movement – and the Schumacher policy is being successfully unmasked, and reactionary efforts in the bourgeois parties are being successfully countered." Quite proudly, he added that the second meeting of the People's Congress, on 17 and 18 March, had been a "great success" and had made a "strong impression on [the] masses, in the West too".[72]

After hearing this, the "tearing up of Germany" and the "creation [of a] western state", which he nevertheless addressed as dangers, appeared by no means inevitable. A week earlier, Grotewohl had explained to the Party Executive that the efforts to establish a western state would "probably" mean that the Soviet Occupation Zone would "not be able to avoid in the longterm" the tendency to "act on its own as a state".[73] With his typical mixture of fear and fascination in the presence of Stalin, Pieck forgot to draw such conclusions and instead reported exactly what the leader of the Communist world movement wanted to hear. Stalin for his part saw no reason even to discuss with his German *Genosse* the possibility of organizing the Soviet Zone separately. Without any modification of their strategic orientation, the SED delegation returned to Berlin on 1 April. In June 1948, Pieck still noted as the strategic line: "Consultative council from above / Control Council remained / people's movement from below."[74]

Stalin reacted to the currency reform in the Western Zones in accordance with the line of argument he had constructed: by making a claim to the currency authority over all of Berlin. Sokolovskii had to instruct the municipal authorities in Berlin to introduce the East Mark, whose creation had now become unavoidable, into all four sectors of the city. He rejected a compromise proposal from the three Western military governors, who agreed to the adoption of the East Mark in the Western Sectors provided it occurred under the supervision of all four Allies. When the Western powers replied to this rejection by deciding on 23 June to introduce the West Mark into their sectors alongside the East Mark, all surface connections between the Western Zones and Berlin were blocked. Simultaneously, West Berlin's energy and food supplies from the Eastern Sector and the Soviet Zone were cut off. The measures were initially justified only by citing the necessity of protecting the Eastern currency. The *Tägliche Rundschau*, however, declared at the same time that the Western powers had now forfeited their right to a presence in Berlin.[75]

The Soviets named the price for lifting the blockade only after having been asked and only hesitantly. Cutting off the connections to West

Berlin was obviously supposed to have an effect first and make clear to the Allies in what a precarious position they found themselves. When the three Western military governors sought to negotiate, Sokolovskii declared to them on 3 July, diplomatically veiled, that in consideration of the "growing difficulties" between the Western Zones and the Eastern Zone, he regarded "resolution of the general question as appropriate; the special question of transportation links would then resolve itself".[76] In separate notes, the three Western powers then turned to Moscow. They first received an answer on 14 July: Conversations "could be effective only in the event" they did not remain confined to the administration of Berlin; negotiations on the general question of four-power control in regard to Germany should be undertaken.[77]

Under these circumstances, it took until the end of the month for the three Western governments to agree to push for a discussion with Stalin. First of all, the three ambassadors of the Western powers had to present their request to Molotov. On 31 July, he impressed upon them once again that "conversations regarding Berlin were not possible except within the framework of conversations regarding all of Germany".[78] When they were then allowed to see Stalin on the evening of 2 August, toward 9:00 p.m., he too began the conversation by asking if they were authorized to speak about the German problem as a whole.[79]

He thereupon presented to them his view on the development of Berlin's status more or less officially: "Berlin has ceased to be the capital of Germany because the three Western powers have split Germany into two states. The Allied powers have lost their right to maintain troops in Berlin." With feigned generosity, he added that this did not mean "that we want to drive the troops of the three powers from Berlin. . . . Even if no kind of unanimity can be re-established among the four powers in the decision over the fate of Germany, even if the Soviet government alone would have to supply Berlin, we would never have the intention of driving the Allied troops from Berlin. Because of this, one must make a distinction between juridical arguments regarding the legitimacy of the presence of Allied troops in Berlin and the desires of the Soviet government."[80]

After he had granted the three representatives of the Western powers a presence in Berlin through the grace of the Soviets, as it were, he finally named his price for lifting the blockade: "Abolishing of the special currency for Berlin and a temporary suspension of the resolutions of the London conference" on establishing a west German state. Clarifying the second condition, he stated that "assurance must be given,

that the fulfilment of the resolutions of the London conference be deferred until representatives of the four powers have met and have come
to an agreement over the most important questions regarding Germany".[81]
When US Ambassador Bedell Smith and the British representative Frank
Roberts attempted to limit the price to an agreement in the currency
question, Stalin insisted that the establishment of a government for the
Western Zones as decided in London was for him "the only real issue
he had in mind".[82] After he had announced that the sought-after conference of four must address all questions left open at the Moscow
and London foreign ministers' meetings, he declared once again that
"the Soviet Union will set up no government in the Eastern Zone. The
three powers had compelled the Soviet Union to put a new currency in
circulation. They want to compel the Soviet Union to form a new government in the Eastern Zone. The Soviet government does not want to do
that."[83]

When the representatives of the three Western powers still found it
difficult to accede to the demand to suspend the London resolutions,
Stalin opined that it would suffice if an oral agreement to defer formation of a western German government could be reached; one did not
necessarily need to make it public. The Western ambassadors did not
want to accept that either. After more than two hours of negotiations,
he conceded that an agreement could limit itself to withdrawal of the
Western currency from Berlin in return for the lifting of the blockade.
It then only had to be formally noted that it was "the insistent wish of
the Soviet Government" that the London resolutions be suspended.[84]

After Stalin had in this way at least seen to it that the thread of
negotiation did not break again right away, Molotov made it unmistakably clear to the ambassadors during following discussions over an
agreement that Four-Power authority over Berlin and the implementation of the London resolutions were not to be had simultaneously,
however. During a further top-level discussion on 23 August, Stalin
altered his compromise proposal to this effect by seeking to have the
four powers declare that the question of forming a western German
government had been discussed "in an atmosphere of mutual understanding".[85] Molotov finally agreed to a directive to the four military
governors on 30 August that the introduction of the East Mark to the
Western Sectors of Berlin as sole legal tender would be put under the
control of a Four-Power finance commission.

In the negotiations among the military governors over the implementation of this directive, it very soon became apparent that the Soviet side had not thereby given up its claim to sovereignty over currency

in all of Berlin. The discussions became difficult; and since at least the American government had in the meantime lost interest in introducing the East Mark into West Berlin as the price for lifting the blockade, the discussions were broken off without result on 7 September.

THE TURNING POINT IN THE BLOCKADE

Stalin presumably did not know how close he was to his goal in negotiations during the summer of 1948. The French military governor Koenig, who had as little liking for his nation's concessions in the London resolutions as he had for the prospect of a confrontation with the Soviet Union, pleaded as early as 26 June in a démarche to his two Western colleagues that they postpone issuing instructions to the western German prime ministers to summon a parliamentary commission for 1 September to work out a constitution for West Germany.[86] On 12 July, his British colleague Robertson suggested to his government that the Soviets be offered the withdrawal of all occupation forces to certain border regions, participation in control of the Ruhr, and the formation of a central government. Berlin was not to be held in the long run, and if one attempted to do so with force, it would lead to war.[87]

George Kennan, head of the planning staff of the American State Department, argued along similar lines: when asked how the American government should act in the crisis, he presented a plan on 12 August which provided for an agreement on the departure of all occupation forces and, connected with this, the re-establishment of an independent German state. "We could then withdraw from Berlin without loss of prestige, and the people of the Western sectors would not be subjected to Soviet rule because the Russians would also be leaving the city." Despite complications which it would cause for the Marshall Plan, such a solution was nevertheless better than the lasting burden of the Berlin problem, of a West Germany which, lacking a connection to the East, would not be economically viable, of West Germans thinking only of reunification with the East, and of the perpetuation of the division of Europe.[88]

Such reflections, which in the moment of confrontation naturally could not be discussed publicly, definitely met with a positive response. Within the French government in particular, fear of the negative consequences of a division of Germany and of Europe was widespread. But the American Secretary of State Marshall was also convinced that time was on the Soviet side and Berlin was in the long run not to be held by the Western Allies. That is why he feared that, despite Truman's vigorous exhortations to hold out, either Berlin must be given up or the London resolutions suspended.[89]

That Stalin's calculation did not work out, however, resulted mainly from the success of the Berlin Air Lift. Important too was that the US Congress had meanwhile come to a decision by issuing the Vandenberg Resolution of 11 June, which cleared the way for a permanent US military engagement in Europe. This reduced French fears of standing alone should a conflict with the Soviet Union ensue. Likewise of significance was that Clay was energetically carrying out the London resolutions against the reservations of his colleagues as well as those of the western German prime ministers. Also, the support of Berlin's Mayor, Ernst Reuter, for the founding of the western state played an important role, helping overcome the prime ministers' reservations against summoning a parliamentary council.

All these moments of decision, however, would have led to nothing if it had not been possible to provide supplies for two million West Berliners from the air on a long-term basis. That such an operation would be at all technically feasible, especially through the winter when the need for coal increased significantly, was initially anything but certain. Likewise, it was not at all foreseeable whether the Soviets would also block the air routes to West Berlin. Only in the second half of August did American experts become increasingly confident that the transport capacities were sufficient to ensure supply of the city. And the longer the Air Lift continued without the Soviets' intervening, the greater grew the confidence that they would not intervene at all.

In fact, Stalin did not consider hindering the air routes between the West Zones and Berlin. They were much better secured by treaty than the land routes, for which only oral agreements existed. The air routes were, moreover, only to be blocked with military force, through use of the Red Air Force. The risk of setting off a war by obstructing the air routes was consequently much higher – much too high for the cautious master of the Kremlin, who knew only too well the military vulnerability of his imperium. There is no trace in the files of any consideration of whether or how to proceed against the Air Lift.

The blockade of roads, canals, and other surface lines of supply thus became a blunt weapon as of the end of August. The American leadership no longer felt itself under pressure to choose between two evils. The other two Western powers also gradually became confident of withstanding this test of strength without making concessions. Still more: the instrument with which Stalin sought in the last moment to prevent the establishment of a western German state now directed itself against him. The blockade appeared as an attempt to abandon two million people to the danger of starvation, an attempt made only to achieve some sort of political advantages in Germany. And it fed the flames of the wildest speculations about Soviet goals. The necessity of standing together against Soviet extortion grew accordingly, and existing misgivings over the founding of a western German state as well as the creation of a European–American military alliance dwindled. "The Russians", as Marshall ruminated on 21 September, "are retreating."[90]

They themselves certainly had not yet realized this at the time. In order to give credence to their claim to sole sovereignty over Berlin against the municipal authorities too, whom they now discovered had deserted to the camp of the "war mongers", the Soviets had the SED organize demonstrations against the city council from the end of August on. This led to regular interruptions of its sessions. At the same time, higher civil servants adjudged to be "insubordinate" were declared to be dismissed. After the assembly had reacted by transferring its sessions to the Schöneberg borough hall in the British Sector, Semyonov presented the SED leadership on 13 September with a detailed plan for "overthrowing the municipal authorities".[91] In accordance with it, the "SED and the bloc" were to "call the population in the Western Sectors not to participate in the elections on 5 December, through which the anti-democratic and openly reactionary elements sought to carry out the division of Berlin". At the end of November, a "well prepared" mass assembly would "resolve to depose the reactionary majority of municipal authorities and to install a provisional city-wide authority".[92]

Obviously, it was believed in both Karlshorst and Moscow that it would be possible in this way to achieve the "re-establishment of the unity of the municipal authorities"[93] under Soviet sovereignty. No one perceived that another resort to a combination of repression and mass agitation would only lead to a strengthening of the repulsion felt by West Berliners and of the suspicions held by the West as a whole. The disappointment was probably all the greater when, five days after proclamation of the "provisional city-wide authority", some 86.3 per cent of West Berliners went to the polls in the West Sectors on 30 November. This time too, it did not dawn on the Communist authorities that the German population, including a large majority of the "working class", saw little value in the protection of the Soviet Union. And only a few in authority wanted to admit to themselves that the forced struggle for unity had in reality hastened the process of division.

5 Zigzag to the Eastern State

The more remote the possibility of a republic encompassing all of Germany became, the more freely could totalitarian tendencies unfold on the soil of the Soviet Occupation Zone. Stalin's call to evince more readiness for battle against the presumed imperialist danger, with which he reacted to the Western powers' refusal to cooperate, promoted thinking in the categories of class conflict. Accordingly, those functionaries in the SMA and the SED who had never known particularly well what to do with the concept of completing the bourgeois revolution gained influence from the summer of 1947 on. They quite easily identified the required defence against reactionary elements with the establishment of their own monopoly on power. For them, the struggle for democracy was synonymous with the struggle for socialism. Without completely understanding the consequences of their actions, they worked very actively for the establishment of a Soviet-controlled separate state, objectively contradicting Stalin's intentions.

ULBRICHT AND TULPANOV

Walter Ulbricht played a key role in this process. He combined an unshakeable faith in the omnipresence of class conflict with an outstanding instinct for power, obsequiousness, and personal ambition. This combination of traits had led to his becoming go-between for the SMA in its Occupation Zone. From this position, he now worked to organize the territory over which the administrative competence of the Soviets extended according to Stalinist principles. "The opponent is intensifying the class struggle," he declared at a meeting of the Party Executive in July 1948. "He wages the struggle with all the means at his disposal and therefore we permit ourselves to prepare for this struggle and to orient ourselves correspondingly."[1]

According to his understanding, the party had to be developed into a closed battle formation in order to be armed for the confrontation with the class enemy. The party had to offensively assume its leading role in the Soviet Zone, had to "unmask" and "defeat" the "reactionary forces". Administration of the Zone had to be centralized and put under the control of the party; the police and security forces had to be stiffened up and strengthened, the bases of their opponents' power had to be taken from them. Ulbricht did not ask himself the question whether it would still be possible to secure the unity of Germany through such measures. It was alone decisive that the Soviet power and the Unity Party assert themselves in the "struggle" carried on by these class opponents "against the democratic order" in the Soviet Zone.[2] Only on the basis of such a victory, in his view, could the struggle for the unity of Germany be waged.

Whether Ulbricht could use his position of confidence with the SMA to initiate his own directives through the occupying power or whether his influence could only make itself felt in the implementation of Soviet directives still cannot be determined in detail. What is certain is that his influence grew with the implementation of the Cominform Line and that under the protection of the top SMA leadership, he was gradually able to establish a control system which passed over not only the state governments but also the Party Executive and the Central Secretariat itself. In the Central Secretariat, he was an outsider apprehensively avoided; and in the elections to the Executive at the Second Party Congress, he almost lost. On the ground, however, "Ulbricht and his growing apparatus" increasingly gave "politics in the Eastern Zone the stamp of dishonesty", as Gniffke formulated it in his letter of resignation in October 1948.[3]

Ulbricht was supported above all by Sergei Tulpanov, a protégé of Zhdanov heading the "Administration for Information" and directing the party work team of the CPSU in the SMA apparatus. In contrast to his devoted German charge, this self-confident and energetic occupation officer holding the rank of colonel definitely had in view "the rapid establishment of the unity of Germany as a democratic republic which could not be killed off by reactionary forces again".[4] With self-evident loyalty, he time and again carried out directives in the spirit of the Stalinist programme. Also unlike Ulbricht, he associated with all members of the Central Secretariat, even those of SPD provenance, "with emphasized camaraderie"[5] and impressed middle-class politicians as well with his thoroughly obliging manner. He spoke excellent German and had an obvious penchant for German culture.

Neither theoretically nor empirically was he familiar with the distinction between a democratic and a socialist order, however. Securely entrenched in class-struggle thought, he put both under the rubric of "progress" and unreflectingly took the Soviet Union to be the model on which the societal and governmental development of Germany had to be oriented. As he explained at the Second Party Congress, "The situation gives your country far-reaching possibilities to help a higher socio-political system achieve its triumph."[6] He accordingly pressed for the SED to organize itself following the example of the CPSU, and his ears were open to all suggestions which amounted to erecting the structures of the Soviet Union in the Eastern Zone.

In conflict situations, moreover, he made himself the one charged with carrying out a historically-inevitable mission. "Take note," he barked to Gniffke, who had been summoned for some admonishing in early June 1948, "I am a Bolshevik. I am a revolutionary." He felt himself all the more drawn to a reliable German functionary such as Ulbricht, who not only carried out all his tasks with as much obligingness as effectiveness but also similarly understood himself to be charged with carrying out the historical mission of the working class. Such a man had to be shown favour, and advice could also be taken from him. "We find ourselves in crisis-plagued times" he also said to Gniffke during a conversation. "The party needs a steadfast and experienced man, a man such as Walter Ulbricht. The other secretaries must orient themselves toward him."[7]

It was completely in keeping with Tulpanov's taste that Stalin demanded greater fighting power in the face of the Marshall Plan and preparations for a western German state. With genuine enthusiasm, he spoke in the middle of April 1948 to the staff of the SED party school "about an upcoming intensification of international relations and a 'more rapid development' of the Soviet Zone".[8] A few days later, he appealed to party leaders to "overcome the fear of decisive measures when it's a matter of entering into a conflict against outspoken enemies of the new democracy to be built in the Soviet Zone – against the enemies of the SED and of the democratic development of Germany".[9]

Whereas among the SED leaders and apparently among the Moscow leadership too a kind of helplessness predominated initially after the failure of the London foreign ministers' meeting, Ulbricht and Tulpanov immediately went over to the offensive. The Eastern Zone now had to "follow consistently the path of people's democracy", as Ulbricht declared to the departmental directors of the Central Secretariat. There were "comrades who believe that we already have ourselves a people's democracy, isn't that so? That is, however, an error, isn't it? Many prerequisites for this still need to be created. We must first fortify the mass organizations, split the bourgeois parties, and then set up a 'National Front'".[10] Before the interior ministers of the states, he argued that the struggle for the unity of Germany meant "that we must take in hand the new construction of Germany there where we have influence".[11]

Fully concentrated on conditions in the Soviet Union, he instructed the lecturers in the party school that a new phase of the class struggle had begun in which one had to see to it "that our party is the leading and fundamental force in the state".[12]

A first decisive success was achieved by the partisans of the "new line" through SMA Order No. 32 of 12 February 1948, by which the DWK received the right to "decide upon, issue, and review the implementation of decrees and instructions which will be binding upon all German organs in the area of the Soviet Occupation Zone in Germany".[13] With this, the dogged resistance of the states against the hollowing out of their competencies had been broken; and the path had been cleared for a centralized organization of the zone. After the DWK had been reorganized, a process completed on 9 March, it began working out a production plan for the second half of 1948 and drew up a two-year plan for 1949 and 1950, which was passed by the SED executive on 30 June. In the course of concluding the sequestrations, the executive at the same time put through wide-ranging dispossessions once again and took from the states competence in the area of economic policy.

Parallel to this, the SMA with support of the SED orchestrated the founding of the "National-Demokratische Partei Deutschlands" (NDPD), the "National Democratic Party of Germany", and the "Demokratische Bauernpartei Deutschlands" (DBD), the "Democratic Peasants' Party of Germany". They were supposed to take away the monopoly in representation of the old and new middle-classes heretofore enjoyed by the CDU and LDPD, thus weakening those two parties vis-à-vis the SED. It may well have been the case that the authorities envisioned that at least the NDPD would be active in the Western Zones as well. Since both parties were, however, orchestrated by the occupying power (Pieck even noted about the DBD explicitly: "near to the SED"[14]), their function after having been licensed on 16 June confined itself de facto to furthering SED hegemony. Alongside this activity, the occupation forces also practised more manipulation so as to render the CDU and LDPD submissive. They then supported the formation of a non-partisan "People's Committee for German Unity and a Just Peace" within the framework of the Peoples' Congress movement. Through this new organ, Ulbricht attempted to get around the resistance of "reactionary elements" in the bourgeois parties.[15]

On 8 May 1948, the SED leadership was officially sworn to the new line. Rendering Stalin's theory of two camps geographical, Tulpanov now declared[16] that "in actuality" a "division of Germany into two parts developing according to different laws has come into existence". The SED found itself "on the border between two worlds, there where the world of capitalism meets the world of socialism". The development of the Soviet Zone, he added, was "a development following the model of the new democracy", and the SED "took up a dominant role in the state"; it was "actually in power". This was a line of argument developed a few days previously by Ulbricht speaking to the party lecturers.[17]

As a consequence of this crude application of the Leninist revolutionary outline to the situation in Germany, which was somewhat in advance of that situation, Tulpanov demanded "the welding together of a firm, disciplined party work team" which would overcome the "weaknesses and incompetencies in the organizational and ideological work of the party". It was also to provide all party members with "a clear conception as to the development and decline of capitalism, as to the inevitability of the victory of the proletariat, as to the state, democracy, and dictatorship". Furthermore, it was to "unleash hate against the imperialism of the US, which was quickly developing along fascist lines, as well as against the allies of the US". On the other hand, Tulpanov demanded that "through its members, [the party] carry on the struggle for securing the zone as a whole, for boosting the morale of the populace, and raising the economic level etc."

The orientation toward a united Germany, which still constituted the official programme of Stalinist policy, was not lacking in this definition of tasks. Admittedly, this now became "the struggle for the conquest of all of Germany" since "the immediate goals and the final goals", according to Tulpanov, were "only to be achieved by means of class struggle". In other words, the "dominant position" of the "party of workers and peasants", which could already be considered as having been achieved in the Eastern Zone, was not only supposed to be the basis of the struggle for unity but was also to be sought in western Germany as well. For him, the "acute struggle for the whole of Germany and for socialism" collapsed into each other.

In the vision of Tulpanov, Ulbricht, and their fellows at least, the party of German unity had all of a sudden thus become the avantgarde of the proletarian revolution. From the leading role it had been supposed to play in bringing about German unity, the claim to hegemony was now derived; from the completion of the bourgeois revolution, the breakthrough to socialist revolution was now derived, into which according to Tulpanov every people's democratic development had to flow anyway.[18] Ulbricht had been able to push through his hegemonic fantasies as a programme; and Tulpanov, under the impression of East–West confrontation, had let himself be influenced to equate the struggle for unity with the conquest of power.

In practice, the programme of the Ulbrichts and the Tulpanovs amounted to the establishment of a cadre dictatorship on the basis of Soviet military power. Since this power existed only in the Soviet Zone, however, the division of Germany was in this way simultaneously furthered. Ulbricht had at most a shadowy perception of this, Tulpanov none at all. Neither saw, though, that the supposed hegemony of the party of the working class in reality rested upon Soviet bayonets. The fatal tendency toward self-deception, inherent in the Soviet system from the beginning, intensified itself in them to a mad vision of the "intensification of the class conflict" which only became concrete in its ramifications upon the Eastern Zone. In contrast, the "struggle for all of Germany" remained a pale chimera, a programme point. Further measures were neither implemented nor prepared on its behalf.

ULBRICHT SEIZES POWER

Fixated on class struggle, Ulbricht and Tulpanov blatantly ran amok without Stalin's perceiving the consequences. Semyonov, who had always avoided Ulbricht,[19] repeatedly expressed to Grotewohl his apprehension "that some of the measures introduced by Tulpanov and Ulbricht go beyond the goal of Moscow's policy and will further complicate the present situation, which is in itself difficult already".[20] This demonstrates that Tulpanov's programme was neither unequivocally nor in all its dimensions Stalin's programme. Given that there had been no talk either of a new phase of the class struggle or of a new set of tasks for the party during the visit of the SED leadership in Moscow at the end of March,[21] it is likely that not even the main slogans of the new course had been agreed upon with Stalin.

Meanwhile, the transformation from the idea of a struggle between two opposing tendencies in world politics to the idea of a capitalist–socialist conflict between classes had been a smooth one. Fear of attack by the "class enemy" was widespread at all levels of the Soviet administration, and the reversion to Leninist methods, as preached by Ulbricht and Tulpanov, was only too familiar to the Soviet officers and functionaries. Sokolovskii too had seen the struggle for democracy from a class standpoint: "Between the camp of socialism and the camp of declining capitalism there is no middle ground," as he had said at the first reception of the Central Secretariat after its installation in April 1946.[22] He was thus receptive to Tulpanov's inducements. It was similar in the case of many high functionaries in the Soviet bureaucracy. Because Stalin only sporadically concerned himself with and was only selectively aware of German affairs, it was possible, despite the absence of any delegation of authority, for a course to assert itself which was no longer in harmony with the master's intentions.

In Tulpanov's argumentation, Wilhelm Pieck detected above all elements which amounted to state-defined systemic opposition and proceeded to develop these further: "Through the establishment of the western state, Germany is being torn into two parts," he declared at the tenth meeting of the Party Executive on 12 May, almost word for word depending on Tulpanov, "each of which is developing according to its own laws, which diverge markedly from one another. The Western state is developing according to the laws of capitalist conditions and finds itself completely dependent on the Western powers." In contrast, the development of the Eastern Zone was orienting itself toward the Soviet Union and the nations of people's democracy. Certainly more future-oriented and more concrete as to the actual possibilities open to Communist policy than was Tulpanov, he then explained what had to happen "if a large part of Germany is torn off from the East", and consequently "an independent state construction encompassing the current Soviet Occupation Zone were to come into existence": "Life and politics within this state would not be the same as before but rather on their own would develop their own particularities." The SED, "as the party of the workers, the peasants, and the progressive intelligentsia, will become the leading force, which will assume responsibility for the shaping of political, economic, and cultural conditions". It would therefore become a "party of a new type" (here, the concept was used for the first time), which was to "take leadership into its hands" and was "to see to it . . . that not only economic life would develop in a socialistic direction".[23]

Differing from that of Ulbricht and Tulpanov, this was now an Eastern-state orientation without offensive elements: If a Western state was to be created – and in the view from East Berlin during May 1948, there was little to indicate that it could be prevented – then those in the East at least wanted to make socialism a reality. Tulpanov's declarations seemed to signal that Moscow was in agreement with these new tasks. Consequently, Pieck quickly announced as an introduction a "strategic alteration in our struggle", one "resulting from the changes in the political and governmental situation in Germany". In their comments on Pieck's presentation of basic principles, Franz Dahlem and Fred Oelßner spoke of a "turning point".[24] Pieck clearly gave no thought as to how the new task of the party was to be harmonized with the

higher goal of Soviet policy on Germany. Only very broadly and in a
rather muddled fashion did he explain that the SED must at the same
time naturally continue to "carry on the struggle for all of Germany
and in the process always work toward the necessity of the unfolding
of democracy and the realization of socialism".

In contrast, Otto Grotewohl initially persisted in wanting that the
"programmatic lay-out [be] still more insistently geared toward all of
Germany".[25] As he said, "Perhaps we cannot avoid the temporary separation of a Western German state. In that case, one should avoid creating any institutions which could possibly exclude a later unification
of the separate parts".[26] As late as early June, he declared in a conversation with Gniffke that he wanted to "prevent a development through
which Ulbricht would become general secretary and put through his
conception". He was still optimistic that this could be done: "If Ulbricht
continues to act as he does, he will eliminate himself."[27]

In the run-up to the Party Executive meeting of 29 and 30 June, at
which the two-year plan was to be adopted as the party plan, Grotewohl
nevertheless yielded for a second decisive time – the first being his
consent to unification of the workers' parties in the Eastern Zone. As
Ulbricht's "great day"[28] dawned, Grotewohl not only remained silent
about its appeal to intensify the class struggle but in his closing remarks also sided with the supporters of an Eastern orientation:

> The division of Germany seeks of us a clear answer to the question
> on which side is the Soviet Occupation Zone to be in the coming
> years. . . . If there were a possibility of implementing the fantastic
> ideas of the bourgeois politicians who always talk of our needing to
> regard ourselves as a bridge between East and West, then such a
> compromise solution would at best permit us an alignment with capi-
> talism and at best the reestablishment of a normal bourgeois repub-
> lic. . . . That, however, is not a political goal we have in mind,
> comrades. We do not want that. From the situation created by Lon-
> don ensues a clear answer to our question such that the alignment
> of our party in the implementation of this economic plan, clearly
> and without reservation, is to be toward the East.[29]

That Grotewohl characterized the "compromise solution" as impossible and undesirable suggests in itself that he was under pressure. This
became still more obvious in the further justification for the Eastern
orientation. As he explained,

The development which has manifested itself in the nations of people's democracy is the sole possibility for development which remains to us *in connection with this economic plan* [author's italics] in our zone and which we as a Marxist–Leninist party must clearly acknowledge in order to draw clear conclusions as to the policy we must pursue in the next two years alongside this economic plan.[30]

In other words: Grotewohl had capitulated, and Ulbricht had won out.

Like Pieck, Grotewohl had come to the conclusion that Stalin stood behind Ulbricht. What that meant for future conditions in the Soviet Zone could not have remained hidden from him after the graphic instruction offered by the people's democracies and especially the recent events in Czechoslovakia. His speech certainly betrayed the opposite of enthusiasm. He presumably preferred to remain in power rather than suffer humiliation in the West for the role he had played in 1946. His embitterment toward Western politicians was unmistakable and not without justification. And he probably said to himself that at the head of the SED he could prevent the worst from happening – the classic justification of the easy way.

In any event, Grotewohl's acquiescence heralded Ulbricht's definitive breakthrough. Three days after the decisive speech in the Executive, which was also promptly published in *Neues Deutschland* owing to its strategic meaning, Ulbricht pushed a resolution through the Central Secretariat. It stated that the "most important lesson of the events in Yugolsavia" (meaning Stalin's break with Tito, which had led to the exclusion of the Yugoslavian Communists from the Cominform on 28 June) was "for us German Socialists with all our power to set about making the SED a party of a new type which unshakeably and uncompromisingly rests on the foundations of Marxism–Leninism". Only Erich Gniffke and one of his Social Democratic colleagues in the secretariat, August Karsten, dared vote against this resolution.[31] The majority of the Social Democrats in the Central Secretariat, already in a mood of resignation for weeks anyway,[32] regarded further resistance as senseless after Grotewohl had yielded; and a segment of the Communists fell back into their old habits.

Accordingly, quick progress was made in establishing the Ulbricht system: under the Ulbricht-confidante Kurt Fischer, who was named president of the enhanced German Central Administration of the Interior on 13 June, a central police administration was created; the control of all police forces through Polit-Culture organs of the party was introduced, and the raising of billeted Volkspolizei, People's Police, was begun. All this in order "to secure the dominance of the working class" in the "intensification of the class struggle", as it was formulated by Fischer at a conference of the interior ministers and higher administrative functionaries on 23 and 24 July in Werder.[33] The interior ministers were urged to "unmask" and remove "enemies of democracy, agents, Schumacher people, spies, saboteurs, etc. who have crept into the administrative apparatus".[34] In the SED executive on 29 July, a resolution was made over the "organizational consolidation of the party and its cleansing of hostile and degenerate elements".[35]

While the cleansing was going on and the Yugoslavian Communists' defence against their condemnation by the Cominform office gave occasion to painstaking professions of loyalty to "the great Soviet example",[36] the leaders of the "bourgeois" parties yielded a bit further to the continual pressure. After the Bloc Central Committee had not met for over five months owing to its numerous differences with the SED, it accepted a mass organization as a member by taking in the FDGB on 5 August. The DBD was simultaneously accepted as an additional party, and on 7 September, the NDPD was as well. The CDU's and LDPD's previous possibilities of blocking the SED's proposals were in this way significantly limited.

Grotewohl began to retreat once again. Possibly swept along by the completely different context of discussion, he declared on 7 August to the "People's Council" of the People's Congress movement that the future constitution of the German republic could "not grow in accordance with the opinions of the occupying powers", but rather must "with complete independence orient [itself] toward German points of view", toward "a middle way acceptable to all of Germany, toward a unification of both the most left-leaning and the most right-leaning views within the realm of progressive and democratic principles".[37] However, after this speech was criticized in a conversation among Semyonov, Russkich (Semyonov's deputy for political affairs), Pieck, and Ulbricht, for containing "many distortions" and indulging in "objectivism",[38] Grotewohl brought himself into line for good.

Inspired by success and receiving additional encouragement from the Cominform tirades against Tito and the Polish Communist Party leader Gomulka, Ulbricht forthrightly called for the completion of the Bolshevik Revolution at the next session of the Party Executive on 15 and 16 September: "It is our task to pursue the complete elimination and liquidation of capitalist elements in the countryside as well as in the cities. This task is, in short, that of building socialism." He then attacked Ackermann, whose theory of a "special German path to socialism" hid the fact that "the transition to socialism [can] only be victoriously carried on in the most intense class struggle through the elimination of the last capitalist classes".[39]

Pieck vainly reminded him that Ackermann's analyses had at the time been "party line". Furthermore, "these formulations did not develop only in the narrow ranks of the leadership of the Communist Party but were also regarded as useful. The WKP (B)[40] never once raised an objection to this formulation." Grotewohl's soothing statement that these "small family affairs from the past . . . really do not interest us" did not help either. Ulbricht and Fred Oelßner, who now defined himself as the new party theoretician, persisted in their correction of Ackermann. Eight days later, Ackermann engaged in self-criticism by publishing a confession in *Neues Deutschland* that the "theory of a special German path to socialism has proven absolutely false and dangerous". It gave "manoeuvring room to antibolshevism instead of combating it decisively with its full power". In actuality,

> wherever in the world freedom and socialism are being fought for, . . . the Soviet Union is the basis of this struggle. For all revolutionary workers' parties, regardless of whatever nation they are in, the teachings of not only Marx and Engels but also Lenin and Stalin are the plumb line of political action. The CPSU (B) is the exemplar for the genuine Marxist–Leninist workers' parties of the whole world.[41]

With this – and only at this point – did the implementation of the Soviet model on the soil of the Soviet Occupation Zone become the primary and overriding goal of the SED. One can only speculate as to when and to what extent it had become clear to Ulbricht that he was striving toward this goal. Incontestable, on the other hand, is that it was *his* goal and that in the moment when Stalin's policy on Germany had been lamed, he introduced an independent factor into events. The GDR had a de facto existence from 16 September 1948: the state structure established by Ulbricht with the help of SMA was now supplemented by a conception of the state, and there was a growing number of people who had much to lose if one thing or another were once again called into question. Gniffke, faced with the approaching "dictatorship of Ulbricht, to which both of you are also subject in the end" (as he said in his last conversation with Pieck and Grotewohl),[42] left in late October for West Berlin.

STALIN STOPPED

The occupying power supported the transition to the "party of a new type" with didactic and detailed criticism. In a conversation with Semyonov and Russkich on 16 August, Pieck and Ulbricht heard that the Party Executive's resolution for "organizational consolidation" contained "positive and negative points": the organizational form and tasks were too "abstract", "positioned independently of the practical tasks of the day"; party functionaries were emphasized to much; "hostile and damaging elements" were falsely equated "with passive elements". To be sure, only the incorporation of Lenin's works, the resolutions of the CPSU, and "resolutions of the Cominform on the fundamentals of parties" were agreed upon in order to correct such "errors". Semyonov, who had either adapted or, in this question alone, also supported the "new course", was given the task of "passing along points" which corresponded to the criticism.[43] Two and a half months later, Russkich again gave detailed information as to the CPSU's organizational principles and modes of operation.[44]

The SMA carried on "cleansing" as well. Pieck discussed the "cleansing" of the party "from agents and speculators, corrupt members" with among others General Kovaltschuk, chief of the MGB apparatus in the Soviet Zone. On this occasion, he noted numerous cases of presumed "sabotage and terroristic activities" by an "anti-Soviet underground movement", against which the secret service had made arrests. Also discussed were "anti-Soviet activity and propaganda" as well as "espionage" by "Schumacher people", whom they saw working almost everywhere.[45]

In contrast, the SMA authorities clearly applied the brakes in the question of a governmental organization of the Soviet Zone, even though such an organization was a consequence of the Tulpanov programme. Pieck did indeed note in a conversation with Semyonov on 10 June that "unity [must come] through connection East" (which undoubtedly meant linking up with the East).[46] When the SED leaders asked two weeks later, on the first day of the Berlin Blockade, "whether [a] government [in the] Eastern Zone" should be formed, they were, however, turned down: "Temporarily [only] Economic Commission."[47] At a top-level discussion with Sokolovskii on 30 October, the establishment of an Eastern state was only considered as a consequence, probable or possible, of the development of the international situation. Pieck noted: "Perspective – development of the international situation – Western powers – Western state – Soviet Zone – autonomy / government – parliament."[48]

Still less did the SMA want to further "socialist construction" as proclaimed by Ulbricht in the Party Executive. The theme "socialism in the Soviet Zone" reared its head only a single time, and that on a subordinate level in a conversation between Pieck and Major Smirnov, Head of the Department of Public Security in the Soviet Military Kommandantur of Berlin during the first week of September. It remains unclear from Pieck's notes as to how the Soviet representative stood on the issue.[49] At most, there was talk at the top level concerning the "intensification of the class struggle".[50] The development of the social order in the Soviet Zone was not discussed between the SMA and the SED leadership.

When, in the middle of October, the SED leaders were asked to prepare a "report" on "evaluating the situation" and on a further "perspective" for a new "meeting in Moscow with Stalin",[51] they thus cautiously made the formation of a "German government for the Soviet Occupation Zone" dependent upon whether "the formation of a government in the West has occurred". The People's Council, which had approvingly taken note of a draft constitution for the – viewed as nationwide – "German Democratic Republic", was not to be brought into the formation of such a government. Rather, the plenum of the DWK was to be expanded into a "people's chamber for the Soviet Occupation Zone", and in connection with this, an "administrative law for the Soviet Occupation Zone" was to be passed.[52] This would be a "kind of constitution", as Pieck later explained orally in a meeting with Stalin, admittedly only a provisional one, just as the whole affair was to have only a provisional character so as to leave room for the later realization of the People's Council project.[53]

The SED leaders dared not speak at all of "socialist construction". As they emphasized in their report, "The working class has the decisive influence in the new state apparatus, but still does not have the prerequisite experience [for] the definitive elimination of the remnants of the reactionary bureaucracy. A significant segment of industry is the property of the people, but capitalist forces still have large portions of industry, trade, and agriculture in their hands. . . . In the bloc with other parties, the SED directs the state; but reactionary elements in the bourgeois parties are still not beaten. Under these circumstances," as the conclusion was drawn, "we regard it as correct to retain the two-year plan's characterization of the present order as a 'higher democratic order'".

The justification for this reserve let the actual intention shine through clearly enough; and the measures suggested by the SED Executive in connection with presumed "sabotage" on the part of "class opponents" meant in reality the "transition to people's democracy": direction and control of "private capitalist facilities with special significance", "removal of big farmers from the administrative bodies of agricultural cooperatives", systematic limitation on "private capitalistic wholesaling", "nationalization of facilities with over fifty employees". The "leading role of the SED" was supposed to be "strengthened", its "development into a Marxist–Leninist party" hurried along, and "the right wing in the bourgeois parties . . . was to be exterminated". As to the "political elections in the Eastern Zone" which were in the planning, Pieck gave two possible dates: "Autumn 49", the regular date of the state parliamentary elections, or "spring 50". In any event, the voters would be presented with a "bloc list" of the parties of the Unity Front. Consistent with all this and in a radical break with the goals in the founding phase of the party, the executive then formally applied for "acceptance into the Information Office of the Communist Parties".

Next to this detailed programme for "intensifying the class struggle", a concept which was also employed by Pieck in his presentation to Stalin, the suggestions for "intensifying the unity of Germany, against the colonization of western Germany" looked particularly modest. Cited in the written position on the issue were only the "formation of discussion groups against the Schumacher policy within the SPD", as well as the "concentration of party work on winning over union members in the factories". Pieck orally added the creation of the "widest possible National Front", admittedly without elucidating how it was to come into existence.

When Pieck, Grotewohl, Ulbricht, and Oelßner were received by Stalin on 18 December – the journey originally planned for the end of November had been somewhat delayed – they certainly learned that the leader of the Communist movement still placed his priorities elsewhere. As Pieck noted, "No transition to people's democracy yet," "Right wing, not struggle against it yet, do not beat, people's democracy to wait." After the four-hour discussion, he emphasized further "no dispossessions, still too early", "do not take action against groups of owners, but rather only against individual ones if they sabotage", "not direct interventions, but rather zigzag", "don't insist on plan, make distinctions". As justification for the reminder to pursue a "cautious policy", Stalin stated that the "situation" in Germany was "not the same as [in the] people's democracies": "No unified state yet – not yet in a position to take power." Then he once again impressed upon his German *Genossen* that in Germany it was first of all a matter of bringing about "unity [and] peace",[54] and accused them, "like your ancestors the Teutons . . . [of] always being above board in your dealings". "That is perhaps courageous, but often very stupid. In enormously difficult conditions, there is discussion among you . . . of a people's democratic order, of a dictatorship of the proletariat, or of a bourgeois-democratic order. That discussion is extremely stupid and harmful. It must be put to an end. The analysis of what kind of order there had been in Germany can be done later, if one has triumphed in Germany. Instead, one should now work."[55]

Not a word of the "dominant position in the state" for the party of the workers and peasants, as had been proclaimed by Tulpanov as early as May. Also, no explanations of the different development in the Western Zones and the Eastern Zone. Instead of that, Stalin continued to insist on, or insisted again on, the sequence on which he had oriented himself since the spring of 1945: first, the realization of "unity" and "peace", that meant the Potsdam programme, everything else only after that. The division of Germany was for him by no means definitive, and the thought of incorporating the eastern portion into the camp of the people's democracies was obviously rather far from his mind. Socialism for Germany was still not on the agenda. Under these circumstances, the application for acceptance into the Cominform had no chance: Pieck only dared present the desire as a "question", and he was turned down.

The struggle for "unity" and "peace" was, admittedly, for Stalin too a part of the worldwide class struggle in the final analysis. He too agreed that in this realm an "intensification" had occurred in recent years. He now considered the theory of a parliamentary path to social-ism as finished: it did not succeed without the dictatorship of the pro-letariat, as he declared to a delegation of the Bulgarian party leadership also visiting him in December 1948. This was "an axiom".[56] Conse-quently, his contradiction of Ulbricht's new course was indeed brusque in form, but somewhat diffuse in regard to content. Taking a balance, Pieck noted, "Path to socialism is zigzag".[57] Developing the party "into the leading force" was accepted by Stalin without objection, likewise the announcement of the desire to go into the elections with a "unified bloc list". He did not want to allow the elections to occur "before spring 1950". As for the sought-after transformation of the SED into a "party of a new type", he even provided an additional argument: the "Gniffke affair", which at the very beginning of the meeting had led to an embarrassing inquiry ("how possible?"). He also introduced a new element into the draft of resolutions for the "First Party Conference", one which was intended to secure the new party organization: Introduction

of "candidacy" for membership without voting rights ("deadline different
– factory worker with 10 years in the firm 1 year; others, peasants,
intellectuals, 2 years").

Added to this, Stalin was in the meantime no longer able to close
his eyes completely to developments which did indeed amount to the
founding of a western German state. It just might not necessarily have
dawned on him that the Berlin Blockade had achieved the opposite of
what it had been intended to achieve. After supply of the West Berlin
populace had been conducted by air for a period of six months, he
was, however, no longer sure of the blockade's success. So he agreed
to the formation of a "people's chamber" and a government on the
basis of the DWK "if in the West [a] government" were to be established. As the possible date for this breakthrough in the Western negotiations, Pieck noted "February/March" 1949.

That this would be only a "provisional German government" was
explicitly held to. Beyond this, Stalin insisted that "leading politicians
of the . . . People's Council" belong to this government as well and
that they be confirmed either by the People's Council or by a new
People's Congress. These determinations were not contained in the SED
draft. For Stalin, such a government had nothing to do with forcing
through a special Eastern German path to socialism. It was, rather, an
emergency measure owing to the force of circumstances, and by no
means would it mean an end to the struggle for German unity.

ALL-GERMAN TWILIGHT

Stalin's objection put a powerful damper on Ulbricht's revolutionary
ambition. After those returning from Moscow had on 27 December
given a report to the Central Secretariat, Pieck began the official retreat in an interview in *Neues Deutschland* on 30 December. In reference to Georgii Dimitrov, who had just defined "people's democracy"
as a societal order with a Soviet stamp,[58] Pieck declared that "Conditions in the Soviet Occupation Zone are entirely different from those
in the people's democracies." He thereupon disputed that the SED sought
such an order: "The SED does not see its task as the transition to
people's democracy, but rather as the consolidation of the existing new
democratic order." And to the question of whether in the People's Council
there was an intention to "create an autonomous government for the
Eastern Zone", he answered that "there is no such intention". Rather,
the People's Council was struggling "for the unity of Germany and for
a just peace and will continue to do so until this goal is achieved".[59]

Grotewohl, who happily got over this disavowal of his public commitment to the "orientation" toward "people's democracy",[60] went a step further. At the "First Party Conference" of the SED from 25 to 28 January 1949, which had actually been summoned in order to give its blessing to the "new course",[61] he settled his score with Ulbricht in a manner hardly veiled. As he said in his opening report to "our Zone politicians", not even "such a beautiful Eastern Germany, whatever it may be called", could "fulfil the task . . . which a unified, progressive, and democratic Germany could fulfil in all of Europe. . . . Such a Germany means the definitive pacification of Europe." To bring this about was for this reason "no tactical but rather a strategic task of our party".[62]

Internally, in a speech to leading economic and government functionaries in early March 1949, Grotewohl bolstered this reminder as to the original task of the SED with the argument that "the great riches of western Germany [must] not fall into the hands of foreign imperialists and monopolists and their German accomplices". Beyond this, he expressed in somewhat irritating syntax, that one must pay attention "that among the new group of states forming in Europe, the German East, devoid of an economic foundation in iron and steel, would be in economic terms only a burden for the southeastern bloc of states, whereas Germany as a whole constitutes a strengthening of this bloc and at the same time, since it represents the economic foundation for armament, it presents the peaceful ordering of Europe".[63]

The party conference had declared the "struggle for the unity of Germany and a just peace" once again to be the primary task of the SED.[64] In the newly-created "Politburo" of the party, Grotewohl was then able to put through a directive to the Party Executive in March which was thoroughly in keeping with its earlier line, which in the meantime had been criticized: The party was not to take division as an accomplished fact and "in the Eastern Zone, so to speak, carry out the transition to socialism immediately. In contrast, we are of the opinion . . ., that we will continue to wage the struggle for the unity of Germany with all the means at our disposal, which means" – and this was the decisive passage – "that we will implement a policy which can be realized in Germany as a whole, of which the majority of the population of all of Germany can be persuaded."[65]

The party did actually increase its engagement for a German-wide solution once again. After the debate on the constitution of a "German Democratic Republic" had received hardly any attention during the winter months – the Constitution Committee of the People's Council had worked into the draft some 129 changes suggested by the People's Committees[66] – a new meeting of the People's Council was called, for

18 and 19 March. It passed the modified draft and at the same time announced the summoning of a "Third German People's Congress", this time to be elected directly by the populace. As had already been discussed in the conversation with Stalin ("If 3. People's Congress/ Constitution – against occupation statutes in West"),[67] this was intended to set a manifestation of German popular will against the presumed diktat of the Western occupying powers. This manifestation was also supposed to have an effect in the West – even if it were "just five minutes to twelve", as formulated in early May in the Party Executive by August Koenen, Gniffke's successor as General Secretary of the People's Council.[68] The Parliamentary Council in Bonn and the Frankfurt Economic Council were asked to meet "if possible as early as 6 April in Braunschweig" with a delegation of the People's Council "in order to conduct talks on the creation of the democratic unity of Germany and the completion of a peace treaty as well as the withdrawal of occupation forces".[69]

Parallel to this, the weight was shifted within the SMA. Whereas Semyonov attained the rank of ambassador in early January, the radio broadcast of a speech by Tulpanov on 25 January, in which he once again pulled to pieces "Anglo-American imperialism" in the sharpest tones, was interrupted after four minutes. Newspaper editorial staffs received a directive not to report on the speech; rumours of an intense conflict between Tulpanov and Semyonov made the rounds. On 29 March, Sokolovskii was dismissed without explanation. His position was then taken over by the army general Vassili Tshuikov. After this, little was heard of Tulpanov. In early October, the Soviet news service reported that he had been ordered back to Moscow "some time ago".[70] Obviously, it had become clear to Stalin during the visit of the SED delegation that developments in the Occupation Zone had strayed off course and so he had pulled the responsible parties out of circulation.

The measures for transforming the SED into a "party of a new type" were, though, carried out as planned. As observer at the party conference, Stalin sent – of all people – the ideological zealot Michael Suslov, who after Zhdanov's death in August 1948 had directed the Cominform campaign against Yugoslavia.[71] Centralization of the power structure was not reversed; mobilization for the two-year plan continued. In the party leadership, there was no conclusive discussion as to whether these measures did not after all amount to realization of the Soviet model in the Eastern Zone. Rather unwillingly, Grotewohl made clear in his speech to the party conference that the possibility still existed: in the Eastern Zone, "the working class [could] not exercise dominance, in contrast to the people's democracies, because the majority of the working class still does not stand committed to the struggle behind the party".[72] That for Stalin this was neither the sole nor the first priority, but rather, the realization of unity was of greatest importance, was lost in the strain of the debate over the meaning of his "pieces of advice".

The constitution thereupon presented by the People's Council was for Western democracies not particularly attractive. Owing to a request made by Semyonov,[73] it did accommodate western German federalist conceptions in so far as it envisioned a chamber with suspensive veto for the provinces, in contrast to the SED draft of 1946. The separation of powers was, however, still missing to the benefit of parliament. Economic planning attained constitutional status. Also, the stipulation that "all factions having at least forty members" were to be made participants in the government meant that, de facto, the bloc principle was constitutionally established.

Above all, however, the direct elections to the Third People's Congress were not able to overcome the deficit of legitimation suffered by the People's Council. The first two People's Congresses stemmed from arbitrarily assembled delegations of parties, mass organizations and firms, and had been subject to diverse sorts of manipulation. This time, the citizens of the Soviet Zone and of East Berlin were to choose the delegates. Only for those seats earmarked for delegates from the Western Zones, amounting to one-quarter, was the earlier process retained. In order to avoid endangering the "leading role" of the SED, which in consideration of the continuing "dissatisfaction of the workers" was an outcome to be feared,[74] the party leadership and SMA insisted, however, that in each electoral district, only one predetermined "unity list" of parties and mass organizations be presented to the voters. Moreover, a vote for this list was linked with affirmation of the "unity of Germany" and to a "just peace treaty".

Under these conditions, the result of the election on 15 and 16 May approached a catastrophe. Comprehensive cooperation among authorities and intensive mass agitation did indeed bring about a participation rate of over 95 per cent of those eligible to vote. Despite the suggestive question about unity, the percentage of no votes was so high, however, that after an intervention by Kurt Fischer's Administration of the Interior in many places, "generous" interpretations of negative expressions of opinion were made. None the less, 34.2 per cent no votes and 6.7 per cent invalid ballots were registered in the end. The People's Congress, meeting on 29 and 30 May and "adopting" the draft constitution, could claim only the most diffuse of mandates.

It was no wonder that the West Germans for the most part saw the whole People's Congress enterprise as an instrument of Soviet expansionist policy and let their politicians get away with the declaration that they would not sit down at a table with "slaves of the Soviet Union".[75] No wonder either that "among many comrades, a false conception of the present political regime in the Soviet Occupation Zone still" existed, as Pieck wrote or had someone write in *Einheit* in March. This referred to the false equation of that regime "with the regime in the nations of people's democracy". If, after Stalin's reprimand, the majority among the SED leadership and also at the SMA no longer wanted to "give the impression that we had come to terms with the division of Germany",[76] the reality looked different.

Stalin clearly did not perceive such subtleties. Through the informal conversations which the American delegate to the UN Security Council, Philip Jessup, had carried on in loose succession with his Soviet colleague Jakov Malik, the Soviet leader had to note that no more pressure at all could be exerted through the blockade. In late April, he made up his mind to agree to lift it even without the postponement of the formation of the western German government; the sole condition was that the Allied Foreign Ministers' Council be summoned again.[77] All the more important for Stalin was mobilizing the German public: it alone could still prevent the establishment of the western state, if this were still possible to prevent at all. At the same time he approved the lifting of the blockade, he entrusted Semyonov, who had been ordered back to Moscow specifically for this purpose, with the creation of a "National Front for Unity". It was now "necessary", as he let the SED leadership be told, to go a "step further than [the] People's Congress".[78]

It is clear that he also had in mind the creation of a "battle formation" for "reinforcing the national liberation struggle", as he had once already requested through Semyonov in June 1948.[79] It was also supposed to appeal to and accommodate "former Nazi[s]" and "former officer[s]". Grotewohl, to whom Semyonov first reported after his return from Moscow on 6 May, held fast to the concrete measure that "voting rights" must be given "to Nazis without exception". As he had done for the first time in June 1948, Stalin proposed once again to the Allies that all occupation forces be withdrawn within one year of the signing of a peace treaty. In so doing, Soviet diplomacy naturally did not neglect to emphasize the contrast with the undetermined duration of the occupation statute of the future Federal Republic.

It is definitely possible that Stalin hoped to have success with this altered tactic as early as the foreign ministers' meeting which began on 23 May in Paris. In any event, Pieck, who since 14 April was in Moscow for medical treatment and a health cure, noted down for a meeting with Molotov on 11 May as "prospect of development in the near future" and "possibility at the Paris conference" the "resumption of the work of the Control Council" and "of the Allied Kommandantur." He noted further "no Western state – no occupation statute", but rather "unified government – constitution – parliament" as well as "peace treaty" with a "unified Germany". He expected that the Ruhr statute would be changed ("international control") and that an agreement would occur on the basis of the introduction of the "Eastern currency" in Berlin. In "new elections of city council members", which he regarded as possible in this case, it became clear to him that the "SED [would win only a] minority".[80]

Stalin was not discouraged by the fact that in Paris, where the foreign ministers negotiated until 20 June, nothing more was achieved than an affirmation to "continue efforts to restore the economic and political unity of Germany" and that at the next UN General Assembly in September, a date would be agreed upon for a further meeting of the council.[81] As he let Pieck know through Semyonov, it had not in fact been possible to achieve in the "German question" a "decision similar to [the one in the] Austria" question, in which agreement had been reached on the basic articles of the state treaty. The conference was "not, however, insignificant because of that": "The very fact of its being called" meant for a "strike against the dividers", still greater "recognition for [the] policy of the S.U. . . . than Potsdam". At the council meeting in London, the attempt had been made to "exclude [the] S.U." It was "now different – S.U. not to exclude". The Western powers had "reacted very nervously" because of the "risk peace [would] ensue". Additionally, the agreement in the Austria question meant "progress in the peace arrangement for Germany too". Stalin expected the "next Foreign Ministers' Conference", which would "concern [itself] with unity and the peace treaty", to be in the autumn. After having now achieved "1 step forward", he saw general possibilities "to find [a] modus vivendi among the occupying powers". He thereupon reaffirmed yet again his conviction that "war [is] not possible".

As "Stalin's directive", Semyonov communicated to the SED leadership that they should "continue [their] efforts to achieve economic and political unity". He requested once again that they set up a National Front. As the reason for this, he impressed upon them that the "peace treaty" with Germany could not be set aside "because [the] peace of the world" is dependent upon it. "Therefore", the "struggle [must] go on."[82] Far from regarding the eastern state as an acceptable partial success after the failure of the blockade, which has been the view commonly taken by Western interpreters, he sought new ways to prevent the western state and was persuaded that this could be achieved at least in the long term. Despite the proclamation of the Basic Law on 23 May, he still did not want to give consideration to preparations for a government in the Eastern Zone, which since the December meeting with the SED leadership he no longer excluded in principle.

The SED leadership could hardly understand this optimism, a mindset which indirectly emphasizes once again how important the German-wide solution was for Stalin and how far removed he was from thoughts of a "socialistic" state extending over only part of Germany. The success of the threefold breakthrough of the Western powers in the negotiations over the occupation statutes, the North Atlantic pact, and the Basic Law was too clear. Also, the interest in not giving up power was too strong. The alternative to which Stalin referred was too little conceivable, his demand for creation of a National Front even caused significant difficulties. After his return from Moscow on 23 May, Pieck noted: "What is that supposed to mean?" "Not prepared." And "motto questionable", because it echoed a "Nazi slogan".[83]

After not reacting at all to the first call in June 1948 for creating such a "battle formation", the SED leaders supplemented the programme of the Third People's Congress at short notice with the passage of a "Manifesto to the German People", containing a call to form a "National Front for unity and a just peace".[84] Beforehand, however, they had agreed with the SMA leadership that no organized institution should grow out of this.[85] When "resistance [by] the bourgeois parties against [the] creation [of the] National Front"[86] manifested itself during a session of the People's Council Presidium on 28 May, they raised few objections. Even Semyonov's admonition of 19 July, which suggested that Moscow was not satisfied with the efforts up to that point,[87] led to no concrete engagement: the SED leaders did find themselves ready per force to work out a programme for the National Front through the People's Council, and declared that further "dispossessions or compulsory administrative measures" did not represent "the main component of the democratic task in the Eastern Zone at the present time", but rather, merely the "consolidation of previous progressive achievements".[88] In regard to organizing the movement, which was to have its "main weight [in the] West", there was nothing more than the vague formulation that "many forms" of work were necessary.[89]

The "National Front" received much less attention from the SED leadership than did a project they themselves had developed in early May: the formation of a "German government" by the Third People's Congress. As Pieck noted on 11 May in Moscow, this would occur if the Paris meeting of the Foreign Ministers' Council would not halt the preparations for a western state at the last moment.[90] The People's Congress was not only to approve the constitution of the "German Democratic Republic" but also to appoint a government right away. The People's Council newly chosen by the congress was to constitute itself "as [a] parliament". On 23 May, Pieck therefore pledged "to postpone [the] People's Congress – until after [the] close [of the] Paris conference", which he already on this first day of negotiations presumed would probably fail. He presented the formation of a government connected with this as part of a big campaign which would give "more meaning to [the] National Front slogan as well".[91]

It can be assumed that the members of the Politburo associated more with this founding of a government. In Moscow, Pieck thus had the draft of a cabinet list with him: Grotewohl was envisioned as prime minister, CDU chairman Otto Nuschke and his LDPD colleague Hermann Kastner as deputies, LDPD Prime Minister of Saxony-Anhalt, Erhard Hübener, as foreign minister – but also Kurt Fischer as minister of the interior. A total of ten out of sixteen ministries would go to the SED. Ulbricht at least may have seen in this proposal a way to get around Stalin's resistance to the establishment of an Eastern government. For Grotewohl, and perhaps for Pieck as well as others, Stalin's ambivalence corresponded to their vacillation between German-wide interests and insight into the reality of the division.

Moscow certainly wanted to hear nothing of the attempt. Using the argument that the Third People's Congress should again send a delegation to the meeting of the Foreign Ministers' Council,[92] the quick summoning of the congress was insisted upon, which would have to content itself with the "adoption" of the constitution and the election of the People's Council. But after the Paris conference there was still no green light for the formation of a government. Instead, Stalin made reference to the next meeting of the Foreign Ministers' Council in the autumn,[93] so that the SED leaders per force had to wait before taking action. "I believe, however", Pieck explained on 17 June in the bloc's *centrale*, "that we should take no position on the issue of forming a parliament and a government in the East until this process has fully run its course in the West. As long as that is not the case, the struggle for maintaining Germany's unity should be waged. We would do our struggle very great harm if we let ourselves be led astray by taking the same steps now as are being taken in the West."[94] Grotewohl perhaps even gained new hopes. As he noted during a session of the Politburo on 28 June, "Formulating Germany's economic and political unity [is] the new task." Further: "Modus vivendi = preparing the situation for Potsdam."[95]

As the election campaign for the first German Bundestag was in high gear in the Western Zones in early August, Ulbricht and Grotewohl sounded out Semyonov once again regarding implementation of the GDR constitution.[96] The answer was negative this time too, and Ulbricht once again had to postpone into an uncertain future what everyone expected after the implementation of the Basic Law. "Political issues regarding the state are not at present so very much in the foreground", as he declared in the presidium of the People's Council on 11 August.[97] The undecided situation between the nascent SED state and Stalin's continued ambitions for all of Germany lasted the whole summer of 1949.

DECISION IN SEPTEMBER

Stalin reconsidered his position on the issue of his own separate state only in early September, not only after the Bundestag had been elected on 14 August but also after a new meeting of the Foreign Ministers' Council had failed to materialize. On 15 September, Konrad Adenauer had been elected first Chancellor of the Bonn-based Federal Republic of Germany. As had been prearranged in the event of a Western government's being formed, Pieck, Grotewohl and Ulbricht, with Fred Oelßner as interpreter, flew to Moscow the next day. In their luggage was a "plan for the formation of a government" from 8 September. This emphasized that it concerned itself "not with the formation of an Eastern German state or with an Eastern German government ... but rather with a government for all of Germany". In their luggage too was a paper of 15 September bearing the title "Short-term Procedure for the Formation of a Government", which emphasized an "immediate three-week intensive campaign to discredit and unmask the federal parliament and the federal government of the Western state as organs of the Western occupying powers betraying German interests".[98]

In conversation with Stalin, the SED leaders again justified "the necessity of going forward with forming a German government in the Soviet Occupation Zone". The justification consisted exclusively of required "political education" and deepening of the "struggle against this policy of the Western powers". They drew an additional argument from the results of the Bundestag elections, in which the KPD had received a disappointing 5.7 per cent of the vote:

> If one adds the votes for Social Democracy to the bourgeois votes, since Social Democracy supports the same policy of colonial enslavement of the German people, it is thus clear that the tremendous majority of the voters has opted for these parties and thereby enables the Western powers to declare that their policy has received the approval of the mass of the people. . . . This electoral decision demonstrates the great danger through misleading the masses which threatens national autonomy as well as the economy and even to a greater extent the peace.[99]

It is possible that this blunt reference to the actual mood of the western German population was what first moved Stalin to agree definitively to the establishment of the eastern state. Pieck's records report that first on 27 September, in the context of a "discussion in the Politburo of the Central Committee of the CPSU", an "answer" was received from the Soviet side.[100] Stalin agreed that the People's Council should declare itself a "provisional Volkskammer" and set the process of forming a government in motion following the constitution of the "German Democratic Republic". He further agreed that the government thus formed would assume "all administrative functions" which "up to that point had been exercised by SMA, whereas SMA [would be] reorganized as a Soviet control commission". And in order to ease the takeoff of the new government, he also conceded the dissolution of Soviet prison camps in Germany as well as release of all German prisoners of war by 1 January 1950, "with the exception of those convicted by military courts".[101]

Finally having been permitted to come into existence, the government was not allowed, however, to term itself "German government", which would implicitly raise a claim to the sole representation of all Germans. Stalin persisted in the formulation "Provisional Government of the German Democratic Republic", leaving open the issue of what territory this GDR covered. He was clearly little persuaded by the argument that a government of the People's Council would rouse the Western Germans. Above all, though, he did not want to let his possibilities for negotiation become too restricted by the new regime in East Berlin which had been forced upon him.

The SED leaders had once again to issue a denial of what they had originally sought. At a joint session of the People's Council Presidium and the Central Bloc on 5 October, at which the programme agreed upon in Moscow was proclaimed, Pieck declared that "provisional government" was not to be understood as "a government for all of Germany but rather one for the German Democratic Republic".[102] Because the founding of the GDR, which now followed in the shortest possible interval on 7 October, was none the less accompanied by expressions of desire for unity, Grotewohl had to insist again in the Party Executive on 9 October:

> There is too much talk of a government for all of Germany. Comrades, we are forming no government for all of Germany. Rather, the foundation of our work is the constitution of the German Democratic Republic; and the government which is being established here is the government of the German Democratic Republic. It is another question as to what extent it will have an effect in Germany as a whole.[103]

Grotewohl implicitly limited the "German Democratic Republic" to the territory of the Soviet Zone, in contrast to what had been intended in the People's Congress campaign. Not only in actuality but also according to its self-understanding, it was more the embodiment of separate statehood than the core of the sought-after Potsdam republic. To this extent, the founding of the state on 7 October 1949 was actually "a turning point in the history of Europe", as Stalin wrote in his congratulatory telegram of 13 October. From his perspective, it was certainly not a turn for the better. What was for Ulbricht the first satisfaction for the setbacks suffered since December 1948, and what was for Grotewohl a necessary step, was for Stalin a defeat – not the first one but a rather painful one. That he himself did not take part in the foundation ceremony should be seen as symbolic.

6 Between Two Goals

After the founding of the GDR, Stalin had not given up his hopes for a Germany as had been envisioned at Potsdam. In his congratulatory telegram, there was still no reference to socialism in Germany but much rather to a "unified, independent, democratic, and peace-loving Germany". In an extremely effusive hommage to the German people, he declared that

> the experience of the last war has shown that the German and the Soviet peoples have made the greatest sacrifices, that these two peoples possess the greatest ability of any in Europe to bring about great actions of global significance. If both these peoples evince the same resolution in struggling for peace with the same exertion of their power with which they waged war, then the peace of Europe can be regarded as secure.

The founding of the GDR was only one stage in this struggle. The goal remained of "rendering impossible the enslavement of the European nations by the global imperialists".[1] On 10 October 1949, Commander-in-Chief Tshuikov declared that "the Soviet Union [sees] the meaning of the resolutions of the People's Council" for founding the GDR as making a contribution to the "re-establishment of the unity of Germany" and to its "rebirth on a democratic and peaceful foundation".[2]

In the first year that the new state existed, Stalin clearly harboured no doubts that this could be achieved. As he wrote in his congratulatory telegram, "You need have no doubts that if you enter upon this path [meaning the struggle for peace] and strengthen the peace, you will enjoy the great sympathy and active support of all the peoples of the world, among them the American, English, French, Polish, Czechoslovakian, Italian peoples not to mention the peace-loving Soviet people." In December 1949, Malenkov published a birthday hommage to Stalin in which he quoted a long passage from the interview with Harold Stassen in April of 1947. In contrast to the treatment of the text at that time, it was now quoted as direct discourse, as if the doubts of that earlier time as to whether cooperation among states with different systems were really possible had in the meantime resolved themselves.[3] Numerous reports from the Soviet Control Commission (SCC) over the deep enmity with which the "oppressed West Germans" regarded their "American colonialist masters", over the growing opposition to Adenauer, and over the decline of the "pro-American wing" of the SPD,[4] certainly strengthened Stalin's conviction that the struggle for a democratic, unified Germany had not come to an end with the governmental organization of the Eastern Zone.

SILENT COUP

The SED leaders initially had a completely different goal in view: safeguarding their power over the eastern part of Germany achieved during 1948 in the course of the "intensification of the class struggle". This power was threatened above all by the elections which would have to occur after the end of the current legislative period – to the local and district parliaments in the autumn of 1948, and to the provincial parliaments in the autumn of 1949. The greatest threat, however, was presented by the elections to the Volkskammer foreseen in the new constitution. The leaders of the middle-class parties were expecting an overwhelming victory, up to 70 per cent of the vote according to a situation report made by SED spies in June 1949,[5] a victory which would push the SED to the margins and would allow these other parties to establish themselves as the main partners in a Soviet policy oriented towards all of Germany.[6] The SED leaders were likewise conscious that on election day they would have to pay for all the violations committed by the occupying power.

To escape looming defeat, they developed two ideas as early as 1948: initially, postponement of the elections; and when it became clear that this alone promised no salvation, offering on the ballot only a unity list comprising all the parties brought together in the bloc. After the occupying power had granted a delay of the local and district parliamentary elections (in June 1948)[7] and then also of the provincial parliamentary elections (reception by Stalin in December 1948),[8] SED functionaries pressured the middle-class parties to accept the principle of the unity list. In the process, they ran up against stubborn opposition. When the Soviet Foreign Ministry asked in early March 1949 if the SMA and the SED regarded it as possible to hold the planned elections in the autumn of 1949, Semyonov answered that the SED was interested in carrying out the elections with a unity list; in regard to this, however, not everything had as yet been prepared.[9]

In early August 1949, Pieck and Grotewohl presented Semyonov with a new proposal: implementing the GDR constitution with the stipulations on elections bracketed off. During the period of the provisional government, which itself constituted a postponement, the occupying power was to bring about a perceptible improvement in the supply situation. This would allow them, as they hoped, in a year's time to defeat the CDU and LDPD in union with the "new" parties, the NDPD and DBD.[10] During negotiations in Moscow in September, Pieck and Grotewohl developed yet another argument for the postponement of the elections "for up to one year": "Further developments in the western part of Germany" would by that time have "clearly demonstrated" that "the situation there had continually worsened, in contrast to the advance in the Eastern Zone. This fact would bring about the failure of the rabble-rousing carried on by the West and Berlin in the Eastern Zone."[11]

It may be the case that the expiration of the provincial parliamentary terms in October 1949 had played a role in Stalin's decision finally to accede to the urging of the SED leadership for a governmental organization of the Eastern Zone. It is in any event clear that the looming election date inspired the SED leaders to solicit the founding of the state with all their energy. As a partial victory, they could return home with Stalin's agreement that "autumn 1950" would be "taken into consideration" for the elections and that for this "the drafting of joint election lists of the SED and the other parties [was to be] sought".[12]

To push this through among the middle-class parties caused, as Pieck had predicted, further "great difficulties".[13] Their leaders, who were worked on by Pieck and others in separate talks, showed themselves stubborn in both questions.[14] After it was "from the highest places" (that is, from Tshuikov or Semyonov) "intimated that elections could not be held for reasons of foreign policy",[15] they accepted the postponement immediately before the joint session of the Central Bloc and the People's Council Presidium on 5 October. They did so with the vague but to an extent definite hope that the unity lists would thereby be dropped. They were also influenced by appeasement in the form of government posts which the SED offered or let themselves be talked into offering. Above all, they regarded it as an important victory when CDU General Secretary Georg Dertinger was named foreign minister, a move which had not originally been intended.[16] In the joint session of the Bloc and People's Council, only the deputy CDU chairman Hugo Hickmann still raised objections to the postponement of state parliament elections. When, in closing, Pieck noted general accord on the rescheduling of all the elections for 15 October 1950, there were no more objections at all.[17]

Under the influence of strong protests from the base and the various formations of the middle-class parties against this decision, Nuschke (CDU) and Kastner (LDPD) both resisted further attempts by Tshuikov and Semyonov regarding unity lists over the course of several months.[18] The SCC thereupon introduced a campaign in January 1950 aimed at "cleansing" the middle-class parties of "reactionaries". The SED received a commission to work on deposing Hickmann and other prominent opponents of unity lists. Semyonov told Kastner directly that "one tenth of the members [were to be] removed"; there would be "no future" for the party if it came out in support of "monopolists and Junkers" and came out "against people's own enterprises".[19] Tshuikov admonished Pieck and Grotewohl on 7 March not "to ease up" in the "unmasking of reactionary elements in the bourgeois parties",[20] and the continual pressure wore down the opposition. The party members gave up; and in the second half of March, the party leaders did so as well. Nuschke, who in January had initially wanted to resign,[21] agreed "in principle to joint lists" during the initial visit he paid to Pieck as president on 15 March. On 20 March, LDPD Co-Chairman Karl Hamann followed suit; and on 25 March Kastner did so as well.[22] When the SED leaders sought the signatures of the party chairmen on an agreement over unity lists three days later, Kastner got ruffled up again, but after being worked on by Pieck, finally gave in.

With this – and only at this point – the backs of the middle-class parties had been broken after more than two years of continual and in the end intensified pressure. Against many thoughtless assessments connected with the deposing of Kaiser and Lemmer, it must be stressed that only at this point did the parties give in. Even with all the problems which had not remained hidden from them, they had rightfully been able to regard their participation in the People's Congress movement up to the implementation of the GDR constitution as a contribution to a project democratic in nature and oriented toward Germany as a whole. From this point on, however, their participation predominantly contributed to the consolidation of the SED cadre-dictatorship, even if it only served to provide legitimation. Of course, there were still vague hopes that the Soviet Union could once again orient itself toward Germany as a whole. Likewise, there remained the task of not leaving the field completely open to the SED cadres and so perhaps preserving some freedoms which threatened to disappear as the Leninist ideologues marched through. This was all now unavoidably connected with individual corruption and led not infrequently to embarrassing expressions of obedience made without having been solicited. In the Central Bloc, Nuschke presented as his very own the idea of doing without the possibility of choosing between "yes" and "no" on the ballot, which was still a given during the elections to the Third People's Congress.[23]

With the definitive exclusion of free elections and the permanent safeguarding of SED hegemony ensuing from it, the resolution binding SED ministers and deputies to the Politburo, issued as early as 17 October 1949 by the Small Secretariat of the Politburo, took on in retrospect the character of a coup d'état against the GDR constitution. It decreed that

> laws and ordinances of significance, materials of other kinds concerning governmental decisions, furthermore proposals regarding the issuance of laws and ordinances . . . [must] be directed to either the Politburo or the Secretariat of the Politburo respectively for issuance as resolutions before passage by the Volkskammer or by the government.

Moreover, "the ruling of the responsible department of the Party Executive [is to be] obtained before the implementation of all other important administrative measures. . . ." Comrades in governmental positions were required to cooperate with the Party Executive. Beyond this, party groups in the ministries were to report "errors and incompetence in work".[24] As chairman of the Small Secretariat, and since the Third Party Congress in July 1950 as General Secretary, Ulbricht was thus de facto master of the situation in so far as events were not determined by the intervention of the SCC. The government and the parliament were, from this point on, organs doing prepatory work for and carrying out the will of the Politburo.

Applying these stipulations to the Ministry of State Security, established through a resolution of the Volkskammer on 8 February 1950, was of special significance in safeguarding power. As an autonomous apparatus, it was subordinate only to the SED Politburo, and with a rapidly expanding net of agents, it provided for surveillance and intimidation. Initially, this by no means covered all areas but in union with the mobilization actions of the party, it was effective none the less. A whole range of measures – including inspections, instances of manipulation, arrests, collective pressure on households, on the staffs of firms, and on village communities as well as the propagation of voting in public and, on election day itself, the use of "tractors" – ensured that when the voters went to the polls on 15 October 1950 protest could not make itself heard as it had in the almost traumatic elections to the People's Congress. Approximately 90 per cent of the voters cast ballots. Falsified vote counts rendered an official participation rate of 98.73 per cent and an approval of the unity list of 99.72 per cent.[25]

It must be stressed that it was the SED leadership which undertook this silent coup with great energy and not the Soviet occupation forces. For Ulbricht and the Leninist ideologues of his coloration, it was a matter of achieving the decisive breakthrough in the class struggle. Having just returned from exile in the US, the former Comintern functionary Gerhart Eisler declared with great openness in the Party Executive session of 4 October 1949 that "as Marxists, we must know: If we found a government, we never give it up either through elections or through other means." This moved Ulbricht to call out "Some still haven't understood that!"[26] This statement betrayed as much about his true thoughts as it did about the fact that not all SED leaders thought in this way.

Those who, like Grotewohl – now Prime Minister of the new state – still had the German-wide perspective in view, brought themselves into line. In light of the polarization which meanwhile had arisen between the regime and the population, the only alternative remaining to them was loss of power. Neither would they accept this for themselves personally, nor did they believe that the occupying power would accept the loss of the SED's monopoly on power. They were not aware that they thereby underestimated their scope of action. They certainly did not at all dare to grope around on its limits. Instead, they participated highly actively in repressive measures to forcibly achieve what they had originally hoped to gain through an improvement in the supply situation. For his part, Stalin accepted postponement of the elections and establishment of unity lists not in regard to the SED power monopoly but rather because he believed that a defeat at the polls for the SED would cost him his most important instrument for German policy.

Tshuikov and Semyonov, who essentially continued to carry out their old functions under new titles ("Chairman of the SCC" and "Political Advisor to the Chairman of the SCC" respectively), were nearer to events. At the Moscow meetings in September 1949, the introduction of a five-year plan was decided upon to succeed the two-year plan set to expire in the middle of 1950. This was to be implemented "in close cooperation with the Soviet Union and people's democracies".[27] After this, the two Soviet officials probably became convinced that the founding of a state in the Eastern Zone constituted the prelude to the establishment of a socialist state confined to only a part of Germany rather than constituting a roundabout way of achieving the German-wide solution. At any rate, Pieck noted during a discussion with Semyonov on 14 February 1950 that the "class struggle" in the GDR had "intensified" and that the "parties [will] disappear": "We are heading for socialism – but zig-zag / We don't talk about it."[28]

"GERMANS AT A SINGLE TABLE!"

Not only concern about the loss of their hegemonic position lay behind the zeal with which the SED employed all the instruments of power at their disposal in order to achieve an election result of nearly 100 per cent for the "National Front" list. Long after the division of the seats in the new Volkskammer had been established, the SED did not shrink from using diverse forms of manipulation to raise the voter turnout of 90 per cent to nearly 100 per cent. This can only be explained in that it was – naively – believed that the West German population would be impressed by such a result. From "high voter turnout" and "greatest possible unified yes-votes", they expected, according to Pieck at the next Moscow visit in early May 1950, a "great impact on the West".[29]

The German-wide engagement of the SED leadership certainly confined itself to this – in fact counterproductive – effort. Everything else served to secure its power in the East and could be justified as German-wide only in so far as a suction effect was expected upon the doubly-exploited West Germans, victims of both "predatory foreign monopolies" and "German monopolists", who "once again [had come] to power in the Bonn government".[30] As Grotewohl said at the Third Party Congress, "The example of peaceful, honest work will serve to convince the working class and the population of West Germany. They will recognize who is the friend and who is the enemy of the German people."[31]

The "National Front of Democratic Germany", initially nothing but a slogan and only since the renaming of the People's Congress Secretariat as Front Secretariat on 7 January 1950 an actual organization, from the beginning served more as a means of eliminating resistance against the SED than as a means of agitation in the West. Even in that function, it found little success. "The restructuring of the People's

Congress Committees into Committees of the National Front is going very slowly", as Semyonov complained on 24 January. "Some organizational units of the SED are carrying out no work at all in regard to propaganda for the National Front. . . . As a rule, lively agitation is lacking."[32] Six weeks later, Tshuikov insisted that the "National Front movement" was still "weak" and "not [anchored] in [the] masses".[33]

It was no wonder that Pieck, Grotewohl, Ulbricht, and Oelßner once again had to listen to harsh criticism when they met with Stalin in early May to get approval of the Five-Year Plan.[34] In a meeting at the Kremlin on the evening of 4 May, Pieck referred in vain to the great achievement which lay behind the agreement of the "parties of the old middle classes" to the Unity List. ("There were, however, some difficulties and strong countercurrents."[35]) Stalin unequivocally emphasized "that the policy and the practical work of the SED are insufficiently oriented toward the solution of the tasks regarding all of Germany".[36]

The *Genossen* vowed improvement. In an internal "resolution on strengthening the struggle in West Berlin and West Germany" on 2 June, the Politburo determined, "self-critically" as it said, the insufficiency of the work in the West up to that point. It agreed with Stalin "that the main task lies in the development of a policy for all of Germany" and declared that "the leading organs of the party [must] not limit themselves to the tasks within the GDR".[37] The draft resolution of the Third Party Congress was accordingly reformulated in such a way that the struggle for peace and national unity appeared unambiguously as the highest priority. The Party Congress embraced Stalin's reproach by characterizing the insufficient German-wide orientation of the party as one of "the main causes for the insufficient success of the National Front for Democratic Germany in West Germany and West Berlin". It also obliged the newly-elected organs of the party "to regard themselves as directly responsible for . . . the unfolding of a German-wide policy".[38]

In actuality, the SED leadership now sought, as Franz Dahlem phrased it, "to throw" all available forces "toward West Germany and to popularize the policy of the GDR there" in regard to the "National Front".[39] Hundreds of full-time instructors and voluntary assistants went to the West under various pretexts in order to "expose" the "rabble-rousing" of the "imperialistic warmongers" and to arouse "national resistance" against the "Anglo-American imperialists and their German accomplices". Huge quantities of brochures were printed and to an extent via adventurous routes smuggled into the Federal Republic. The "National Front" activists directed millions of letters, telegrams, and telephone calls to

West Germans. The KPD and moreover diverse front organizations sponsored rallies and discussion groups. West Germans were invited to tours and encounters, sometimes also for schooling and vacations.

As is well known, the success of this actionism in the West was modest. The West Germans felt themselves by no means as oppressed or exploited as the SED leaders presumed in their increasing loss of reality. All the more, they perceived the dubiousness of an allegedly "national" and "democratic" policy which ultimately rested upon the presence of the Red Army and had nothing more to offer in material terms than did the Marshall Plan. Reinforcing old stereotypes, they could perceive the call to resistance only as an attempt to unleash a revolution in the service of the Soviet Union, something which had to be countered energetically.

In accordance with this, the heads of the SCC and the SED again and again had to acknowledge that the propaganda campaign in the West was falling flat. As Pieck noted during a meeting with Tshuikov and Semyonov on 3 July 1950, "struggle for peace (Stalin commission) very bad in West Berlin / in West Germany". As the reason for the insufficient response in the West, he noted "apparent fear, cowardice".[40] Those responsible could console themselves that "such a silence suffered . . . [is] for the imperialist oppressors sometimes more dangerous than open demonstrations", as *Neues Deutschland* wrote picking up this assumption. The hoped-for "outbreak" of "dissatisfaction" and "indignation"[41] still failed to materialize, and soon the enthusiasm of the base decreased in regard to promotional efforts whose prospects of success were clearly minimal. "Even in the GDR", as the Politburo had to acknowledge in March 1951, "the peace movement by no means possesses the depth and national momentum corresponding to the special and especially conspicuous threat to the German people and which for the effect on West Germany is so necessary."[42]

A few weeks after the New York conference of the three Western foreign ministers, meeting from 12 to 19 September 1950, had paved the way for the incorporation of the Federal Republic into the Western defence system, Stalin finally made up his mind in October on a new initiative. He had the Prague conference of foreign ministers issue a proposal. This group met on 20 and 21 October and for the first time included the representative of the GDR along with his colleagues from the states which were part of the East Bloc at that time. The proposal amounted to a compromise between the GDR and the Federal Republic: the creation of a German-wide constituent council to be composed equally of representatives from East and West Germany, which would pre-pare the formation of a provisional, democratic, peace-loving, sov-ereign government for all of Germany and which must submit its proposals to the governments of the USSR, the US, Great Britain, and France for joint confirmation.[43]

Grotewohl's government declaration of 15 November, which had been agreed upon with the SCC,[44] supplemented this proposal with the idea "that this constituent council for all of Germany could take on the preparation of conditions for the holding of free, German-wide elec-tions for a national assembly".[45] In the form of a letter from the GDR's prime ministers bearing the date 30 November, both proposals were handed to Federal Chancellor Adenauer.[46] It remained unclear, how-ever, as to what "conditions" in the view of its authors needed to ob-tain in order to permit free elections. Nor was it clear as to whether the "formation" of a government for all of Germany was to occur be-fore or after the elections.

With this proposal, Stalin indirectly signalled that hopes of an "up-rising" of the West Germans against the Western occupying powers and against the regime installed by them had been deceptive. The in-stitutions of the Federal Republic had become a power factor which could no longer be disregarded in the struggle for German unity. The operational goal was thus no longer "erection of the German Demo-cratic Republic on the territory of all of Germany", as *Neues Deutschland* had written in March,[47] but rather the agreement of both German govern-ments upon a regime which satisfied Soviet ideas on security. In Moscow's view, the West German government certainly had to be compelled to reach such an agreement. It is beyond doubt, however, that the FRG government and the Bundestag were to have a part in the results of negotiations just like the GDR government and the Volkskammer.

Implicitly, this brought the order in the GDR as much into question as that of the FRG – certainly no very pleasant prospect for Ulbricht. After he had, as late as August, threatened Adenauer that he would "be put before a court of the people",[48] he now, however, found himself needing to declare in the Central Committee that "furthering the ouster of the Bonn government [be] put in the foreground". He also had to warn against domestic political measures which "could be a hinderance to a future free decision of the population of all Germany, which would block the establishment of the unity of Germany". On the same occa-sion, Rudolf Herrnstadt issued the watchword to concentrate "our fire essentially on the American aggressor" and that the FRG government be attacked only in so far "as we can be certain that our attacks find support among the broad masses in West Germany who want an agreement".[49]

Naturally, the contours of the order to be negotiated among the two German states and the four Allied powers remained rather vague. It was, however, no longer clear that the elections would take place only after the departure of the "Anglo-American intervention troops" and the admission of the GDR parties and mass organizations into the West. These had been conditions demanded by the GDR government in early March to counter the American demand for German-wide elections on 15 October 1950.[50] It is not clear (and was not at all to be foreseen) that the principle of the Unity List, to whose pushing through the SED had dedicated so much effort, would also govern the system for the German-wide elections, in which "the proposals of the Bonn government too just as the proposals which can be made by the representatives of the German Democratic Republic, [should] be taken into account". And it was not guaranteed either that in the negotiations over the "creation of an order embodying the rule of law and a free form of government for all of Germany", as was offered by the Volkskammer in reaction to a first negative position by Adenauer on 30 January 1951,[51] nothing other would emerge than an affirmation of the order of the GDR. In the Central Committee, Herrnstadt admonished that "some of us would . . . do well, to free ourselves from the undialectical conception that the coming unified, democratic Germany would simply be an enlarged copy of the present German Democratic Republic".[52]

The Prague proposal held so many risks for the SED regime and also for the socialist perspective of the future which its protagonists had in mind, that the suspicion immediately arose in the West that it was not seriously intended but was, rather, a cheap propaganda manoeuvre designed to prevent the West Germans from participating in the defence of the West. In actuality, it corresponded not only to Stalin's unchanged objective; there was more or less confidence in Moscow that this approach to West German institutions would meet with success. The "Bundestag will not say no," as Pieck noted at a meeting with Tshuikov and Semyonov on 21 February 1951. Delays and "tricks by the FRG government [had to be] reckoned with", but then the constituent council "eventually" would indeed "discuss the 8 Points", which the Volkskammer had sent to the Bundestag with the slogan "Germans at a single table!"[53]

It is likely that Stalin was driven to this de facto recognition of the Federal Republic by a concern that the resolutions for mustering West

German troops and creating an integrated defence organization for Europe indicated that the US was indeed preparing a military attack on the Soviet Union and its allies. According to the account of the Italian Communist leader Pietro Secchia, he characterized the world situation in a meeting with the top representatives of the Italian Communist Party (Secchia, Luigi Longo, and Palmiro Togliatti) as "serious, tense, and full of danger" in the winter of 1950–51. Giorgio Amendola, Secchia's colleague on the executive, reported that in this conversation, the participants were of the opinion "that the Cold War in internal and foreign affairs had reached a turning point. . . . The hypothesis of a general conflict no longer appeared to have been pulled out of the air."[54]

What Khrushchev emphasized in his *Memoirs* fits with this: it was believed in Moscow "in the days leading up to Stalin's death, that America would invade the Soviet Union and we would go to war. Stalin trembled at this prospect. How he quivered! He was afraid of war. He knew that we were weaker than the United States. . . . Our victory in the war did not stop him from trembling inside."[55] On another occasion, Khrushchev declared that a regular "war psychosis" reigned in the Politburo. Molotov had repeatedly made calls back from international conferences warning of the immediate danger of a new world war.[56]

In the context of these accounts, it is likely that Pieck was not simply emphasizing a propaganda slogan when he noted at the beginning of a conversation with Tshuikov on 4 April 1951 "Adenauer's plans to fail, only in this way prevent war."[57] In public, Stalin clearly appeared somewhat more worried now than he had been at the time of the founding of the Cominform. To the question of whether he held "a new world war to be unavoidable", he answered in an interview published by *Pravda* on 17 February 1951 that the "aggressive forces panting for a new war" are faced by peoples "who want no new war and are for the maintenance of peace". He added in warning that war could "become unavoidable if the warmongers succeed in beguiling the masses of the people through lies, deceiving them, and drawing them into a new world war".[58]

STALIN'S NOTES

After the Bundestag had rejected the appeal by the Volkskammer on 9 March, the campaign for the Federal Republic reverted for the time being to an attempt to mobilize the West Germans against their government.

Ulbricht, for whom the restraint of the previous months had clearly been difficult, presented a plan in early May for a plebiscite in both German states by which power would be seized from both Adenauer and Schumacher: "In the struggle against remilitarization and for a peace treaty, those men and women who are patriotic and aware of their responsibility will step forward who are in a position, after the overthrow of the Adenauer clique, to establish an agreement with the representatives of the German Democratic Republic".[59] With these "representatives of a West German democratic coalition", he then wanted to carry on those talks on the formation of a "Constitutive Council for All of Germany" which had been rejected by the government and parliament of West Germany.[60]

It must remain an open question as to whether Ulbricht actually believed that he could reach his goal in this manner. It is in any event clear that he preferred to enter upon this course, along which fewer dangers for the existence of the SED regime lurked, rather than Moscow's course via elected representatives of the West German state. It can be assumed that he had quietly speculated from the very beginning that Adenauer and Schumacher would see to it that the Prague Initiative was rejected so that a further argument for seeking their "overthrow" could be constructed.

Whatever expectations those responsible in the SED may have held regarding the campaign for the plebiscite, they had to realize very soon that the "mood for German-wide talks", which they had correctly diagnosed in the Federal Republic,[61] could not be turned against Adenauer or Schumacher. As Pieck reported in a meeting with Tshuikov on 11 May, "movement in the West for plebiscite still weak". "Of ten thousand committees," which had obviously been planned, "only one thousand" had come into existence; the KPD was "not in action", was "separated from the masses", and "weak".[62] Declarations against "remilitarization" and for the conclusion of a peace treaty "as late as 1951" were only collected with difficulty. Some 1.7 million signatures, corresponding to 6.7 per cent of West German voters, had been registered by the SED to the end of July[63] – measured against the popularity of the question, no exciting result. It was not made public.[64]

Grotewohl drew the conclusion from this that he and his comrades had wound up on the defensive: "Initiative early with us – up until the vote – now with the opponent." To the question of "What to do about it?" there were certainly few convincing answers at the top-level discussion on the evening of 30 July in Karlshorst. Ulbricht wanted to know how one could make "understandable" to the "masses" "that SU wants peace, USA war". Perhaps, he thought, a "special letter to [the] SPD workers" should be published, in which they would be called to "unity of action". This then took place on 1 September. Grotewohl nevertheless moved in the right direction when he referred to the fact that the Federal Republic could achieve "equality in remilitarization", and thus there must be more substantial talk about the "content" of the sought-after "peace treaty". He too refrained from more detailed explanations as to what the concessions on the West German side were to be like.[65]

Initiative from Moscow was needed once again for an approach to the Federal Republic. After rather long consultation with Tshuikov and Semyonov in which the Moscow centrale was also involved,[66] Grotewohl presented on 15 September in the Volkskammer a proposal for a "joint German-wide meeting of the representatives of East and West Germany". This was to "decide" "firstly, on the holding of free elections for all of Germany", and "secondly, on the acceleration of the conclusion of a peace treaty with Germany".[67] In an appeal which took up Grotewohl's proposals, the Volkskammer called for the Bundestag to cooperate.[68]

With this, as Grotewohl specifically emphasized in his government declaration, the demand for equal composition of the preparatory body was given up. At the same time, the holding of elections to a national assembly for all of Germany came very much into the foreground of the proposals as to the process. That they should take place *before* the formation of a government for all of Germany was still not explicitly stated; it could be assumed to be likely since there were no other specifications as to the means of forming a government. When, among other conditions, the Bundestag demanded the "guarantee of free political activity in preparation for the election", the "guarantee of a secret ballot", and the "preparation and holding of the election under international control", Grotewohl declared the "majority" of these proposals to be "acceptable".[69] In a letter agreed upon with Semyonov,[70] Pieck specified to Federal President Heuss that the government of the GDR was "in agreement with the review of the prerequisites for carrying out free elections . . . in all parts of Germany". He insisted, however, that this review be conducted "by a commission composed of representatives from East and West Germany under the four-power control of the USSR, USA, England, and France".[71]

The goal of the undertaking was to move the representatives of the Federal Republic to press jointly with the GDR for the rapid conclusion of a peace treaty with the four powers.[72] Despite the negative experience with the Prague Initiative, the Soviet authorities did not consider the possibility of achieving this to be without prospect. Semyonov, now once again at the very head of the "whole-Germany" line, informed the SED leaders on 1 November that the demand for supervision of the elections by the United Nations, as made by Adenauer in his government declaration of 27 September, was "not [a] hopelessly contentious question".[73] He let Ernst Lemmer, a potential ally on the West German side, know confidentially via the latter's old party friend Georg Dertinger that "Soviet policy wants to concern itself seriously with reunification without consideration of the SED, insofar as all of Germany is made neutral; Moscow is prepared to pay a high price for a neutral Germany."[74]

In order to give the offer of free elections more substance, Semyonov instructed the SED leadership to take the "Weimar electoral law as the basis" for the draft of an answer to the Bonn electoral law of 30 October.[75] And this was done: the electoral law passed by the Volkskammer on 9 January 1952 did foresee the participation of "mass organizations" in the election but otherwise followed by and large the proportional electoral law of the Weimar Republic. The only thing that remained open was the issue of who determined whether a party were "democratic".[76]

The Bundestag also refused to participate on this basis, which in Moscow had been regarded as the more likely result from the beginning. In late January 1952, Stalin then agreed to Gromyko's proposal to let the government of the GDR approach the four powers alone. The Soviet government was then to answer with the publication of fundamental principles for a peace treaty, which were to be communicated to the Western powers via a note. An alternative proposal of the SED leadership whereby the principles for the peace treaty would initially be presented by the GDR government received no further attention at Gromyko's instigation. It threatened to emphasize unduly the role of the GDR and thus offer the opponents of a conjoint arrangement in the West unnecessary points at which to attack.[77]

The "draft for a peace treaty with Germany", in whose preparation especially Gromyko and Molotov were involved after preliminary, very piecemeal presentations by Foreign Ministry Departmental Director Gribanov, retained on the one hand essentials which Stalin in all events wanted realized in a peace agreement. On the other hand, it was formulated consciously to attract and its contents accommodated the Germans in a series of points. Essentials were giving up the areas beyond the Oder and Western Neisse, a ban on "organizations inimical to democracy and the maintenance of peace", as well as the condition "to enter into no kind of coalition or military alliance directed against any power which took part with its armed forces in the war against Germany".[78] The last item was aimed not only at the security of the Soviet Union; as Daniil Melnikov, a co-worker in the Foreign Ministry, explained, it was also intended as an offer to the "traditional enemy" France, whose trauma was still Rapallo. The concept of "neutralization" was consciously avoided because the issue was not one of "pushing Germany away from the West".[79]

Deviating from the line still held to by the Prague Initiative, Stalin for the first time in this draft offered the Germans their "own national armed forces (land, air, and sea) which are necessary for defence of the country" as well as the production of "war materiels and equipment" required for that purpose. In contrast to the bureaucrats' preliminary draft of 8 September 1951, there was now no mention of reparations.[80] Instead, the Germans were assured that "no kind of limitations" would be placed upon the development of the peace economy. Also unlike the preliminary draft, there was no reference to "democratic transformations in industry, in agriculture, and in other sectors of the economy". Further, denazification was presented as having been concluded: "Civil and political rights equal to all other German citizens . . . must be made available to all former members of the German army, including officers and generals, all former Nazis, excluding those who are serving court sentences for commission of crimes." Finally, the united Germany's membership in the United Nations was promised – and thereby, beyond the withdrawal of all occupation forces, an end to any kind of special rights reserved by the victorious powers.

With the note published on 10 March, the Soviet leadership signalled its willingness, reacting to the gains made by the West Germans in the negotiations on the "general treaty", to depart from the Potsdam agreement at essential points or at least to interpret them in a very restrained fashion. The magnitude of their concessions was not sharply defined in every respect; in accordance with the situation in the talks, they could be made broader or narrower. The Soviet Union, furthermore, did not want the proposal in all points to be regarded as the last word: in the accompanying notes to the Western Allies, it declared itself "at the same time ([ready]) to consider other possible proposals on this question". At the presentation of the draft by the SCC head on the evening of 9 March, Pieck noted "also other possibilities".[81]

What still remained unclear and a possible point of contention was what was to be understood under the concept of "democratic parties and organizations" and who was to rule on this criterion. In a second note of 9 April in answer to a query by the Western powers, the Soviet government gave the assurance that "free elections for all of Germany" could be carried out "in the immediate future".[82] This, on the other hand, actually left hardly any doubt that the "formation of a government for all of Germany" was to precede the elections. The SCC instructed the GDR foreign ministry to draft a plan for carrying out separate elections in each German state for the joint national assembly.[83] Reservations on the Soviet side regarding security were now limited to the demand that a four-power commission alone have the right to review "whether the prerequisites for such elections exist". They rejected a review of the prerequisites by the UN, as demanded by the Western powers. The Soviets saw the UN as a tool of the US and feared an uncontrollable "imperialistic" influence in the part of Germany occupied by the Soviets.

It can be seen unambiguously from the history of the preparation of the 10 March note that the Soviet leadership did indeed clearly want to mobilize the West German population for the peace treaty. This is also confirmed by the commentaries with which Soviet diplomacy accompanied the initiative. On 28 January, Gromyko wrote to Stalin that now the point had come "for supporting the German democratic forces in their struggle for the unity of Germany and for accelerating the conclusion of a peace treaty with Germany". In the draft of a communication to the governments in Warsaw and Prague, there was talk of the "necessity of developing still more widely the movement of the German people for peace and against war as well as to counter the aggressive plans of the three powers regarding West Germany with a positive programme of a peace arrangement with Germany and of the conclusion of the peace treaty with Germany".[84]

As can be seen in the subsequent disappointed reactions,[85] there had been hopes in Moscow that through mobilization of "patriotic" forces, the FRG government and Bundestag could perhaps after all be moved to come over to the side of the GDR organs for the peace treaty. If this were not successful, the hope still remained that the effect of the manifestation of the German desire for unity would not be lost on the Western powers. One way or another, the serious engagement of the Western powers with the proposal for a peace treaty still remained the operational goal of Soviet policy. Gromyko addressed this explicitly in a communication to Stalin.[86] Pieck asked during his next encounter with Stalin on 1 April if he regarded a "four-power conference" as likely and "what possible results" were to be expected. At the same time, he reported that "the proposal by the Soviet government" had "unleashed a great movement of the masses – through which the Western powers and their Adenauer government are getting into great difficulties".[87]

The internal files thus confirm what Stalin told the Italian Socialist leader Pietro Nenni at a meeting on the evening of 17 July 1952: that with the first note, the Politburo "was really willing to make sacrifices to obtain unification".[88] That the willingness to sacrifice also had its limits indirectly underscores once again that for Stalin it was not only an issue of having a propaganda effect – that could have been really much more effectively formulated. If Moscow actually wanted to negotiate, however, then it had to be certain that in making accommodations, the essential objectives of its own programme were looked after. Under the impression of his conversations in the Soviet foreign ministry, Melnikov thus had good reason to assume "that this note says very much about Stalin's thoughts at the time and that he was honest insofar as he really wanted reunification".[89]

As we know from its long prehistory, the note did not signify for Stalin the fundamental turn which it was held to be in public, if it was given any credence at all. Since in his view there was no socialism in the GDR, it was not a matter of having to give up socialism there. On the other hand, the SED leaders, in so far as they had established themselves in the "leading position in government", had to ask themselves more poignantly than at the time of the Prague Initiative whether they now had to start over from the very beginning again. In fact, there are some indications that this question was discussed. Nenni had heard from Pieck and Grotewohl as early as the beginning of 1951 "that the Soviet government is pursuing a policy which will demand great sacrifices from them and that soon they in Germany could be brought into a situation comparable to Nenni's in Italy".[90] According to testimony of former colleagues after his fall in August 1953, State Security Secretary Wilhelm Zaisser had said in a meeting of the provincial heads of the Ministry for State Security in April or May 1952 that it was "not [to be] excluded that in the interest of preserving the international peace, the Soviet Union would enter into a compromise and pull back from the German Democratic Republic".[91] In May 1960, Ulbricht told SED district delegates at a conference that

> our proposal in 1952 was also associated with a risk for the GDR, for the working class. At that time, the GDR was still not so strongly consolidated, and the questions of securing peace and of reunification and the character of Western domination were not so clear in the whole population as they are now. But we were ready to carry

on the struggle on a level field. That would have become a long path of struggle in Germany. In the end, however, the progressive forces would have predominated.[92]

In the Politburo, a consciously optimistic assessment was drawn from the discussion of 25 March: "To the question of how the single Germany will look, the answer is: As the German people wants it to look. Democratic elections in all of Germany will lead inevitably to Adenauer's fall because in West Germany too the patriotic forces are becoming stronger and stronger."[93] Accordingly, Pieck presented the problem to Stalin on 1 April: "For Germany question of elections, without UN Commission, as mass struggle for the overthrow of the Adenauer government."[94]

Differing conceptions lay hidden behind this consensual formula. For Grotewohl, it was still without a doubt more a matter of unity than a matter of the SED's monopoly on power. To that extent, he greeted the Soviet initiative without qualification and supported it by coming out on Semyonov's side as the author of the confidential message to Ernst Lemmer.[95] Many of his Communist *Genossen*, however, were able to believe that they would acquit themselves well in free elections – with the premise that they were not "manipulated" by the UN. As Pieck stated in a conversation with Stalin in May 1950, their starting point was the rather bizarre idea that "in West Germany and West Berlin" there were up to that point "no democratic rights for free elections – but rather occupation statutes and suppression of the progressive press and organizations".[96] Whoever did not let his or her view of power-political realities be warped by such ideological delusions, had to "reckon . . . that we no longer have the majority of the people behind us", as did Zaisser according to his colleagues' accounts. Then "he [would] not [be] minister any longer and Mielke no longer State Secretary".[97]

Everyone knew, however, as Oelßner explained to worried party comrades, that "some concessions" had to be made in the interest of unity.[98] One could not refuse an unambiguous commission from Stalin, even when one had meanwhile abandoned oneself to other ideas. In January 1952 in the Central Committee Secretariat, Ulbricht too stated that one would have to do without the "dominance of Communism"[99] – even though according to his understanding only temporarily. Visibly irritated, he had explained to the SED county secretaries two months earlier that it was "not true that these proposals [meaning the second appeal by the Volkskammer] are, so to speak, only formal offers".[100]

Having been forced to do without a short-term perspective on social-ism clearly did not prevent Ulbricht from continuing to count on the mobilization of the "German people" against the supposed "warmon-gers" in Bonn and Washington during the sought-after elections for all of Germany.[101] Additionally, he pursued the extension of the existing order in the GDR so that it would be optimally armed for the elections and the period thereafter. He probably did not perceive that in this way he was directly assisting the opponents of a German-wide com-promise in the West. The idea of permanent class struggle had become such a part of him that he could neither adequately grasp the situation in the Federal Republic nor was he in a position to adjust himself to that situation.

The answer to the question of the century as to whether in 1952 there had been a chance for unity in freedom is thus obvious: Accord-ing to the records, there was a chance to seize onto the conditions roughly outlined by Stalin in the note of 10 March, and these included elections without Unity Lists as the basis for organizing German state-hood. Just as he had in the previous years, Stalin wanted a compro-mise, and he was prepared to pay the Germans a significantly higher price than he had initially had in mind. This chance was nevertheless limited by the fact that large segments of the Communist apparatus still thought exclusively in the categories of class struggle and con-sequently could imagine unification only under their leadership. Con-flicts over the content of the concept of democracy were thus programmed in, and the failure of the negotiations, if they actually were to take place, could not be excluded.

SOCIALISM IN PLACE OF UNITY

After the three Western powers, in their answer of 25 March, persisted in demanding that a UN commission investigate the prerequisites for free elections and that the future German state be free to enter into coalitions, the Soviet leadership itself strengthened Ublricht's counter-productive agitation. The leader of the Diplomatic Mission of the USSR in the GDR, Georgii M. Pushkin, declared to Foreign Minister Dertinger on the evening of 27 March that it was now clear that the "general treaty with the Bonn government" was completed and that "shortly" also "the signing of the Pleven Plan" of the European Defence Com-munity would follow. West Germany would then "find itself unequivo-cally in the front of the North Atlantic pact". The West Germans could "now only through great propaganda efforts be brought to the point of strengthening their opposition to the Adenauer government and finally to bring about its fall".[102] Pieck expressed himself in the same vein to Stalin on 1 April: The SPD Executive would "probably" reject the proposal to form an "action unit for the peace treaty" as had been put forth by the SED Central Committee on 27 March. Further, the general treaty would "probably [be] adopted in the middle of May". Consequently, what was needed was "protest strikes in firms, demonstrations, calls for peace, collection of signatures", and a "national programme [for] peace, unity, democracy".[103]

Stalin obviously assessed the meaning of the Western answer in exactly the same way. Pieck noted by the Soviet leader's remarks at the closing meeting with the SED delegation on the evening of 7 April: "Up to this point, all proposals rejected." And further: "no compromises / ... Atlantic pact – autonomous state in the West." Likewise, Stalin at least accepted that now there would be intensified calls for the "overthrow" of the Bonn government. "Unity – peace treaty – agitate further," as Pieck recorded at the close of the meeting.[104] After Ulbricht, as early as 28 March, had gone ahead with an appeal to "struggle against the Bonn clique [of] henchmen of American imperialism",[105] the first calls for "mass strikes and mass struggle" which were "to topple Adenauer's general-war treaty and bring about the rapid conclusion of a peace treaty".[106]

Unlike many ideological zealots, Stalin may well not really have believed any longer in the short-term success of this agitation. In any case, he told Nenni on 17 July, he "expects that split between two Germanies will continue for some time". The Italian Socialist leader got the impression in this conversation that Stalin "had written off the hope of a successful four-power conference at which Germany would be unified via an agreement".[107]

Safeguarding his East German provisional arrangement was now all the more important to Stalin. On 1 April, Pieck cautiously mentioned "steps toward formation of the Volksarmee instead of police", which was clearly at Soviet suggestion since there was no mention of such steps in the "proposals of the Politburo in connection with preparations for the Second Party Conference".[108] Stalin replied by immediately ordering comprehensive armament: "Not steps, but rather immediately." He thereupon even began to deal in specifics: "9 to 10 army corps – 30 divisions – 300,000 [soldiers] / training in SU / youth corps" and so forth. In the closing meeting on 7 April, he not only spoke more precisely of "military training for infantry, navy, aviation, submarines", but also pushed for fast action: "Armament must be gotten, immediately Russian rifles and ammunition." To justify this haste he said that the "demarcation line" is a "dangerous border": "We must figure with terrorist acts."[109] He explained to Nenni that "he intends to maintain a military equilibrium between West and East, by matching strength of NATO forces in Western Germany with an equally strong East German army".[110]

Still more important for further developments was that when Pieck reported on "increasing activity by the enemy" and mentioned especially "big farmers" and "church", Stalin advised him to create "production communes in villages in order to isolate big farmers" and in the context of these "collective farms" spoke for the first time of the "path to socialism".[111] Ulbricht and his brothers in arms thereupon not only prepared the formation of the first agricultural production communes. They also drew the conclusion from the clearly spontaneous inspiration on the part of the master of the Kremlin that pushing through socialist conceptions of order in the GDR had now become possible.

Therefore, immediately after the return from Moscow, it was decided in the Politburo on 11 April, within the framework of measures for "improving the work of the state apparatus", not merely to undertake just more stringent "direction and supervision of the provincial governments", as had been planned in the run up to the Moscow visit,[112] but rather to eliminate the provinces with their federalistic remnants completely. They were to be replaced by fourteen districts formed according to economic criteria.[113] The fact that this widened the gulf between the GDR and the FRG no longer played any role.

After the SCC had raised no objections to this break from the regional structure of the rest of German territory, which at the same time served the Politburo by making more effective its efforts to push through its decisions,[114] Ulbricht ventured another decisive step. The upcoming Second Party Conference was originally only supposed to deliberate over the "conclusion of the peace treaty, bringing about the unity of the fatherland on a democratic basis, and fulfilling the economic plan in the most important year of the Five Year Plan".[115] On 30 May the Secretariat of the Central Committee resolved that the central motto for that gathering would be the slogan "Forward for peace, unity, democracy, *and socialism.*"[116] On 24 June, the Politburo agreed to this expanded slogan.[117] On 1 July, Stalin was asked to "make a statement" on the view that the government power in the GDR had "developed from anti-fascist democratic order to democratic people's power, to people's democracy", and that it was now the task of the party "to lead the working class forward along the path of constructing socialism".[118]

In order to obtain Stalin's consent to a public proclamation of the socialism perspective, Ulbricht appealed to the Soviet dictator's obsessions in a letter sent on 2 July:

> In the German Democratic Republic, such an evaluation of our present level of development will significantly develop the initiative of the working class. This is of great importance for securing the German Democratic Republic against hostile sabotage and diversion measures and for organizing the armed forces of the German Democratic Republic.

At the same time, he claimed that with the declaration of the "transition to socialism", "the working class in West Germany [would also be] taught class consciousness". Moreover, "working farmers and the petty bourgeois would come to the conclusion that they can live better with us than in West Germany".[119]

Seen in the light of day, this was an attempt at extortion: Ulbricht told Stalin that the GDR could only avoid becoming a victim of the class enemy's offensive if the SED were allowed to lead the GDR to the emergence of socialism. That this worked is attributable to two factors: first, after the disappointment over the ineffectiveness of the Soviet compromise offers, it seemed reasonable to Stalin that he now put his money only on the magnet effect of a more attractive GDR; secondly, bringing about German unity had in the meantime lost its urgency in his mind. He told the SED leaders in April that the "Europe army" was directed "not against [the] Soviet Union", but rather had been created by the US "in order [to preserve its] power in Europe".[120] That was no particularly discomforting perspective if one assumed that "[West] Germany and Japan" would attempt "to get back on their feet again, to break out of the US 'regime', and to advance along the path of autonomous development", as Stalin had noted under the date 1 February 1952.[121] In the meantime, it was sufficient that "a strong East Germany under Soviet control . . . protect Russia's Western flank". Given this premise, "there will be no war", as he explained to Nenni.[122] He declared to American journalists on 31 March that a "third world war" was at the time no more likely "than two or three years ago".[123]

Agreeing to the proclamation of the "transition to socialism" was the price Stalin payed for securing his western flank. On 8 July, the Politburo of the CPSU approved the "course of forcing the construction of socialism in the GDR as had been begun by the SED".[124] On the very same day, *Neues Deutschland* published, perhaps a bit too rashly, an appeal for a mass demonstration under the motto "Forward for peace, unity, democracy, and socialism." In the Central Committee, Ulbricht presented the draft resolution for the party conference with the announcement "that constructing socialism has become the fundamental task in the German Democratic Republic"; there had not been enough time to copy the text beforehand.[125] The next day, the equally surprised delegates of the party conference learned from Ulbricht that the Central Committee was "to propose that Socialism will be constructed according to plan in the German Democratic Republic".[126]

Strictly speaking, Stalin's last-minute consent referred only to the public announcement of the status of a "people's democracy" and not to the commitment to "constructing socialism" as the *main task* which Ulbricht had made it into. It certainly did not mean that Stalin now saw the GDR as being on the path to a socialist state. In a telegram sent to the Second Party Conference by the CPSU, the socialism perspective was not mentioned at all. Instead, the unchanged wish from Moscow was "further success . . . in fulfilling the historical task, creating a unified, independent, democratic, and peaceful Germany".[127] It was exactly the same in Stalin's congratulatory telegram and the address of his representative, Nikolai Shvernik, on the third anniversary of the founding of the GDR on 6 October 1952.[128] An informant even reported to the Eastern Office of the SPD on 18 July that the SCC had curtly criticized the resolutions of the party conference.[129]

Important to Stalin were only the stabilization of the GDR and its catching up to the Federal Republic in creating an army. According to statements to Nenni by high-ranking Soviet leaders, Stalin expected in the "near future", "a new balance of power resting upon the success of both sides in their efforts to rearm the Germans".[130] If these efforts were successful – and Stalin had no doubt about this for the East side as well – it was possible to bear "that the split between two Germanies will continue for some time". As he told Nenni, he was prepared to accept a Cold War for ten or fifteen years since he was confident that the East Bloc could better bear the economic strain thereby obtaining than could the Western powers. Stalin had clearly come to the conclusion, as Nenni summarized his impressions, that Germany was "no longer" the "supreme danger spot but just another area where a long term must be persued and the exchange of notes on Germany [is] losing significance".[131]

That he had become a prisoner of Ulbricht's through his interest in a military balance in Europe, was not perceived in its full scope by Stalin, convinced as he was that the West Germans had been blinded by American imperialists. Stalin saw little prospect of success in the calls for "overthrow of the Bonn vassal-regime" (according to the resolution of the Second Party Conference) and for the "irreconcilable and revolutionary overthrow of the Adenauer government" (according to a resolution of 11 November 1952), promulgated by the SED in consistent application of Ulbricht's policy.[132] These appeals were so vague and corresponded so poorly with realities in West Germany that, internally, Pieck and Ulbricht in a conversation with the SCC had no answer to the question as to how the "overthrow [of] Adenauer" was to be brought about.[133]

Given the concentration on "constructing socialism" in East Germany, the SED's strategy on German policy atrophied into a vague hope of revolution in western Germany. This policy was no longer put into operation, and it determined the SED's actions less and less. Many members of the inner leadership circle did not take it all seriously. As a Communist intellectual, Rudolf Herrnstadt was to a certain extent more capable of realistic assessments than the majority of his colleagues on the Politburo. He drew the conclusion from the consent of the "comrades in Moscow" to the proclamation of "constructing socialism",

> that in their view, the perspective of "peaceful unification" is to retreat into the background vis-à-vis the perspective of armed confrontation. Their agreement to this solution at the same time signifies . . . an extremely negative assessment of the work of the KPD and SED in regard to the decisive question, the question of Germany: It signifies the determination that the KPD and the SED have not been in the position to change the power relations in Germany to their benefit at the historical moment available to them, a moment which is essentially past".[134]

Stalin clearly gave not a moment's thought to the alternative of an armed struggle for the unity of Germany. Consequently, from the summer of 1952 on, his policy on Germany exhausted itself in maintaining the status quo. De facto he thereby bowed to the logic of bloc confrontation even though he was not prepared to admit the defeat and refused to see in that defeat anything more than an intermediate stage. The status of a member of the "people's democratic" bloc was thus withheld from the GDR. Stalin simply did not want to admit that the orientation of the East German provisional arrangement toward a state on the Soviet model definitively undermined the hope for a "unified, independent, democratic, peace-loving" (and not just yet socialist)

Germany. He avoided looking too carefully. Furthermore, he was now mainly preoccupied with the exposure of "Jewish conspiracies" in his immediate vicinity and declared that the problem of Germany had lost significance.

In the final analysis, Stalin had to ascribe to himself his defeat on German policy and the resulting formation of blocs in Europe, a development he did not desire. It was not only that the Ulbrichts were products of his claim to domination of the Communist world movement, pushed through with relentless cruelty. He also carried the mistrust against all actual democrats so far that in the end only those willing to submit themselves unconditionally remained as allies. At the Nineteenth Party Congress of the CPSU, the first held since 1939, he declared on 14 October 1952:

> Earlier, the bourgeoisie succeeded in presenting itself as liberal; it came out in favour of bourgeois-democratic freedoms and gained for itself popularity among the people. Now, not even a trace of liberalism remains. . . . The banner of bourgeois-liberal freedoms has been thrown overboard. I think that you, the representatives of the Communist and democratic parties, will have to raise this banner and carry it forward, if you want to gather the majority of the people around you. There is no one who can raise it other than you.

Amid "tumultuous applause", he added:

> Earlier, the bourgeoisie counted as the head of the nation. They came out in favour of the rights and the independence of the nation, placing it "above everything". Now, not even a trace remains of "national principle". Now, the bourgeoisie sells the rights and the independence of the nation for dollars. The banner of national independence and national sovereignty has been thrown overboard. Without a doubt, you, the representatives of the Communist and democratic parties, must raise and carry forward this banner, if your are patriots of your country, if you want to be the leading force in your nation. Other than you, there is no one who can raise it.[135]

The master of the Kremlin, grown lonely, was unable and unwilling to see that these flag bearers were extremely unsuited to make democracy and national independence a reality.

7 Ulbricht's Revolution

According to a report in *Neues Deutschland*, the delegates to the Second Party Congress of the SED reacted with "rapturous jubilation" to Ulbricht's suprising "proposal" to construct socialism in the GDR "according to plan": "The delegates rise to their feet, they call out, clap. Walter Ulbricht has uttered the decisive words of this conference. . . . Unbounded enthusiasm radiates from the faces of the delegates. How often socialism has been talked about. Now, for the first time in German history, this greatest goal of humankind will be turned into a reality on German soil."[1]

It remains difficult to assess how great the enthusiasm actually was. The only thing certain is that in the face of the difficulties which developed in the spring and summer of 1952, this enthusiasm yielded to disillusionment, and that out of this disillusionment grew another chance for the German-wide option. After the proclamation of the "construction of socialism" in the GDR, now unequivocally understood as an Eastern state, that option had seemed completely lost.

THE CRISIS OF SOCIALISM

The crisis of the SED regime brewing since late autumn 1952 could on the one hand be traced back to the fact that in his "methodical construction", Ulbricht gave no consideration to actual interests, moods, or power relations, but rather employed every form of persuasion in order to achieve as quickly as possible the socialistic state in its final form as he conceived of it. Although Stalin had explicitly impressed upon the SED leadership "not to compel anyone [in] the creation of production co-ops in the villages",[2] strong pressure was exercised by the lower party organizations on the farmers to join such co-ops. Farmers against whom accusations were made of alleged violations of the "regulations on proper cultivation" were forbidden to cultivate their land independently any more. Additional taxes were required of middling and big farmers. The state party dealt in the same way with artisans and other members of the commercial middle class: they too were to be driven into the system of collective property as quickly as possible.

Parallel to this, the ideological screws were tightened: the churches, regarded as the stronghold of "reaction", were forbidden to carry on religious education in the schools any more. Pupils, teachers, and lecturers loyal to the church were expelled; pastors who stood out politically were arrested. Efforts were increased to push through the "leading role of the party" in the schools and universities. The promotion of "socialist realism" led to numerous conflicts with artists and intellectuals. The state apparatus was now organized according to the principle of "democratic centralism", as had already been done within the party. The cult of personality around the "wise master", the "flag bearer of peace and progress in the whole world", the "great Stalin" (as he was dubbed in Ulbricht's speech setting out basic principles at the Second Party Congress[3]) reached fatuous climaxes.

The consequences of this forcing of the Soviet model – flight, refusal, and the resulting loss of production – took on an even more dramatic dimension when the GDR at the same time had to bear the burden of re-arming as decreed by Stalin. An additional sum of approximately 2 billion Marks had to be raised within the period of a year, corresponding to 10 per cent of the total revenue of the state. Likewise, the establishment of district administrations and the promotion of agricultural production co-ops resulted in costs unforeseen in the current Five-Year Plan. Initially, the government sought to make up the difference by levying additional taxes on those "classes [which are] dying out". These measures included raising the income and artisan tax, exclusion of the self-employed from the general health and social insurance, as well as making loans more difficult. These served only to increase dissatisfaction. Cuts in social services also hit the workers, who as a consequence of the all too ambitious goals of the plan already had an increasingly tense relationship with the state as employer.

A further intensification of the situation stemmed from the fact that as soon as difficulties began to become apparent, the Ulbricht apparatus increasingly employed repression. The number of trials against "agents" and "saboteurs" grew by leaps and bounds, and for the most part, draconian punishments were handed down. In the middle of December, Trade Minister Karl Hamann of the LDPD was arrested together with two state secretaries for "sabotage". Four weeks later, Foreign Minister Georg Dertinger of the CDU was arrested because of "hostile activity" against the GDR. In late December, the Central Committee formulated "lessons from the trial against the conspiratorial centre Slansky" in Czechoslovakia. Prominent Communists were taken into custody, over 150,000 members and candidates were excluded from the party. When during the exposure of the "doctors' conspiracy" in the middle of January *Neues Deutschland* had to join in the campaign against "demoralized bourgeois Jewish nationalists",[4] Herrnstadt too began to tremble.[5]

Accordingly, the number of refugees increased dramatically. Between 15,000 and 23,000 people were leaving the GDR bound for West Germany each month at this point. In March of 1953 the flow reached 58,000. Especially fatal for the food-supply situation was the flight of almost 20,000 independent farmers. But also 8,000 members of the billeted Volkspolizei and 2,700 members of and candidates for membership in the SED headed west. Among those who remained behind, "enormous energies of resistance" gathered, as the agitation secretary of the Berlin SED district direction at the time, Heinz Brandt, assessed in looking back. Ulbricht brought "all classes of the people, but especially the workers, to direct opposition against the SED and to the verge of revolt".[6]

This development did not remain hidden from the Soviet Control Commission. If one is to believe Heinz Lippmann, at the time deputy chairman of the Free German Youth (FDJ), the SCC as early as autumn 1952 commissioned special investigatory teams with the participation of Soviet functionaries to find out about the mood of the people and about various organizations' methods of operating. Newer sources demonstrate that a "group of responsible functionaries from the Central Committee of the SED and the government of the GDR" concerned itself with an analysis of the difficulties from the middle of February to late March 1953. The findings were in any case alarming: the first phase of the investigation determined that the population was "disinterested" in the work of the SED; that the workers were "hostile" to the measures taken by party and government; and that the functionaries of the firm organizations and the district administrations carried out their work without engagement. The investigation for the months of February and March 1953 led to the conclusion "that a retention" of the existing policy "could only be endured in the short term" and "that the limits of the burden on the population of the GDR [had been] breached".[7]

Ulbricht rejected these warnings as tendentious concoctions hostile to the party. Beyond the intensified repression, he sought his cure alone in material relief from the Soviet Union. As early as the end of 1952 he asked Stalin, in a communication, for additional deliveries. In early February 1953, he pressed for a "loan" and for "procurement of material". A new "trip to Moscow" was to be organized in order to get these.[8] After this plan was invalidated by Stalin's death on 5 March, Grotewohl presented the request for help to the new Soviet Prime Minister Georgii Malenkov and his deputy Lavrenti Beria at Stalin's funeral ceremony. In early April, the SED leadership sent a further communication to Moscow in which they, as Grotewohl in late June explained somewhat euphemistically to the Central Committee, "asked for a review of the situation which had developed and for support in word and deed".[9]

Moscow was neither willing nor able to supply substantial financial support. After Ulbricht's letter to Stalin had gone unanswered, the new master of the Kremlin issued a negative decision.[10] In answer to its April petition for help, the SED leadership was "urgently" advised to moderate its course.[11] The deputy director of the Soviet Commission for Economic Planning, Nikitin, declared to his GDR colleagues during a visit to East Berlin: "The Soviet leadership is planning a new course which aims at improving the living standard of the population. For this purpose, it must employ all available reserves. It is recommended that the SED likewise alter its economic policy and employ measures which would result in an improvement of . . . living conditions."[12]

In the face of the Soviet refusal, Ulbricht gave a green light to two rigorous cost-cutting measures which caused dissatisfaction to grow further: on 9 April, the Council of Ministers decided as of 1 May not to issue any more cards for food supplies to independent traders, owners of "devastated" agricultural concerns, and owners of rental property – a total of about two million people; on 14 May, there followed the resolution of the Central Committee to increase "the average work rate by at least 10 per cent altogether." In the sectors "decisive for production", these increases were to be guaranteed up to 30 June 1953 through a further resolution of the Ministerial Council as early as 28 May.[13] Since, with this measure, the possibility of overtime largely disappeared, it meant a severe drop in real wages for many industrial workers.

At the same time, Ulbricht intensified once again the ideological and power-political pressure. "The German Democratic Republic", as he declared now, for the first time without any consideration of the Soviet position in the German question up to that time,

is in its present developmental stage a power of the workers and peasants, in which the leading role belongs to the working class. The state of the German Democratic Republic successfully carries out the functions of the dictatorship of the proletariat. This means that it accomplishes the fundamental task of the transition period from capitalism to socialism – the construction of the economic and cultural bases of socialism as well as suppression of forces hostile to the people; it also organizes the protection of the homeland.[14]

In the cleansing campaign unleashed by the Slansky trial, Ulbricht accused his old rival Franz Dahlem of sharing responsibility for the "capitulatory behaviour" of the Paris KPD leadership at the beginning of the war in 1939. In the same session during which the increase in average work rates was decided upon, Dahlem was excluded from the Central Committee.[15] At the same time, a "Commission to Prepare for the Sixtieth Birthday of Comrade Walter Ulbricht" on 30 June 1953, under the leading participation of Lotte Ulbricht and Fred Oelßner, was creating a pompous cult around the "German worker's son".

BERIA'S REVISION

In the Kremlin, meanwhile, the alarm bells sounded. Semyonov was summoned to Moscow on 20 April to report. Initially, the report he brought along gave rise to no particular reactions among his direct superiors in the Foreign Ministry.[16] It was different with Beria, who as chief of the secret police was most familiar with Stalin's world of ideas. And in the position of Interior Minister, which he had regained after the death of the dictator, Beria was also the principal aspirant to be Stalin's successor. Beria immediately recognized the necessity of exorcising the spectre of the "construction of socialism" in the GDR and of orienting German policy once more toward bringing about unity. According to testimony by the chief of the First Office in the Ministry for State Security at the time, Pavel Sudoplatov, Beria wanted to approach the Western powers in the process and mobilize Western assistance for coming to terms with the developing economic crisis in the Soviet Union. In late April, Sudoplatov was commissioned by Beria to sound out through confidential channels in Bonn and Washington whether support could be won in the West for such a programme.

"The Beria Plan", according to Sudoplatov,

foresaw a reunified German state with a coalition government. The four Allied powers were to participate equally in the unification. For Beria, however, it was primarily a matter of the political and economic interests of the Soviet Union. For the sounding-out conversations in the West, he produced the following points: 1. Stretching out German reparations to the Soviet Union; 2. A rebuilding programme for Russia, the Ukraine, White Russia, and the Baltic States; the costs were to be met by Western sponsors, primarily the Germans. New industrial regions were to be created and a large rail and express-way net to be laid out in the Soviet Union. Beria contemplated technical assistance with German participation to the extent of ten billion dollars. If the Soviets wanted to support the illusory socialist construction of the GDR, he argued, they must invest not less than twenty billion dollars within the next ten years, including deliveries of raw materials and food to the GDR and Poland. He wanted to be rid of the heavy burden. Instead, he sought a wide-ranging economic agreement with the West. Through political arrangement with America, England, and France, he wanted to get this agreement blessed under the patronage of the United Nations.[17]

This project lay completely in line with Stalin's policy on Germany, right up to the sum to be mobilized for Soviet rebuilding; in the course of its further implementation, in the middle of May, Beria inquired of the "Small" Information Committee of the Foreign Ministry, what would be the attitude of the Social Democratic opposition in the FRG should it take over the government after the coming Bundestag elections. He was not satisfied with the answer that an SPD government too would continue the consolidation of the Western course oriented toward division. He expressed his doubts as to this evaluation, and demanded a more careful review of the situation. The officials of the Foreign Ministry defended their pessimistic assessment by making reference to the fact that the SPD had rejected all efforts of the KPD and SED for joint action against the Western treaties.[18]

Prime Minister Malenkov clearly was made aware of Beria's plan early and initially participated without reservations. The former NKVD Colonel Sergei Fedosseyev, whom Beria wanted to send to Yugoslavia, attests that Malenkov agreed to the reconciliation with Tito, which was being pursued simultaneously.[19] This makes the later accusations by Khrushchev and Molotov that Malenkov also shared Beria's position in the German question[20] seem thoroughly credible. In contrast, the Foreign Ministry did not concern itself with the affair for the time being.[21] After Stalin's death, Molotov had reassumed the post of Foreign Minister. First, on a Sunday in the second half of May, either the 17th or the 24th, he summoned his deputy Gromyko to his home in order to speak with him about the further course of action pertaining to the

GDR.[22] It cannot be determined whether he did this on his own initiative or whether it was a task assigned by Malenkov and Beria.

As can be gathered from Molotov's explanation to the Central Committee plenum from 2 to 7 July 1953, Beria had then introduced on 27 May a "draft resolution" in the Presidium of the Council of Ministers demanding a fundamental correction of the course taken up by the SED beginning in the spring and summer of 1952. In this document, "the course oriented toward the construction of socialism entered upon by the German Democratic Republic" had been characterized as "incorrect under today's conditions". It had further demanded that "at the present point in time, the GDR refrain from the course toward the construction of socialism". According to Khrushchev, who likewise reported on the Presidium session to the Central Committee Plenum, Beria had also announced that he wanted to conclude a "treaty" with the Western powers guaranteeing "a neutral, democratic Germany".[23]

In connection with the text passed by the Presidium at the close of the session,[24] it can be gathered from the statements to the July Plenum that Beria's attempt had not met with undivided approval. Afterward, Khrushchev warned of the danger "of giving eighteen million Germans over to the domination of American imperialists". Molotov said that "the traces of Hitlerite influence have still not been eliminated in all of Germany". The deputy minister for medium machine-building, Avraami Savenyagin, added to the discussion by making reference to the fact that "much uranium [is] mined in the GDR, perhaps as much as is currently available to the Americans". According to Molotov, Beria defended his position in the Presidium session with the argument "that a Germany reunited on a bourgeois basis would thoroughly satisfy the Soviet Union since a bourgeois Germany at the current time could only come into existence without close ties to other imperialistic states, since under present conditions, only a bourgeois Germany which is neither aggressive nor imperialistic could exist". Gromyko's memoirs make him out to have been still more clear: "The GDR? What does this GDR mean? It's not even a proper state. It's propped up only by Soviet troops, even if we call it the German Democratic Republic."[25]

Clearly, not all members of the Presidium were familiar, as Beria was, with the aims of Stalin's policy on Germany. Some had let themselves be so captivated by the fear of American imperialism that they were no longer capable of flexibility in the German question at all. For reasons of egotism connected with their departments, some feared losing the concrete advantages brought to them at the moment by the GDR. Beria did not possess enough authority in order to push aside these doubts easily. After some further attempts to win over the others,[26] he therefore finally agreed that the "construction of socialism in the GDR" was not to be condemned in general but rather, as Molotov had suggested during the course of the discussion,[27] only "the *forcing* of the construction of socialism".

The resolution "on the measures for recuperation of the political situation in the German Democratic Republic" clearly did not represent a "rebuff" for Beria, as the victors in the power struggle of 1953 wanted to have believed after his fall.[28] Under the rejected "course", he understood unequivocally and without any limitation the resolution of the Second Party Conference of the SED on the "construction of socialism", which, as was explicitly retained, "had been approved by the Politburo of the Central Committee of the CPSU in its resolution of 8 July 1952". This course correction, which "was recommended to the leadership of the SED and of the government of the GDR", was justified not only by the necessity of a "recuperation of the political situation in the GDR". Also cited were the goals of "bolstering our position in Germany itself as well as in the German question on an international level" and of "securing and expanding a mass movement for the creation of a unified, peace-loving, independent Germany". The "struggle for the unification[29] of Germany on a democratic and peaceful basis" was again unequivocally termed the "main task" in the document. There was no mention of other tasks, such as "more cautious action against the capitalists", as Molotov characterized the goal of the document after the fact.[30] Rather, it unmistakably decreed: "The propaganda carried out up to this time about the necessity of the transition of the GDR to socialism [is to be] regarded as incorrect."

The measures introduced in the course of "constructing socialism" were condemned one and all: the "artificial start of the agricultural production co-ops", the "restrictions on and the driving out of medium and small private capital", as well as the reprisals against the church and clergy. Instead, the Presidium demanded "measures for strengthening legitimacy and the guarantee of civil rights" as well as the "decisive eradication of naked administration devoid of political sense and social feeling". The SCC under military command was dissolved, and Semyonov, as "high commissar" now top representative of the Soviet Union in Germany, was to see to it "that the presence of the Soviet occupation forces harm the interests of the civilian population to the least extent possible". Lastly, the "totally hostile position" of the SED toward the SPD was condemned: the German comrades were much rather to "attempt, where and when possible, to organize joint actions against the Adenauer policy of division and imperialistic enslavement of Germany", although the officials of the Foreign Ministry had characterized this as without prospect.

Naturally, these measures did not suffice actually to bring about a democratic Germany. The problem of the Unity Lists and "democratic centralism" were not addressed at all, the demands for "strengthening legitimacy" and eradication of "naked administration" were not sufficiently implemented. Beria, like Stalin, clearly lacked an appreciation for the problem here: and he was presumably as poorly informed about the real dimensions of the "SED state" as Stalin had been. All the same, it is unmistakable that with the Presidium resolution of 27 May, course was once again energetically set for a democratic Germany. Neither in the short term nor the medium term was socialism in Germany on the agenda, and war had been declared on the solidification of the provisional arrangement which was the GDR as it had been emerging since the spring and summer of 1952.

No differences among the members of the Presidium were to be perceived when on 2 June the Soviet leadership instructed the SED leadership – Ulbricht, Grotewohl, and Oelßner as interpreter, had been summoned to Moscow – about the resolution on the course change. Grotewohl noted down not only Beria's demand "quickly and forcefully to correct" but also Malenkov's warning: "Don't fear [for] prestige; if we do not correct now, a catastrophe will follow." He further noted an explicitly German-wide reason of Molotov's: "So many mistakes, therefore to correct so that all Germany sees."[31] After "all Soviet comrades" had "rejected" the SED's initial position on the Presidium document "as inadequate",[32] Ulbricht, Grotewohl, and Oelßner while still in Moscow drew up a draft of a Central Committee resolution of the SED which to a great extent drew from the Presidium resolution and accordingly confirmed that "the main task at the present time is the struggle for the national unification of Germany on a democratic and peaceful basis. The fulfilment of this task requires that economic and political measures in the GDR be subordinated to this task."[33]

Having returned to Berlin, Oelßner delcared to his confused Politburo colleagues: "It's clearly a matter of a course change in some decisive questions which involve not only the GDR."[34] On 6 June, Semyonov explained to the SED Politburo, which had "consulted" him, that the "SED does not stand alone in the peace camp. GDR must become a magnetic field for West Germany, France – Italy. . . . Dangers of eliminating not just the avantgarde but also others. Hence, re-unification."[35] He had the *Tägliche Rundschau* announce on 13 June that the resolutions on a "New Course", which the SED Politburo and the GDR Council of Ministers had in the meantime adopted, possessed

> great international significance. They are oriented toward the great goal of the reunification of the German people in a single unified national German state. In the resolutions of the government of the GDR, the good will and the wish is expressed to achieve in the near future decisive progress in the struggle for the peaceful reunification of Germany, for the creation of a unified, sovereign, and economi-cally-strong German democratic state.[36]

Looking back, Semyonov later confirmed "that it was his task to real-ize Beria's course; and that meant not just renouncing the 'acceler-ated' construction of socialism but rather a rigorous change of course".[37]

THE "NEW COURSE" OF THE SED

Consequences for personnel were not initially drawn by the Soviet leadership from the disaster created by the SED leadership under Ulbricht. Beria explicitly assured the German visitors: "We all have made mis-takes; no reproaches."[38] In the Politburo session of 6 June, Fred Oelßner initially and then Wilhelm Zaisser as well went beyond the "recom-mendations" of the Soviet Presidium and called for a "general review of the entire policy", and thereby without further ado addressed "Ulbricht's dictatorship" with the assistance of the Politburo.[39] Semyonov then pushed to bind Ulbricht into the collective leadership: "Sekretariat must be improved. Walter must review. Jubilee modest. Big celebra-tions are wrong. No quotes. Work in the Politburo – collective." And then, directed against the forcing of the cult of personality by Lotte Ulbricht, as Oelßner had already criticized: "Don't employ wives of responsible comrades in the husband's apparatus."[40] Beyond this, Semyonov intimated that the Soviet leadership could also find other partners if the SED did not change itself fundamentally: "If the SED leadership is not in a position to understand the mentality of the working-class population and to address it in the proper form, then the bour-geois parties must be brought in to a greater degree."[41]

Ulbricht sought to take the wind from the sails of these attacks by engaging in self-criticism: "I must bear responsibility, and will change my work."[42] When the attacks nevertheless continued, he showed himself piqued: "Yes, do you think that after this criticism I'll summon the Secretariat again?"[43] In fact, the Politburo resolved to employ a commission "for the preparation of a new organizational order for the mode of operation of the Politburo and the Secretariat". Beside Ulbricht, Zaisser, Oelßner, Herrnstadt, and Hans Jendretzky were made members of this new body.[44] The resolution to announce the revisions "recommended" by Moscow followed three days later. The editorial committee was formed simultaneously, consisting of Ulbricht, Herrnstadt, and Heinrich Rau, who was to work out a more detailed resolution proposal for the next Central Committee meeting. The campaign for Ulbricht's upcoming birthday was abruptly cancelled. His name did not find its way into *Neues Deutschland* any more, and the Secretariat no longer met.

When Ulbricht again paraded high-handedness in the days following, probably under the assumption that the worst danger was past, the Soviet representatives began to look around for alternative personnel. In response to complaints about Ulbricht's behaviour, Ivan Ilyitshov, chief of the Diplomatic Mission of the Soviet Union to the government of the GDR, explained to. Herrnstadt: "Perhaps the best way out is the following. You and Zaisser take a couple of comrades from the Politburo and go as a group to Ulbricht and speak with him. . . . He is after all an experienced man, certainly he'll understand that. Well, and if he doesn't want to understand – then report to us, and we'll become active. This, it seems to me, is the right way."[45] According to the report of an interpreter of the Soviet High Commission on the "Gehlen organization", Semyonov recommended to his superiors on 13 June that in consideration of the growing dissatisfaction of the population, "the supremacy of the SED leadership [be] dismantled temporarily and a new government of a bourgeois character be installed in the GDR". As to the position of head of government, he negotiated with Hermann Kastner, the chairman of the LDPD who had been removed in 1950.[46] One of Grotewohl's co-workers reported of Semyonov's having conversations with Kastner and Nuschke.[47] Other sources report that Semyonov offered the post to the former Reichskanzler Joseph Wirth as a compromise between East and West.[48]

Meanwhile, the situation for Ulbricht intensified more and more in the SED leadership. On the evening of 16 June, the Politburo approved the draft of the Central Committee resolution on the "New Course", essentially formulated by Herrnstadt with the assistance of Heinrich Rau. As the reason for this course correction, it cited the goal of "rapidly creating a unified, democratic, progressive Germany":

The issue is creating a German Democratic Republic which owing to its prosperity, social justice, legal certainty, deeply national characteristics, and atmosphere of freedom, earns the approval of all Germans. This will further agreement among the Germans more effectively than all declarations of good wishes, isolate the warmongers in West Germany and West Berlin, and create a solid basis for negotiations over the new unified Germany.

The draft not only included a reminder about the "task" of "undertaking concrete steps for the creation of the unity of the fatherland and, in West as well as East Germany, to subordinate all individual measures to this great common goal". It also went beyond the points of criticism thematized in Moscow: "That in many cases, measures and forms of organization correct for and possible in the Soviet Union have been mechanically carried over into our situation." Likewise, the Politburo approved Herrnstadt's vision of a "party of the working class" resting on the free development of individual forces, a party which would replace the "cult of personality" with the principle of "collective work".[49] FDJ chief Erich Honecker, one of the few remaining Ulbricht adherents, told his deputy Heinz Lippmann after leaving the session that "everyone is falling upon Walter. He will indeed lose."[50]

The Uprising of 17 June initially changed nothing in regard to the return of the SED leadership to an orientation toward a national-democratic programme. The uprising was unleashed by the characteristic circumstance that when the Politburo announced the withdrawal of unpopular measures, it "forgot" the raising of average work rates because they were not dealt with in the Moscow catalogue of measures.[51] After receiving directives over the telephone from Moscow, Semyonov announced toward noon to the SED leaders summoned to Karlshorst the declaration of a state of emergency. Beyond that, he gave no new instructions.[52] That rolling out Soviet tanks, resulting in at least twenty-five deaths and numerous arrests carried out by the Ministry for State Security in the days following,[53] fundamentally discredited German-wide ambitions was not made into a theme during the unceasing deliberations of the Politburo.

Beria too did not believe – or did not want to admit – that employing tanks on 17 June had damaged his plans. Rather, he set out to his co-workers Fadeykin and Sudoplatov that "after such a convincing demonstration of Soviet strength, the Western powers will now more than ever have to take an interest in new Soviet initiatives regarding German affairs". Sudoplatov's co-worker Soya Rybkina, the sole person who according to Beria's instructions was to be initiated into the project, flew to Berlin on 24 June. She was to meet with the actress Olga Tshechova, who in turn was supposed to make contact with people in Adenauer's circle.[54]

Herrnstadt was thus able to win the approval of Semyonov and Grotewohl too for a lead article in *Neues Deutschland* of 18 June in which he wrote that "serious failings of our party" had to bear part of the responsibility for the unrest. The next day, he announced that the party would "go ahead in reviewing its own activity in the past eight years and its own behaviour in the past two days and will acknowledge the necessary consequences".[55] A Central Committee meeting was called at short notice at Herrnstadt's initiative on the evening of 21 June. In his opening report laying out basics, Grotewohl complained of the "chasm between party, government, and people" as a "result of the incorrect policy of our party", and went on to announce "measures for a thorough repair". He thereupon affirmed once again that the Politburo had "in mind in its resolutions the great goal of bringing about German unity". Anton Ackermann and Kurt Hager demanded to "discuss" in the next gathering of the Central Committee whether a "collective leadership" had existed. Ulbricht spoke only to make a minor contribution to the discussion of procedural questions.[56]

When the Organizational Commission met on 26 June in order to prepare for the next Central Committee meeting, the demolition of Ulbricht went a decisive step further: Zaisser, who had already in March demanded in the Politburo that the Secretariat must no longer be an "organ assisting the collective leadership",[57] moved that the Secretariat be replaced by a "Standing Commission" made up of both party chairmen and other members of the Politburo and that the departmental heads of the Central Committee be subordinated directly to the Politburo. Herrnstadt added that the commission should include "such comrades alongside Walter Ulbricht who will offer the guarantee that if need be they [would] force genuine cooperation, genuine collectivity". He then addressed Ulbricht directly: "I'm sorry, Walter, to have to add the following: . . . Wouldn't it be better if you gave up the direct leadership of the party apparatus?"[58]

As Herrnstadt remembered three years later, Ulbricht turned red and feigned remorse: "If you had not put forward this motion, I would have done so."[59] The commission passed a recommended resolution for the Central Committee adhering to Zaisser's proposals with the further specification that the "Secretariat of the Central Committee [be] dissolved" and the "function of the General Secretary of the Central Committee [be] eliminated".[60] According to the will of a great majority of the Politburo, Ulbricht was to be bound to a collective leadership in which both party chairmen resumed the functions which had originally been intended for them.

Two days later, Wilhelm Pieck, who since April had been in Moscow taking a cure and consequently had only been indirectly involved in the decision process,[61] let it be known that he was a supporter of the reforms. In a message "to the people of the German Democratic Republic", he declared that the Politburo's communiqué of 9 June had been agreed upon with him and that he welcomed the steps announced therein. Like Grotewohl, he termed "overcoming the gulf between the East and West portions of our fatherland" the goal of the "New Course". On 2 July, he confirmed in a radio speech that now "peaceful understanding of Germans among themselves" was on the agenda.[62]

ULBRICHT SAVES HIMSELF

Ulbricht was saved by the arrest of Beria on that same 26 June on which the removal of the SED General Secretary had been initiated. More precisely put, he was saved by the way in which he knew to make use of the fall of the presumptive successor to Stalin and the ideological justifications thereby brought into play, as well as by the shift of power resulting from that fall.

Divergent opinions as to policy on Germany played no perceptible role in the decision for Beria's overthrow. The contrasts were not distinct enough, not widespread enough, and also not important enough. What was decisive was rather Beria's attempts to remove the Interior Ministry and the secret service from the control of the party apparatus and thus forcibly make himself the new absolute dictator. His rivals in the Presidium feared that this could cost them not only their influence but also possibly their lives. Added to this were the party functionaries' concern for the loss of their privileges, the army's aversion toward the secret service, the heavy industrial apparatus's resistance to Beria's favouring promotion of the consumer-goods industry, and the administrators' embitterment over the paring of their influence in the non-Russian republics, a policy pursued by Beria not only in his Georgian homeland.

The rivals' conspiracy was organized by Nikita Khrushchev, who was to an especially great degree threatened with a loss of power due to Beria's action against his "governors" in the Ukraine. Important for their success was winning over Malenkov, who initially had probably seen himself as successor to Stalin. In a conversation with Khrushchev, Malenkov quickly grasped that in actuality he was in danger of becoming Beria's first victim. And what almost constituted a guarantee of success was the support of Marshall Zhukov, the popular hero of the Second World War who exactly because of this popularity was relieved of his post as SMA chief by Stalin in March 1946 and sent off to the relatively insignificant post of commander-in-chief in the Odessa military district. Appointed deputy defence minister after Stalin's death, he now saw to it that Beria was cut off from the troops; they were devoted to the war hero. The would-be dictator stood defenceless when, at a signal from Malenkov, officers loyal to Zhukov came in and arrested him during a session of the Presidium. After a trial before a military tribunal, he was shot on 23 December 1953.

Initially, Beria's fall was of significance for the development of German policy only in so far as the most energetic partisan of a return to the Stalinist line had been declared an "enemy of the state and party", whereas with Khrushchev a politician of the second echellon gained influence, to whom the goals and methods of Stalinist German policy were foreign. As First Secretary of the Central Committee of the Communist Party of the Ukraine until 1949, Khrushchev rarely had the opportunity to hear Stalin's explanations on policy. As he complained after his own fall in 1964, "Stalin never actually discussed issues like these with anyone else."[63] As a result of his ignorance, Khrushchev came to the conviction that at the base of the German policy of his master lay the hope of a "socialist revolution in Germany" and with the founding of the GDR the socialist path had unequivocally been entered upon. In his view, this was no longer to be called into question.[64]

A further limitation upon the German-wide impulse in Soviet policy arose from the circumstance that in their search for charges with which to prove the "criminal" character of Beria, the conspirators made use of, among other points, his energetic defence of Stalin's conception for Germany. Out of the explanation – not comprehensible to everyone – that it was "unimportant" if "socialism arises or not" in Germany,[65] the accusation was now constructed that Beria had wanted to "set course for the transformation of the GDR into a bourgeois state, which would have equalled a direct capitulation to the imperialistic powers".[66] At the Central Committee Plenum from 3 to 7 July, in which the fallen Beria was presented as an enemy of the people, this alleged "treason" was condemned by nearly all the speakers. A typical comment was made by Malenkov in his introductory report: "In light of what we can now learn about Beria, we must re-evaluate his standpoint [on the question of Germany]. It is clear that this fact characterizes him as a bourgeois renegade."[67]

For many members of the Presidium the GDR thus received a value of its own and could not be offered up at will alone for the reason that a basic charge against Beria would thereby collapse. Clearly making efforts to adjust to the new power relations, Molotov explained to the Central Committee Plenum "that the existence of the German Democratic Republic, the people's democratic order now consolidating itself, and the gradual taking up of the construction of socialism is a first strike not only against German imperialism but also against the whole imperialist system in Europe".[68]

All this did not yet necessarily mean an end to the plans for all of Germany reactivated by Beria. In his closing remarks to the Central Committee Plenum, Malenkov expressly avoided including the GDR among the "nations of people's democracy", even though he regarded it as a "bullwark of peace and democracy".[69] The diplomatic initiative set in motion by Beria continued to roll along, and the "New Course" of the SED leadership was not called into question either. Rather, the chances of an arrangement for all of Germany fell definitively to zero with the fact that Ulbricht, acting with a genuinely instinctive sureness, made use of the unhoped-for possibilities offered in the last minute by Beria's fall.

When Beria's name was missing from a routine *Pravda* article of 27 June on a visit by the Kremlin leadership to the Bolshoi Theatre, it was certainly to be suspected that a dramatic change had occurred in Moscow. At that point, it was not possible to recognize exactly what it was about and what it would mean for the development of power relations in the SED leadership. Ulbricht, however, who in the session of 26 June almost seemed as if he had already been beaten, thereupon took courage once again and sought support from Soviet "friends". Perhaps to his own surprise, he had success: when the Organizational Committee met again on 3 July in order to debate the personnel composition of the new leadership body, "a Soviet comrade", Boris Miroshnitshenko, appeared. He proceeded to explain "the top organs of the CPSU in broad strokes", and deemed it "necessary" "to have a group of secretaries of whom two or three must for the sake of expedience be members of the Politburo, the others not needing to be members . . . and it is self-evident that for purposes of summation and coordination the First Secretary must be among them".[70]

It is not fully clear whether this appearance was only a mistake resulting from Semyonov's momentary absence from Berlin[71] or whether Semyonov drew from the first news of the events in Moscow the conclusion that he would be well advised to distance himself from the reforms in the SED leadership.[72] In any event, Ulbricht's fall was prevented for the time being. Zaisser did counter the surprising intervention of Miroshnitshenko with the proposal that Herrnstadt be entrusted with the post of First Secretary: "I have the impression that *Genosse* Herrnstadt enjoys a connection to the masses."[73] No vote on this took place, however. Ulbricht, as if encouraged by the Soviet support, went over to the offensive again: "Your proposal", in retort to Zaisser, "is completely logical! For me, it's the dot on the 'i'!" In contrast, Grotewohl, who led the session, was so irritated by the Soviet attempt that he did not dare to hunt down comrade General Secretary once and for all.

Ulbricht instigated a discussion over who had to quit the Politburo and suggested Friedrich Ebert, who in the Politburo session of 6 June had expressed himself especially malleable to "Ulbricht's dictatorship". Tactically maladroitly, Zaisser thereupon demanded the exclusion of Oelßner: "Often without principles, petty, and in decisive moments also cowardly." Grotewohl, however, demanded the departure of Ulbricht's assistant Erich Honecker: "If I had observed even the smallest tendency toward development in him in all these years, I would not pose the question." Herrnstadt put forth the proposal to release Hermann Matern from the post of chairman of the Central Party Commission in that he had supported Ulbricht to the best of his ability in his disciplinary campaigns. There was, to be sure, no vote on this either. When Miroshnitshenko finally intervened in the dispute over the office of First Secretary by making the remark that further talks could be conducted when Semyonov and his deputy Pavel Yudin were back, Grotewohl ended the session.[74]

The counter-offensive became still clearer when, on 4 or 5 July, Herrnstadt presented the Politburo with the reworked edition of his Central Committee draft resolution, which had been assigned in the session of 16 June. Ulbricht threatened openly: "There are some formulations in there, my friend, that could well cost you dearly."[75] In the discussion of proposals for party reform, initially Matern turned against the excess of criticism. Then Ulbricht launched a general offensive: the draft brought the class character of the party into question; it was the "ideological platform" of the "divisive intentions" of Herrnstadt and Zaisser; Herrnstadt represented Social Democratic views. Only a few Politburo members dared unequivocally to contradict the charges of betrayal, treason and division – the worst violations of the Communist catalogue of virtues. The draft, which in actuality represented only an elaboration of the text already unanimously approved, was rejected. Ulbricht was commissioned to write anew the explanation of the "New Course", and Ackermann was to deliver a new version of the tasks of the party.[76]

Ulbricht was not out of the woods yet, however. When in the next session of the Politburo on the evening of 7 July the personnel question was raised once again, only Matern and Honecker spoke out for Ulbricht as General Secretary or "First Secretary". Oelßner and Erich Mückenberger kept quiet. Everyone else spoke out against Ulbricht, Anton Ackermann with especial vehemence: "For a long time I have remained silent due to discipline, hope, fear. Today, that is all behind me."[77] The session was interrupted because Grotewohl and Ulbricht had to fly to Moscow in order to receive important news from the Soviet leadership. When they returned with the communiqué "On Beria's Criminal Activity Hostile to Party and State", Oelßner and Hans Jendretzky put themselves on Ulbricht's side. That was sufficient in order to reject the version of the draft for party reform as prepared by Ackermann. Grotewohl, Ulbricht, and Oelßner were given the task of producing the next draft.[78]

In the new draft presented to the Politburo on 14 July, Ulbricht and Oelßner included accusations which borrowed from the list of charges against Beria: Zaisser had sought to place himself above the party via the Ministry for State Security, and Herrnstadt as editor-in-chief of *Neues Deutschland* had expressed a "capitulatory, in essence Social Democratic view".[79] Ulbricht thereby succeeded in the decisive trick: those attacked did indignantly deny the absurd accusations, but their comrades-in-arms no longer dared defend them. Still under the spell of Stalinistic purges they assumed without further reflection that a line could be traced between the "criminal Beria" and the "Herrnstadt–Zaisser faction". As soon as they saw this danger, they fell silent so as not to draw the odium of "enmity toward the party" upon themselves. In contrast, the attack on Ulbricht's position lost urgency, and more: no one wanted to participate any longer in such an action "hostile to the party".

When, in the session of 18 July, Grotewohl declared that the accusations against Herrnstadt and Zaisser were "in their fundamental political nature correct",[80] the turning point had been reached. Only Ebert and, somewhat less clearly, Ackermann brought themselves to defend Herrnstadt and Zaisser. No one protested against the arrest of Justice Minister Max Fechner. In continuation of the line represented by

Herrnstadt and Grotewohl, he had stated in *Neues Deutschland* on 30
June that only those who had committed crimes on 17 June would be
put on trial, not those who "went on strike or demonstrated".[81] On 22
July, Ackermann too resigned in that he had to undergo embarrassing
self-criticism. After that, the meeting of the Central Committee from
24 to 26 July devolved into a parade of adventurous charges against
Herrnstadt and Zaisser. It was only a bit less than the CPSU tribunal
against Beria. Ulbricht openly linked them to Beria, and they could be
happy to say that they had not been arrested but merely excluded from
the Central Committee.[82]

Semyonov witnessed this business seemingly unmoved. After Ulbricht
had suggested the existence of a connection between the two energetic
partisans of his demotion and Beria, it seemed smarter to the Soviet
too not to take action any longer against the SED General Secretary.
Additionally, Beria's fall and the accusation of offering up the GDR
let him guess as to where things were heading. When Herrnstadt sought
suport from him against the absurd accusations, Semyonov gave him
the cold shoulder. He remained silent too when on 23 July Ulbricht
presented the draft of his Central Committee speech to the Politburo.
As a result of Semyonov's intervention, Ulbricht had to forgo only the
planned exclusion of Herrnstadt and Zaisser from the party. It was a
matter of solidarity costing little, but very important for those affected.[83]

The final reason that Ulbricht was saved and that the "New Course"
foundered was the insufficient rigour of the reformers. If they had pursued
not just the demotion of Ulbricht but also his exclusion from the Politburo, and had taken less time in so doing, comrade General Secretary would not have received any opportunity to link his opponents
to Beria. But even with that, the failure of the "New Course" was not
inevitable. The reformers needed only further represent their views
assertively in order to make Ulbricht's abstruse constructions risible.
No directive is to be discerned from Moscow for retaining Ulbricht in
all events. In consideration of the confused power relations after Beria's
fall, which made agreement on political questions much more difficult,
such an order could not have existed at all.

Meanwhile, Semyonov feared that such an order could come, and
Herrnstadt and Zaisser thereupon became convinced that there was such
an order. The situation thereby changed for them: instead of carrying
on the struggle for what they recognized as correct and necessary, they
became obedient again, thinking only of saving their personal honour.
"Will you say how it actually was?" Herrnstadt asked Zaisser before
his appearance in the Central Committee Plenum on the morning of 25

July. His answer: "that cannot be done, it could damage the Soviet Union". Herrnstadt felt "a deep satisfaction" over this response.[84] Stalin's system continued to function although the dictator himself had already been dead for more than four months, and a power vacuum existed at the top of the Soviet Union. It was functioning because all involved believed that it would continue to function further.

RETREAT BY INCREMENTS

The deferment of "socialism" in favour of bringing about national unity was thus a mere episode. The resolution finally adopted by the Central Committee Plenum on 26 July did indeed hold verbally to the "New Course" and affirm that it would pursue at the same time the goal of promoting the reunification of Germany. There was, however, no mention of steps for bringing the two Germanies closer together as had been announced in the Politburo's communiqué of 9 June. Likewise, there was no announcement of negotiations over the unified Germany and no criticism of the clichéd transfer of Soviet conditions onto German ones, which had still been part of the first drafts of the Central Committee resolution. Instead, Ulbricht exploited the accusations against Beria's address in order to rehabilitate himself in regard to the main issue: "It was indeed correct," as the adopted text defiantly ran, "that our Party led Germany on the path to socialism and began to erect the foundations of socialism. This general line of the party was and remains correct."[85]

The events of 17 June appeared in the Central Committee resolution exclusively as an attempt at a "fascist putsch" instigated by "West German monopoly-capitalistic and Junker circles as the assistants of American imperialism", with support of a "fascistic underground movement" together with "agents of the Eastern Office" of the SPD.[86] Gone from the text was the self-critical reference to the "consequences of our policy in the past year" as the cause of "discord in some portions of the population", which had been contained in the communiqué of the Central Commitee session of 21 June.[87] Accordingly, all forms of oppositional stirrings were now mercilessly persecuted. The state security service was at all levels systematically subordinated to the party apparatus and its personnel considerably expanded.[88] Simultaneously, the party had to endure a new purge of its ranks. Party gatherings had to express their revulsion for the "Herrnstadt–Zaisser faction"; investigatory commissions examined the political views of each and every party member. About twenty thousand functionaries and fifty thousand ordinary members were excluded from the party,[89] others were demoted. And not a few left on their own because they no longer saw a future for their ideals in such a party.[90]

It was of further benefit for stabilizing Ulbricht's position that in the Soviet government's next note on the German question, issued on 15 August 1953, the formation of a "Provisional all-German government" by the parliaments of both German states was proposed. This government was on the one hand to participate in the negotiations over a peace treaty. On the other hand, it was also to prepare and carry out "free all-German elections", in which the German people would decide for themselves over a governmental and societal order. In the event that the Bundestag was not immediately ready to transfer all responsibility to such a government, "the retention for a certain period of governments of the German Democratic Republic and German Federal Republic" alongside the joint Provisional Government was proposed.[91]

The Soviet government had thereby once again underscored its German-wide ambitions. When Malenkov received the SED leaders on 20 August for talks on the future form of relations to the GDR, he made it clear that he too understood the GDR only as a provisional arrangement – "born in order to create a new, great, peaceful Germany". More distinctly than Stalin or Beria, however, he also let it be known that according to his understanding, the "achievements" of the GDR in the process leading to the creation of German unity were not simply to be offered up as a sacrifice. As he assured Ulbricht and Grotewohl, "The GDR is a bastion and a state for the whole German people."[92] In actuality, the interposition of a "Provisional Government" pushed the risk of free elections into the distant future. In consideration of the dissatisfaction revealed by the events of 17 June, this was certainly no accident.

As is to be assumed from Malenkov's explanation to the SED delegation, he was probably not aware that the proposal for a "Provisional Government" had no chance at all with the Western powers or with the West German population. Conversely, he also did not give the impression that German unity would have to be brought about in any particular hurry. In his understanding at least, it was not a prerequisite for the general détente in East–West relations he was then pursuing vigorously. For the time being, Ulbricht could thus feel relatively secure. This was all the more the case when the agreements of 22 August brought him, beside an elevation of status – the diplomatic missions on both sides being raised to the level of embassies – also significant financial relief: the abolition of all reparation payments and postwar debts to 1 January 1954, limitation of the occupation costs to 5 per cent of the national budget, transformation of the Soviet Aktiengesellschaften (SAGs) into GDR property, and on top of all that, deliveries of goods and a not insignificant loan.[93]

A Foreign Ministers' Conference was held in Berlin between 25 January and 18 February 1954, and after a longish verbal exchange, it turned to the German question again. Molotov assured his Western colleagues "that he in fact wants an agreement"[94] and that he was convinced "that there exists a possibility for some success in regard to Germany". US Secretary of State Dulles then asked wherein this possibility existed in his view. Molotov then inquired "whether some progress could be made along the following lines: A small German army and additionally a German government that was not oriented against the United States, France, Great Britain, or the Soviet Union. He asked himself whether this possibility was completely excluded."[95]

Repeatedly, he attempted to make it comprehensible to his conversation partners that free elections alone could not represent the key to the solution of the German question because "Hitler came to power as the result of free elections." Much rather, it was necessary "to decide on the kind of government to emerge from free elections before these were to take place".[96] "It is a matter of being certain that there would be a government which we could control and which would not work against one of the four powers."[97] He was unable, however, to make a spectacular offer which could have moved the Western powers to accept such a government. Rather, in the official negotiations, he repeated the proposal of beginning with the formation of a "Provisional Government for all of Germany".

This behaviour confirms that the Soviet Union was still pursuing its concept of joint control of Germany by the victorious powers.[98] But it also makes clear that from the Soviet perspective, this goal in the meantime no longer had the greatest urgency. And it demonstrates the inability to make spectacular initiatives in the face of unclear power relations in the Moscow centrale. On 25 March 1955, the Soviet government declared "that the supervision of the activity of the governmental organs which up until now has been conducted by the High Commissioner of the USSR in Germany is abolished". Under these circumstances, Ulbricht could claim at the Fourth Party Congress of the SED, meeting from 30 March to 6 April 1954, that the GDR has "now begun to create the foundations for socialism" without having to fear being once again disavowed. The efforts of the GDR leadership in the realm of Germany policy concentrated on fighting integration of the Federal Republic into the West and to legitimizing itself to its own population. The question of the compatibility of socialism and unity was either no longer asked, or answered completely naively in the sense of a magnetic effect given off by the socialist order.

In the course of its campaign against the Federal Republic's integration into NATO, the Soviet government on 23 November 1954 surprisingly declared its willingness at least to "discuss" the Eden Plan in regard to the procedure for free elections in Germany. At the Berlin conference, the plan had been rejected by Molotov as unreasonable.[99] A few days later, Molotov pleaded once again for an "agreement on the question of carrying out free German elections" without insisting that this agreement be reached by a "Provisional Government for all of Germany".[100] The Presidium of the Volkskammer asked the Bundestag again to "take up negotiations between representatives of East and West Germany over holding free elections for all of Germany", this time for 1955.[101] On 15 January 1955, the Soviet government even officially took the position that it was possible "to come to an agreement about setting up corresponding international supervision over holding elections for all of Germany".[102]

This newfound flexibility, which stemmed from the strengthening of Khrushchev's position and the resultant greater capacity to act on the part of the Soviet leadership,[103] certainly did not last long. When with its acceptance in NATO the integration of the Federal Republic into the West had become irreversible, Khrushchev likewise altered his policy decisively. On 14 May, nine days after the Paris Treaties on the integration of the FRG into NATO came into effect, representatives of the GDR were allowed to sign the Warsaw Pact.

At the Geneva summit conference from 18 to 23 July 1955, the Soviet leaders for the last time sounded out the possibilities for an arrangement encompassing all of Germany. At a meal on 19 July, Nikolai Bulganin, since February 1955 the successor to Malenkov as Prime Minister, declared to his British colleague Anthony Eden that it was certainly not possible to return to Moscow from this conference and "here in Geneva to have agreed upon the immediate reunification"; that would not be understood in the Soviet Union. However, he continued as Khrushchev joined the conversation, he and Khrushchev were prepared to give their foreign minister corresponding directives; the ministers should deliberate over the theme of "reunification", together with corresponding services in return[104] – that is, security guarantees which were still regarded as imperative.

After this feeler remained without tangible result, Bulganin himself in the official portion of the conference referred to the difficulties which meanwhile stood in the way of an arrangement: "In the meantime, two Germanies have formed – the GDR and the Federal Republic of Germany – each with its economic and societal structure. It is clear that under such circumstances, the question of a mechanistic melding of the two parts of Germany cannot be touched upon, since that would be an unrealistic question." As a realistic way to handle the German question, he suggested instead "the creation of a system of collective security in Europe": "Until the unification of Germany, its two parts [could] be members with equal rights."[105]

In order to confirm the new view of things, the Soviet delegation stopped off in East Berlin during the return journey to Moscow. Khrushchev declared that there was no "whole Germany" "at present; two German states exist . . ., nothing else is realistic". And then, amidst "long, continuous applause": "The German question cannot be solved at the expense of the interests of the German Democratic Republic"; "eliminating all its political and social achievements" would not be possible.[106] At their next visit, from 17 to 20 September, he explained to the SED leaders that one had to reckon with two states in Germany for a certain amount of time. Only the Germans themselves could resolve the question of reunification.[107] What Stalin had wanted to prevent, was thereby accepted. Ulbricht's separate revolution, however, finally had the guarantee of continuance upon which it was existentially dependent.

Conclusion:
How the GDR Came to Be

Reckoned from war's end, it was ten years before Moscow gave real existing socialism in the GDR a guarantee of its continued existence. This underscores once again how little the results of Soviet policy on Germany corresponded to the original objectives and how seriously these objectives had been pursued. In the first decade after the war, many hundreds of independent witnesses confirm that Stalin strove for a democratic postwar Germany – a Germany democratic according to *Western* standards, which must be explicitly emphasized over against the perversion of the concept of democracy and the instrumentalization of anti-fascism in the GDR.[1] This Germany, which would have to offer guarantees against renewed aggression and grant access to the resources of the industrial regions in the western areas of the defeated Reich, was to be established in cooperation with the Western powers. To this purpose, the occupation forces were to remain in the Four-Zone area for a limited time.

At no point could Stalin imagine that the occupation forces would remain in Germany permanently. Dividing a nation fitted just as little with his views. Socialism, the socialist revolution in Germany, was for him a task of the future, one for the period after the realization of the Potsdam democratization programme. Even when in the spring of 1952, after many vain attempts to implement the Potsdam programme, he adjusted himself to a long coexistence of the two German states, he did not link this with any transition to a separate socialism: the GDR had simply wound up having to bide its time until the Cold War had been overcome, after which it would be possible to realize the agreements reached at Potsdam.

It is doubtful that the GDR state was ever a part of the "socialist community of states" in Stalin's view. This idea was originally so foreign to Stalin's longtime co-worker Molotov that he initially conceived of the Warsaw Pact in 1954–5 without the East German state. As the reason for his view, he asked Khrushchev, "Why should we fight with the West over the GDR?" Khrushchev was amazed by this.[2] Stalin's successors once again made an energetic attempt to realize his programme before they got to like the idea of "socialism in half a land"

owing to a mixture of insufficient knowledge of the original considerations and pragmatic adjustment to realities.

The history of Soviet policy on Germany in the first postwar decade
thereby not only shows that even with all the monstrosity of his tyran-
nical system, securing the Soviet Union from dangers both real and
imagined took absolute priority over all conceivable ideological objectives. It also demonstrates that he was capable of constructive insights
outside Leninist patterns of thought. In the attempt to harmonize
realpolitical insights with ideological certainties, Stalin became convinced that paths to socialism other than the Soviet one were also
possible and that the path in Germany was via the parliamentary-
democratic system.

From all this, there arose chances for establishing a democratic order, meeting Western standards, for the entirety of occupied Germany.
There also arose chances for containing the East–West conflict, whose
full scope was perceived by almost no one. The internal documents
show that the hopes for an "anti-fascist, democratic republic" and a
"unified Germany" without the Soviet system, hopes with which young
idealists such as Wolfgang Leonhard took up the work of rebuilding,[3]
were based not on illusions as to Soviet objectives but rather on a
very exact feeling for what was possible. There were possibilities not
only in the spring of 1952, but in the entire period from the war's end
to the summer of 1953, and first signs of possibilities in both of the
following years as well. Even if the Soviet authorities and their German favourites again and again resorted to repression and manipulation in order to carry out their commission, this does not change the
fact that an understanding on a republic within the framework sketched
out at Potsdam was at the top level fundamentally possible at any time
– if only the Western powers wanted it.

Close observation of developments within the leadership circle of
the SED underscores that the partisans of Western principles had nothing
to fear. Erich Gniffke reports that during the first two years after the
unification of the two parties, the Social Democrats in the SED leadership could "violate Marxist–Leninist fundamentals to their hearts'
content".

They could hold opinions different from those of the Communists,
they could even oppose the Communists. Ulbricht's continual answer was: "Good, comrades. We must discuss this question." And
the questions were discussed with success in that the Communist
arguments were softened in most instances. A front consisting of

Social Democrats and some Communists formed against the doctrinaire Stalinist Ulbricht.[4]

The same development manifested itself in the spring of 1953: shortly after Stalin's successors had told the SED leaders that the orientation on "constructing socialism" had been wrong, an intensive discussion process began in the Politburo. This process not only aimed to make the GDR once again "ready for unity" but also thereby explicitly criticized the Stalinistic methods standing in the way. Certainly, this criticism did not right away encompass all aspects of GDR realities needing reform; and its partisans did not act decisively enough either in order to be successful in the end. All the same, it must be emphasized that the revision of the situation was actively pursued by the Politburo although the former Social Democrats had in the meantime become a minority in that body. Also, after some orientation problems, the overwhelming majority of the Politburo took aim at the core power-political question: that of eliminating Ulbricht's dictatorship. Furthermore, they did not let the events of 17 June dissuade them from these efforts.

More broadly put: If the perspective for the whole of Germany had only shown itself clearly enough, Ulbricht's revolutionary programme would have fallen behind even under the exclusive control by the Soviet occupier. Under a joint regime of the four occupying powers, regardless of how it were to come about, Ulbricht's programme would have had no chance at all. Conversely, division and the presence of Soviet occupation forces were not sufficient conditions for pushing through the Stalinist system in the Soviet Zone.

Beyond that, what was indispensable for establishing GDR-socialism could be quite vividly seen in Ulbricht's seizure of power in 1948 as well as in his rescue in the summer of 1953: on both occasions the assumption was sufficient that the consolidation of Ulbricht's position corresponded to the desire of the Moscow leadership in order for Communist functionaries, but also politicians of democratic provenance who were ready to adjust, to help him put through his revolutionary fantasies against their better judgement. That on both occasions their compliance rested upon a delusion gives their actions a tragic dimension in hindsight, but also highlights their share of the responsibility. The manoeuvring room of the East German politicians was larger than they believed it was under the impression of the Stalinistic practice of arrest and manipulation. In addition to intellectual freedom, a significant measure of willingness to take risks was, admittedly, also needed in order to perceive this.

Walter Ulbricht, however, must be regarded as the person mainly responsible for real existing socialism in the GDR. As little as the person and politics of Ulbricht are to be understood without the long conditioning through the Comintern, as little as he could have triumphed without like-minded comrades and fewer assistants freely offering their services: it was he who first of all sought to carry out the Bolshevik Revolution on the soil of the Soviet Occupation Zone. The GDR is inconceivable without him. Subjectively only a model student of Stalin's, he was in fact a revolutionary in his own right – one driven by a mixture of ideological sense of mission and thirst for power; since his arrival in Berlin, concerned with submission and control, adaptable but skilfully exploiting every chance to push through his conceptions. That he believed himself to be in agreement with Stalin, did not hinder him from actually pursuing his own course – by interpreting instructions from Moscow in his own way, by accepting stimulus from the SMA in so far as it fitted into his concept, and by using the frequent vagueness of Moscow's signals in order to introduce his own influence.

After Stalin's death, Ulbricht regarded himself as his own master, at least the equal of the various successors in the Kremlin. Only in extreme situations was he aware that his revolution ultimately rested upon the presence of Soviet troops. Apart from those situations, he only too gladly took the appearance of forced adaptation for historical progress – as he understood it. Incidentally, with his cadre regime, which created the fiction of a "workers' and peasants' state", he contributed in a decisive degree to the perpetuation of the division between East and West – and thus to the permanent presence of Soviet troops, which were in turn the prerequisite for maintaining his fiction.

Emphasis on the central role of Ulbricht in the rise of the GDR does not release Stalin from his responsibility. Even if the Soviet dictator did not want the pseudo-socialistic East German separate state – for reasons of the security of the Soviet Union, as must once again be emphasized, rather than out of any sort of weakness for German unity – the GDR was in the final analysis his child, more exactly put, a child of the system he had begotten. Stalin's forcible seizure of the Soviet state and the Communist world movement had not only given rise to the Ulbrichts of all shades, it also resulted in an unbelievable amount of systematic misperception and inability to act. Those in responsible positions at all levels, people who had emerged from the purges, reported to Stalin in a mixture of fascination and fear only what in their opinion he wanted to hear. They were frequently incapable of understanding anything but Leninist dogma and thereby reinforced his latent fear of the machinations of the "class enemy", fears of which he never completely rid himself. Although he continually retained a remnant of realism over against the ideological zealots in his apparatus – above all, because he did not want to admit to having made an erroneous evaluation – he himself again and again furthered thinking in terms of class conflict, treated potential allies as opponents, and sanctioned violations of democratic fundamentals without considering their effects upon the Western side. Because he wanted to control everything himself, much remained uncontrolled; and his subordinates could take steps which ran counter to his objectives.

Shear ignorance and ideologically based misjudgements lay behind all the wrong strategic decisions of Soviet policy on Germany: from forcing the formation of the Unity Party to allowing the creation of Bizonia, and from rejecting the Marshall Plan to blocking access to Berlin. Ignorance and ideological preoccupations favoured an interpretation of the world situation which to a significant extent limited Stalin's possibilities for communication and capability for compromise. By branding every advocate of the Marshall Plan a henchman of American imperialism, he not only presented himself in an extremely unfavourable light, but also developed a need for control which was difficult to harmonize with the unfolding of parliamentary democracy.

Whether Stalin would have allowed a unified Germany to participate in the Marshall Plan must therefore remain open. It is just as questionable whether he would have accepted the integration of the unified Germany in a European combination, as began to take shape with the Coal and Steel Union of 1950–1. It is certain that after the beginning of serious negotiations over bringing about German unity, he would have tracked down presumed opponents of democracy who were to be "beaten". Whether the process of establishing a state encompassing all of Germany could have withstood the resultant conflicts is uncertain.

Of course, "uncertain" also means that the possibility cannot be excluded. The constructive programme with which Stalin approached solving the German problem demonstrates in and of itself that he was capable of learning. This is seen even more clearly in the numerous beginnings as to the revision of errors, and in each of the new offers he developed over the course of time: from the about-face in the question of the German production level, and breaking off the fatal delaying tactic of 1946, and initiating the project of readmitting the SPD, to the step-by-step approach to the West German governmental institutions in 1950–51. A year before his death, he reduced to a minimum the conditions to which a unified Germany would be bound. That the offers often did not go far enough and were not adhered to consistently enough, does not alter the fact that Stalin in individual cases repeatedly knew to free himself of ideological bonds he himself had forged. As unsuitable as class-struggle thought was for making the compromises indispensable in a democracy, Stalin's ability to overcome the class-struggle schemata makes him appear fundamentally capable of compromise. How far this ability to compromise went in individual cases depended not least of all on his experiences with the Western powers.

Stalin's limited ability to compromise thus relativizes the responsibility shared by the Western side for the birth of the GDR, even while not eliminating that responsibility. In particular, the French struggle against the unity of the Reich must be emphasized as an independent factor. Not only did it lead to the veto whereby the establishment of German Central Administrations was blocked. In the disputes at the level of the Control Council and of the Ministers' Council connected to it, the French stance meant that agreements which were within grasp failed to materialize. As little as French policy explicitly aimed at a division between East and West, which evoked the danger of a West German arrangement with the Soviet Union, it did, however, contribute to a decisive extent to the German question's falling into the maelstrom of the East–West conflict.

Important then was that both the American and the British governments rejected the concept of reparations from current production, although Roosevelt had in principle agreed to it at Yalta. Initially, this was as little motivated by efforts to build an anti-Soviet front as was the French policy: at the war's end, Washington had in mind primarily a reduction of the German production level; and that would no longer permit reparations deliveries. London shrank back from additional burdens on an occupation zone which was already running a deficit. Nevertheless, the conflict over the reparations question contributed to the formation of Bizonia and repeatedly blocked negotiations over political unity.

Still more significant over time became the concern that nationwide structures could straight away lead to a Communist seizure of power in all of Germany. This fear drove Kurt Schumacher as early as 1945 to hinder a national SPD organization. Together with other Western politicians, he thereafter successfully torpedoed every kind of representation for Germany as a whole. From the spring of 1946, the same concerns began to make themselves noticeable in the formulation of British policy, and a year later, in American policy as well. In 1947 and 1948, fears of Soviet expansion increased and led to efforts to form a Western security system to which the western portion of Germany belonged as an indispensable component. Adenauer and a growing number of West Germans were so lastingly gripped by this fear that from then on they rejected a reunification which did not allow for the united state to remain unconditionally in the Western alliance.

In assessing the Western role in the history of the origins of the GDR it must certainly be taken into account that in the pursuit of their respective interests, the Western powers had no reason to give consideration to the preservation of German unity. Also to be considered is that the manifestations of Communist class-struggle thought energetically fanned the flames of Western fears and that the outrage over repression and manipulation by the Eastern side was only too justified. And it must be acknowledged too that the organization of a Western community of states became all the more urgent the longer a comprehensive peaceful order for Europe failed to materialize.

However, Western politicians and opinion makers in their overwhelming majority gave in to diffuse anxieties all too quickly. They did not take the trouble to scrutinize the various horror scenarios for the amount of reality they contained. Moreover, they did not expend nearly as much effort in creating a peacetime order for all of Europe as they did in creating the Western community. In consideration of the consequences of the failure of the Potsdam programme, their performance is no example of great statesmanship.

In the case of the West Germans, behind the fear and outrage lay frequently the additional factor of a loss of solidarity after the collapse of the Reich. "Now, our shirt is nearer than our jacket."[5] Only the widespread existence of this view explains why Schumacher could put through his walling-off strategy in the West-zonal SPD, why assertive expressions of a German desire for unity failed to materialize, and why Adenauer's policy of giving absolute priority to integration into the West was sanctioned by the voters in the end. The history of the origins of the GDR is thus simultaneously also the history of a hidden decomposition of the German nation.

This was occasionally registered with bitterness by the Germans in the Soviet Zone, the people who became the victims of this development. The West Germans, however, repressed this by inventing a founding myth of the defence of freedom against the Bolshevist threat. Coming to terms with the problems of the united Germany after the end of the GDR will depend not least of all upon successfully stepping back from this myth.

Epilogue to the English Edition

The German edition of *Stalins ungeliebtes Kind* met with a wide response. Alongside much cordial assent, there was also some criticism, including severe criticism in prominent places.[1] I have not, however, been able to find arguments in this criticism which would call into question the results of my research. Most importantly, no one has produced evidence weakening the testimony of the sources which I have examined. I can thus explain the negative reactions only by supposing that the surprise contained in the book has after all been too great for many reviewers. Also, the message found in the work has perhaps been too unpleasant for some Germans.[2]

I see no occasion for revisions given that, in my view, all the additional sources which have in the meantime been examined by other researchers point in the same direction. To an extent, they allow the picture outlined by me to be presented still more vividly and completely. In each instance, however, these sources confirm the fundamental elements of my sketch.

In regard to the war years, the manifold uncertainties of the Soviet decision makers as to how to treat the defeated Germany and also the permanent orientation toward a joint administration by the victorious powers have been confirmed through research conducted by Alexei M. Filitov. He has examined papers of the Department of International Information of the Central Committee of the CPSU and of the Planning Commissions of the People's Commissariat for Foreign Affairs. In the very first and most detailed document setting out Soviet war aims, signed by Ivan Maiskii and sent to Molotov on 11 January 1944, Germany was treated as one of the countries in which "it may be necessary in order to secure the establishment of democratic regimes, to apply various measures of intervention from outside, by the USSR, the USA, and Britain". Maiskii affirmed that "the USSR is interested in seeing to it that the state structure of these countries shall be based on principles of broad democracy, in the spirit of the people's front idea" and presented the democratization as a joint venture of the Allies: "There are grounds for thinking that, where democratization of the regime in postwar Europe is concerned, it will be possible for the USSR, the

USA, and Britain to cooperate, though this will not always be easy."[3]

Kliment Voroshilov, as chairman of the Commission for Questions regarding the Armistice, warned in April 1944 that it was "impermissible" to regard each Occupation Zone "as property of the Allied power which will occupy it".[4] In November 1944, work was done on drawing up lists of candidates for administrative authorities for all of Germany; "under the joint control of the four victorious powers", all "of Germany's democratic forces were to participate".[5] Maiskii explained that for this purpose, the old laws and the constitution of the Weimar Republic were to be put into effect; democracy had to be built upon this foundation.[6] At the same time, Maxim Litvinov, as chairman of the Commission on Questions of the Peace Treaties and Post-War Construction, recommended the formation of a "neutral zone" in the middle of the European continent encompassing Norway, Denmark, Germany, Austria, and Italy, "wherein both sides [the British and the Soviet] will cooperate on the same footing and with regular mutual consultation".[7]

The effects of this planning on the expectations and orientations of the KPD leadership in exile in Moscow can now be traced thanks to published excerpts from the papers of Wilhelm Pieck and Wilhelm Florin. In many different ways, these texts confirm that by the war's end the path to socialism was not on the agenda of the German Communists. On 24 April 1944, for example, Walter Ulbricht declared unequivocally to the Central Committee's commission responsible for planning the future:

> In the period of opposition to Fascism, of Hitler's war, and in the period of setting up a new democracy, the party defers efforts to realize its final goal. In the struggle in Hitler's war and participation in setting up a new democracy, the extermination of the German reaction, the party sees the creation of the prerequisites for the propagation of its final goal.[8]

Thus, according to this understanding, the "final goal" was not to be "striven for" at all in the democracy phase. Democracy was regarded as the prerequisite for the mere propagation of the final goal, and this was to be achieved solely through propagation. That much remained of the old Communist dream of the "masses" achieving class consciousness.

That Stalin understood "democracy" in this context, as nothing principally different from what his Western allies understood, is once again affirmed by explanatory remarks Anton Ackermann made in 1963, after having been removed from power, to staff at the Institute for Marxism–Leninism of the SED.[9] According to his statements, the concept of "*parliamentary*-democratic republic" was explicitly employed and discussed "as the main orientation of the KPD" in the central meeting between the KPD leaders and Stalin on 4 June 1945:[10] "Stalin too was of the opinion that this motto was appropriate for the situation; a parliament can have various characters. But the hegemony of the working class and its revolutionary party had to be protected. Stalin clearly stated that the Soviet system was not to be transferred to Germany." Even though it remains unclear to what extent subsequent memories and contexts of the GDR have entered into these statements (above all in regard to the emphasis on the hegemony concept), the actual orientation on the contents of the KPD appeal of 11 June 1945 is unmistakable.

In his posthumously-published memoirs, Vladimir Semyonov also leaves no room to doubt that the KPD appeal is to be taken at its word: "The concrete actions foreseen in this document became the practical plan of action for SMA. I remember well that we constantly measured our work against this document." Accordingly, for him, "all important antifascist-democratic reorganization in the Soviet Occupation Zone [was] completed in 1948". Semyonov quotes a statement made by Stalin in a Politburo session in late May 1945:

> The task lies not in destroying Germany but rather in taking away the possibility that it would once again arise as an aggressive power in Europe. That means that the roots of militarism and Nazism in Germany must be eradicated but [Germany] itself must be preserved as a unified, peace-loving, and democratic state.

By way of interpretation, the author added that Stalin had in mind "for a transition period the order and also certain persons of the Weimar Republic".[11]

Subsequently too, Semyonov confirms again and again the orientation of Soviet policy on Germany as a whole. In the reported Stalin quotes, the problem of Germany continually appears as a joint task of the victorious powers ("a question of the grand policy of the states of the anti-Hitler coalition"); never is an East–West division even discussed. For Semyonov, the Stalin Notes of 1952 represent a wholly obvious continuity with the Soviet proposals at the foreign ministers' conferences of 1946 and 1947: "The struggle for a unified, independent, and peace-loving Germany went on for several years after the founding of both independent German states."[12]

It is especially revealing that Semyonov too confirms the unauthorized actions of some leaders of the SMA and the SED who, according to my analysis, contributed substantially to establishing the socialism of the GDR. As he wrote, regarding May and June 1948,

> Some hotheads in the SED overestimate the meaning of the reforms up to this point and are giving out the false orientation that we can go over to the construction of socialism.

And further:

> I heard that at action meetings of the SED, Tulpanov was declaring that in the Soviet Occupation Zone the transition from the antifascist-democratic order to the construction of socialism and to establishment of the dictatorship of the proletariat had now come. I asked him to comment on that. He admitted that he had said things of that sort. But it had been merely a matter of unofficial exchange of opinion in which he wanted to assess to what extent things had been successful in the zone. As befitted the situation, I gave Tulpanov my opinion and stressed above all that it was by no means permitted to make those sorts of declarations without prior approval from the Central Committee of the CPSU (B).[13]

Given his report, we can more precisely imagine how such authorized behaviour was possible. Only the head of the SMA and Semyonov stood in direct contact with Stalin. Tulpanov was responsible for everyday political matters in the Soviet Zone; according to Semyonov, he lacked "the time, also possibly the knowledge, character, and inclination, to raise himself above the current problems of the day – they engulfed him completely". For his part, Ulbricht dealt mostly with Tulpanov only, and so he adopted "tactical methods [which were] not always the best". In a "strictly personal" letter to Stalin in 1952, Semyonov complained of "a host of critical points" concerning Ulbricht. Among them were his directive issued to subordinate SED authorities to report to him on all contact with the SCC, as well as his tendency "simply to copy" Soviet experience.[14]

The autonomous role of Tulpanov is described even more precisely in a study of Soviet occupation policy by Norman M. Naimark. From the files of the Central Committee of the CPSU, it becomes clear not only that Tulpanov was in fact very independently bent on rearranging the Soviet Zone according to the Soviet model, but also that he repeatedly came under fire from investigative commissions of the Central Committee because of this. As early as October 1946, a commission found that he made "serious errors" and was "insufficiently disciplined" in his performance. In late April 1948, a further investigative committee criticized the rash pushing of the introduction of socialism in the Eastern Zone, the neglect of the middle-class parties, excessive meddling in the day-to-day politics of the SED, and the general "inadequate comprehension of the historical perspectives on the development of Germany". A representative of the Main Political Administration of the Army, Colonel Konstantinovskii, reported to Moscow in late August 1948 that Tulpanov was still committing the same "serious political mistakes", which among other things had led many political officers to the incorrect view that the formation of a "socialist republic" was already under way.[15] Nevertheless, he was relieved of his duties only in stages because his knowledge of the land and its people was not so easy to replace.

On the basis of materials from the archive of the SMA and other sources, Naimark furthermore reports on innumerable problems of rivalry and jurisdiction, liberties taken by local commanders, disciplinary problems, and continually-excessive workloads; all this finally making it easier for the SMA to hand over authority to the Germans. It becomes clear that the authorities of the SMA initially did in many cases attempt to implement the democratic programme for Germany as a whole. They pressed for politically-balanced administrations and energetically took action against "revolutionaries", regardless of whether they were members of the KPD, the SPD, or the Antifa committees. SMA authorities and Central Committee representatives also noted what catastrophic consequences the brutal rapes, the capricious arrests, and the endless dismantling had. In the chaos of the Soviet system, however, they were in many cases not in a position to enforce their views. Thus, according to Naimark too, the Sovietization of the Eastern Occupation Zone appears to have been a consequence of the weaknesses of the Soviet system: in overcoming the problems before them, the occupiers acted in accordance with what they had learned; and the contradiction in the tasks of the occupation administration which arose in this way could not be sufficiently corrected given the meagre possibilities to steer the system.[16]

New information as to the prehistory of the Note of 10 March 1952 comes via a memoir account by Georg Dertinger made in November 1967 to which his wife Maria Dertinger has given me access. According to this source, the proposal to augment the calls for negotiations with the draft of the principles of a peace treaty came in 1951 from the GDR foreign minister. Dertinger formulated a draft in accordance with this. As Mrs Dertinger reports,[17] Semyonov pressed for a formulation which would have a chance of being accepted by the West Germans; and he had Dertinger reassure him that this chance did exist. Thereafter, Dertinger heard nothing of the matter for a long time. When the Note was published, he was surprised that it "almost to a letter, with very few deviations, corresponded to my draft, admittedly with a decisive change which I did not have in it: The NVA. In my wildest dreams I had not supposed that an army for Germany could be foreseen in the peace treaty."[18] The rejection of the Note by the Western side, again according to Mrs Dertinger, was registered with great disappointment everywhere.

Disappointment is also to be seen in Soviet records of Stalin's answer to Pieck's question about the prospects of success for the note initiative; the meeting of 7 April 1952 in which these records were made has been investigated by Michail M. Narinskii. It is noted that

> Comrade Stalin considers that the Western powers will not agree to any proposals that we can make on the German question, regardless of what these would be, and that the Western powers will not withdraw from Germany in any case. It would be a mistake to think that a compromise might emerge or that the Americans will agree with the draft of the peace treaty. The Americans need their army in West Germany in order to keep Western Europe in their hands. They say that they have their army there [to defend] against us. But the real purpose of this army is to control Europe. The Americans will draw West Germany into the Atlantic Pact. They will create West German military units. Adenauer is in the pocket of the Americans, as are all ex-fascists and generals too.[19]

This confirms that in his offer of 10 March 1952, Stalin had seen a maximum on possible concessions, and now, after this initiative too had met with rejection, he definitely gave up his earlier optimism regarding success in negotiations.

More clearly than the parallel notes on the conversation made by Wilhelm Pieck,[20] these records show that with the Western refusal of the offer of 10 March 1952, the status of the GDR changed in Stalin's eyes: "In reality, there is an independent state being formed in West Germany. And you must organize your own state. The line of demarcation between East and West Germany must be seen as a frontier and not as a simple border but a dangerous one. One must strengthen the protection of this frontier."[21] Up to this point, the GDR had been for him a short-term provisional arrangement which could at any time be offered up in negotiations. Only now was it to take on the characteristics of a state for a rather long transitional period.

Documents in the Archive of the Foreign Ministry of the Russian Federation show that Stalin's successors began preparation of a new initiative on the German question during the second half of April 1953. The barriers against the neutralization project, which the Western powers erected by demanding prior investigation of the prerequisites for free elections, were now to be eliminated in that the Soviet government proposed that both German parliaments immediately form an All-German Provisional Government. This entity was to take in hand the organization of elections, and in order to guarantee its freedom of action, the Allied troops were already to have left the country and have given up all military bases in Germany at the time this government was to be established. Until a new constitution came into effect, the existing governments were to be responsible for the regular business of government. The experts at the Moscow foreign ministry did not regard it as too likely that the Western Allies would agree to the immediate withdrawal of troops. They were certain, however, that the proposal "would find warm approval with the people of Germany, including Western Germany and amongst well-known parts of [the] German bourgeoisie". They therefore expected that "the great powers will have difficulty objecting to the formation of an All-German Provisional Government".[22] As the final outcome of the initiative, they expected "a four-power conference that they thought could be convened as early as June to conclude with Germany a peace treaty".[23]

These papers confirm that Beria's initiative was in fact supported by a general consensus of the collective leadership after Stalin's death. They underscore the continuity from the initiatives of 1952 to the activities of Beria and the public proposals made after Beria's fall. And they also confirm once again the calculation which lay at the basis of the Note of 10 March 1952: The hope of being able to compel the Western Allies into substantial negotiations over a peace treaty by mobilizing the West Germans and the "German bourgeoisie".

Even with the additional sources, of course, the origins of the GDR have still not been completely reconstructed or wholly explained. The decision processes within the Soviet apparatus require a still more precise reconstruction, as do the decisions within the SED leadership and the interactions between leading SED comrades, Soviet representatives, and the Moscow centrale. Likewise, the social and political processes in the SOZ/GDR itself must be made more clear. For a critical discussion of the structural elements of Soviet Communism, the Western reaction to its appearance in the middle of Europe, and the German way of dealing with the defeat of 1945, enough clues are already at hand now.[24] It should thus not be put off any longer.

December 1996

Chronology

Events in the SOZ/GDR appear in *italics*, and central turning points appear in **bold type**. The trips of the KPD/SED leadership to Moscow are in small capitals.

1945

4–11 Feb.	Yalta Conference of the "Big Three"
7/9 May	Unconditional surrender of Germany
9 May	Stalin speaks out against "dismemberment"
4–10 June	KPD LEADERSHIP IN MOSCOW
4 June	**Stalin approves the programme for "bourgeois-democratic government"**
10 June	*Admission of "antifascist democratic" parties and unions in the Soviet Zone*
11 June	KPD appeal for the "democratic renewal of Germany"
17 June to 2 July	Potsdam Conference of the "Big Three"
14 July	*"Unity Front" of the "antifascist democratic" parties in the Soviet Zone*
27 July	*SMA order for setting up "German Central Administrations"*
7 Aug.	France announces reservations regarding the Potsdam Agreement
3–11 Sept.	*Decrees for implementing "land reform"*
11 Sept. to 2 Oct.	London meeting of the Foreign Ministers' Council
19 Sept.	*Pieck demands "quick unification" of the workers' parties*
1 Oct.	French veto of Central Administration
23 Nov.	Sokolovskii rejects Clay's three-zone proposal
19 Dec.	*Tulpanov orders resignation of Andreas Hermes and Walther Schreiber*
20–21 Dec.	*"Conference of Sixty" of KPD and SPD prepares unification*

1946

28 Jan. to 6 Feb.	ULBRICHT IN MOSCOW
11 Feb.	**SPD Central Committee bows to Soviet pressure in the unification question**
21–22 April	*Founding party meeting of the SED*
25 April to 16 May	Paris meeting of the Foreign Ministers' Council (first session)
3 May	Clay halts reparations deliveries
21 May	*Sokolovskii announces the cessation of dismantling*
15 June to 12 July	Paris meeting of the Foreign Ministers' Council (second session)
12 July	**Molotov misses opportunity to prevent founding of Bizonia**
24 July to 16 Aug.	*Decrees on "Dispossessing War Criminals and Nazi Activists"*

1 Sept.	*Local elections in Saxony*
8 Sept.	*Local elections in Saxony-Anhalt and Thuringia*
15 Sept.	*Municipal elections in Berlin, district and provincial elections in the Soviet Zone*
Oct.	**Sokolovskii offers unity in exchange for reparations**
3 Nov. to 12 Dec.	New York meeting of the Foreign Ministers' Council
15 Nov.	*SED's draft constitution for a "German Democratic Republic"*
2 Dec.	Signing of the Bizonia agreement

1947

30 Jan. to 7 Feb.	SED LEADERSHIP IN MOSCOW
1 March	*SED's appeal for a "plebiscite for the unity of Germany"*
10 Mar. to 24 Apr.	Moscow meeting of the Foreign Ministers' Council
12 March	Truman Doctrine
3 April	**Marshall rejects additional reparations payments**
5 June	Announcement of the Marshall Plan
5 to 8 June	Munich meeting of the provincial prime ministers
2 July	**Molotov rejects Soviet participation in the Marshall Plan**
20–24 Sept.	*Second Party Congress of the SED*
22–27 Sept.	Founding conference of the Cominform in Szklarska Poreba
5 Oct.	Publication of the Cominform Declaration
25 Nov. to 15 Dec.	London meeting of the Foreign Ministers' Council
6–7 Dec.	*First German People's Congress*
19 Dec.	*Jakob Kaiser and Ernst Lemmer removed as CDU chairmen*

1948

12 Feb.	*German Economic Commission receives authority to issue directives*
23 Feb. to 6 Mar.	London Six-Power Conference (first phase)
17 March	Signing of the Brussels Pact
17–18 March	Second German People's Congress, formation of the People's Council
20 March	Soviets leave session of the Allied Control Council
20 Mar. to 2 June	London Six-Power Conference (second phase)
25 Mar. to 1 Apr.	SED LEADERSHIP IN MOSCOW
27 Mar. to 5 Apr.	"Miniblockade"
20 June	Currency reform in the Western Zones
24 June	Beginning of the Berlin Blockade
30 June	**Grotewohl capitulates to the "Eastern orientation"**
late Aug.	**Supply of West Berlin secured**
1 Sept.	Assembly of the Parliamentary Council in Bonn
16 Sept.	*Ackermann recants the "special path to Socialism"*
24 Oct.	*People's Council expresses its support for draft constitution*

30 Nov.	*"Provisional Democratic Municipal Government" in East Berlin*
12–21 Dec.	SED LEADERSHIP IN MOSCOW
18 Dec.	**Stalin halts "socialistic construction"**

1949

25–28 Jan.	*First Party Conference of the SED*
4 April	Signing of the Atlantic Pact
8 May	Passage of the Basic Law of the Federal Republic of Germany
12 May	End of the Berlin Blockade
23 May to 2 June	Paris meeting of the Foreign Ministers' Council
15–16 May	*Elections to the Third German People's Congress*
29–30 May	*Third German People's Congress*
14 Aug.	Elections to first German Bundestag
15 Sept.	Adenauer elected as first Federal Chancellor
16–28 Sept.	SED LEADERSHIP IN MOSCOW **Stalin approves formation of a "Provisional Government of the German Democratic Republic"**
4 Oct.	*Proclamation of the "National Front of Democratic Germany"*
5 Oct.	*Middle-class parties accept postponement of elections*
7 Oct.	*GDR constituted*

1950

8 Feb.	*Formation of the Ministry for State Security*
15–28 March	**Middle-class parties accept Unity Lists**
3–6 May	SED LEADERSHIP IN MOSCOW
4 May	Stalin issues a reminder on SED policy for "Germany as a whole"
25 June	Beginning of the Korean War
20–24 July	Third Party Congress of the SED
15 Oct.	*Elections to the Volkskammer, provincial parliaments, local parliaments, communal representations according to the principle of Unity Lists*
20–21 Oct.	Prague Foreign Ministers' Conference proposes Constituent Council for all of Germany on the principle of parity
18–19 Dec.	Brussels Accords: Integrated NATO armed forces with inclusion of German troops

1951

| 15 Sept. | **Grotewohl proposes "consultation" as preparation for elections** |

1952

10 March	First Stalin Note (draft of a peace treaty)
23 Mar. to 10 Apr.	SED LEADERSHIP IN MOSCOW
1 April	**Stalin reorients himself toward defence of the GDR**
9 April	Second Stalin Note ("Free Elections")

26 May	Signing of the General Treaty in Bonn
27 May	Signing of the EDC Treaty in Paris
8 July	Stalin approves announcement of the "transition to socialism"
9–12 July	**Second Party Conference of the SED approves the "construction of Socialism"**
5–14 Oct.	Nineteenth Party Congress of the CPSU

1953

5 March	Stalin's death
27 May	**Beria demands abandonment of the "construction of Socialism"**
2–4 June	SED LEADERSHIP IN MOSCOW
9 June	*SED Politburo announces "New Course"*
17 June	Revolt in the GDR
26 June	**Organization Commission resolves to remove Ulbricht from power**
26 June	Beria's arrest
2–7 July	Plenum of the Central Committee of the CPSU condemns Beria
8–9 July	GROTEWOHL AND ULBRICHT IN MOSCOW
14 July	**Ulbricht attacks the "Herrnstadt/Zaisser Faction"**
16 July	*Justice Minister Max Fechner is arrested*
24–26 June	*Central Committee Plenum of the SED supports Ulbricht*
15 Aug.	Soviet Union proposes forming a "Provisional Government for all of Germany"
20–22 Aug.	GDR GOVERNMENT DELEGATION IN MOSCOW
22 Aug.	GDR–USSR agreements: Exchange of ambassadors, remission of reparations
6 Sept.	Elections to second German Bundestag support Adenauer

1954

25 Jan. to 18 Feb.	Berlin Foreign Ministers' Conference
30 Mar. to 6 Apr.	*Fourth Party Congress of the SED*
23 Oct.	Treaties of Paris signed
23 Oct.	Soviet government wants to "discuss" Eden Plan for free elections in Germany

1955

15 Jan.	Soviet government declares that unity on international monitoring of elections is possible
14 May	Founding of the Warsaw Pact with inclusion of the GDR
18–23 July	Geneva Summit Conference
26 July	**Khrushchev guarantees the "achievements" of the GDR**
17–20 Sept.	GDR GOVERNMENT DELEGATION IN MOSCOW
20 Sept.	Agreement on the "full sovereignty" of the GDR

Notes

Notes to the Introduction

1. Erich W. Gniffke, *Jahre mit Ulbricht* (Cologne, 1966; 2nd edn 1990).
2. Wolfgang Leonhard, *Die Revolution entläßt ihre Kinder* (Cologne, 1955), quotes here being from the paperback edition of 1979.
3. Rolf Badstübner/Wilfried Loth (eds), *Wilhelm Pieck: Aufzeichnungen zur Deutschlandpolitik, 1945–1953* (Berlin, 1994).
4. For some especially striking examples of problematic interpretations, see Wilfried Loth, "Die Historiker und die Deutsche Frage. Ein Rückblick nach dem Ende des Kalten Krieges", *Historisches Jahrbuch*, 112 (1992), pp. 366–82.

Notes to Chapter 1: A Programme for Germany

1. Cf. most recently Rolf-Dieter Müller, *Hitler's Ostkrieg und die deutsche Siedlungspolitik* (Frankfurt am Main, 1991), and his *Die deutsche Wirtschaftspolitik in den besetzten sowjetischen Gebieten, 1941–1945* (Boppard, 1990).
2. Cf. Dimitri Wolkogonow, *Stalin: Triumph und Tragödie. Ein politisches Porträt* (Düsseldorf, 1989), p. 683.
3. Quoted from Hans-Peter Schwarz, *Vom Reich zur Bundesrepublik. Deutschland im Widerstreit der außenpolitischen Konzeptionen in den Jahren der Besatzungsherrschaft, 1945–1949* (Neuwied and Berlin, 1966; 2nd edn, Stuttgart, 1980), p. 223.
4. Milovan Djilas, *Gespräche mit Stalin* (Frankfurt, 1962), p. 147.
5. Wolkogonow, *Stalin*, p. 682. Cf. also Nikolai Voznesenskii, *The Economy of the USSR during World War II* (Washington, DC, 1948).
6. M. L. Tamarchenko, *Sovetskie finansy v period Velikoi Otechestvennoi voiny* (Moscow, 1967), p. 135.
7. Susan J. Linz, "Measuring the Carryover Cost of World War II to the Soviet People, 1945–1953", in *Explorations in Economic History*, 20 (1983), pp. 375–86.
8. Cf. Laszlo Tikos, *E. Vargas Tätigkeit als Wirtschaftsanalytiker und Publizist* (Tübingen, 1965), pp. 65–79.
9. Jean-Richard Bloch in conversation with Géraud Jouve, at the time information director for Agence France Presse during de Gaulle's trip to Moscow at the beginning of December 1944. Quoted from Géraud Jouve, "Le Retour de Maurice Thorez en France", *Le Monde*, 28 November 1969.
10. Cf. Wilfried Loth, "Frankreichs Kommunisten und der Beginn des Kalten Krieges", *Vierteljahrshefte für Zeitgeschichte*, 26 (1978), pp. 9–65.
11. Directives from Georgii Dimitrov on 6 December 1944, quoted from Karel Kaplan, *Der kurze Marsch: Kommunistische Machtübernahme in der Tschechoslowakei, 1945–1948* (Munich and Vienna, 1981), p. 15.
12. Communicated by Ilčo Dimitrov, "Über den Charakter der volksdemokra-

tischen Macht in Bulgarien", in *Wissenschaftliche Zeitschrift der Karl-Marx-Universität Leipzig. Gesellschafts- und sprachwissenschaftliche Reihe*, 31 (1982), pp. 122–37, here cited pp. 130ff.

13. *Sovetsko-anglijskie otnošenija vo vremja Velikoj Otečestvennoj vojny 1941–1945* (Moscow, 1983), vol. 1, p. 182. Cf. also the British draft of the British–Soviet agreement, ibid., p. 187.

14. Winston Churchill, *The Grand Alliance* (London, 1950), pp. 628ff.

15. Minutes of the 3rd EAC Session, 25 January 1944, PRO, FO 371.405 80, 186.

16. Cf. the analysis of the Yalta negotiations on this question by Hermann Graml, *Die Alliierten und die Teilung Deutschlands: Konflikte und Entscheidungen, 1941–1948* (Frankfurt am Main, 1985), pp. 50–3.

17. Quoted from Josef Foschepoth, "Britische Deutschlandpolitik zwischen Jalta und Potsdam", in *Vierteljahrshefte für Zeitgeschichte*, 30 (1982), pp. 675–714, here p. 691.

18. Vladimir Rudolph, "The Administrative Organization of Soviet Control, 1945–1948", in Robert Slusser (ed.), *Soviet Economic Policy in Postwar Germany: A Collection of Papers by Former Soviet Officials* (New York, 1953), pp. 18–86.

19. FRUS Yalta, pp. 630ff.

20. Cf. Walrab von Buttlar, *Ziele und Zielkonflikte der sowjetischen Deutschlandpolitik, 1945–1947* (Stuttgart, 1980), pp. 43–9.

21. Valentin Falin, *Politische Erinnerungen* (Munich, 1993), p. 308. On Stalin's doubts as to the stability of the coalition against Hitler, see Alexander Fischer, *Sowjetische Deutschlandpolitik im Zweiten Weltkrieg 1941–1945* (Stuttgart, 1975); Vojtech Mastny, *Russia's Road to the Cold War* (New York, 1979).

22. Djilas, *Gespräche*, p. 146.

23. Lecture in the Party school, 10 March 1945, ZPA NL 36/421, fols 112–22 and 130–7, here fols 120 and 130.

24. Wolfgang Leonhard, *Die Revolution entläßt ihre Kinder* (Cologne, 1955, 1979), p. 288.

25. Wilhelm Pieck's minutes of a discussion of 4 June 1945, ZPA NL 36/629, pp. 62–6, here p. 62.

26. Leonhard, *Revolution*, p. 288. In the discussion of the goals of Soviet policy on Germany, little attention has been paid to this element of Leonhard's first-hand account up to now.

27. See note 25.

28. Valentin Beresko, *Tegeran 1943, Moskau 1968*, p. 110.

29. Eugen Varga, *Veränderungen in der kapitalistischen Wirtschaft im Gefolge des zweiten Weltkrieges*, (Moskau, 1946, (Teil-)Übersetzung von Manfred Kerner, Berlin, 1975), pp. 317ff. Essential parts of this study had been published in 1945.

30. Leonhard, *Revolution*, pp. 288ff.

31. See note 25.

32. Cf. Günter Benser, *Die KPD im Jahre der Befreiung. Vorbereitung und Aufbau der legalen kommunistischen Massenpartei (Jahreswende 1944/45 bis Herbst 1945)* (Berlin, 1985), pp. 134–6.

33. As the platform of the KPD Central Committee reads, published in the *Deutsche Volkszeitung*, no. 1, 13 June 1945.

34. Cf. for instance, Dietrich Staritz, *Sozialismus in einem halben Land* (Berlin, 1976), pp. 28ff. and p. 57; with another connotation, also the DDR version by Rolf Badstübner, *Friedenssicherung und deutsche Frage. Vom Untergang des "Reiches" bis zur deutschen Zweistaatlichkeit (1943 bis 1949)* (Berlin, 1990), pp. 110–12.
35. ZPA NL 182/857, ff. 86–99.
36. Cf. Loth, "Frankreichs Kommunisten".
37. Evgenii Varga, *Izmeniia*, p. 8, 11ff.
38. FRUS Yalta, p. 617.
39. ZPA NL 36/735, ff. 204–13 (discussion of 19 July 1949).
40. At the reception of an SED delegation; reported by Erich W. Gniffke, *Jahre mit Ulbricht* (Cologne, 1966), p. 251.
41. FRUS 1945, vol. II, p. 268.
42. The Novikov Telegram (Washington, 27 September 1946), English translation following publication by the Soviet Foreign Ministry, in *Diplomatic History*, 15 (1991), pp. 527–37, cited here p. 536.
43. Leonhard, *Revolution*, pp. 288ff. Cf. also Pieck's directives of 10 March 1945, in which he likewise refers to a rather long period of strict military administration and the founding of KPD local groups "only at a later stage". (See note 23, f. 122.)
44. Cf. von Buttlar, *Ziele*, p. 40.
45. Joseph V. Stalin, *Über den Großen Vaterländischen Krieg der Sowjetunion* (Moscow, 1946), pp. 217ff.
46. Quotes from Pieck's notes after the discussion of 4 June 1946 (see note 25). The course of conversations cannot be precisely determined from the notes. When viewed in connection with later recollections by Ackermann, however, there can be no doubt that the new line was put together at this time and in Stalin's presence. On the uncertainties of Günter Benser's account, see "Quellenveröffentlichungen ja, doch so präzis wie möglich", in *Utopie kreativ*, issue 11 (July 1991), pp. 101–7.
47. Cf. Graml, *Die Alliierten*, pp. 55–60.
48. Leonhard, *Revolution*, p. 344; cf. pp. 337–44.
49. Reported by Otto Grotewohl at the Leipzig SPD district meeting on 26 August 1945, ZPA NL 90/125.
50. Reported by Gniffke, *Jahre mit Ulbricht*, p. 33.
51. "Agitprop-Mitteilungen der KPD-UBL Leipzig 1. Jg.", No. 1 (30 July 1945), pp. 6ff., quoted from Hermann Weber (ed.), *DDR-Dokumente zur Geschichte der Deutschen Demokratischen Republik* (Munich, 1986), pp. 44–7.
52. As the formulation in the platform of 11 June reads.
53. Cf. Staritz, *Sozialismus*, pp. 29–35.
54. Meant here is the idea of the leadership provided by bourgeois-democratic forces in the socialist revolution which he had developed for "backward" nations such as Russia; see V. I. Lenin, "Zwei Taktiken der russischen Sozialdemokratie in der demokratischen Revolution", in V. I. Lenin, *Werke* (Berlin, 1960), vol. 9, pp. 1ff.
55. Quoted from *Berlin: Quellen und Dokumente 1945–1951*, vol. 1 (Berlin, 1964), pp. 792ff. With a few stylistic changes, the passage was incorporated into the resolutions of the Conference of Sixty, published in *Deutsche Volkszeitung*, 23 December 1945.

56. He left Berlin on 28 January and returned from Moscow on 6 February (see Kalendernotiz Piecks, ZPA NL 36/734, f. 159).

57. Quotes from Ulbricht's report with additions by Pieck "on 6 February 1946 at 9 p.m.", ZPA NL 36/631, ff. 33ff. and 49.

58. Reported by Djilas, *Gespräche*, p. 145.

59. Laski's report in the Parteivorstand on the discussion of 7 August 1946, quoted from the copy in the Nachlaß Klement Gottwald in German translation by Kaplan, *Der kurze Marsch*, p. 91. Cf. also the report by Morgan Phillips in *Daily Herald*, 22 August 1946, and the Report on the 46th Annual Conference of the Labour Party, 1947, pp. 218ff.

60. Evgenii Varga, "Sotsializm i kapitalizm za tridtsat' let", in *Mirovoe khoziaistvo i mirovaia politika*, no. 10 (1947), pp. 4ff.; quoted from Jerry F. Hough, "Debates about the Postwar World", in Susan J. Linz (ed.), *The Impact of World War II on the Soviet Union* (Totowa, NJ, 1985), pp. 253–81; p. 270 cited here.

61. Cf. most recently Robert Conquest, *Stalin: Der totale Wille zur Macht* (Munich, 1991), pp. 342–94.

62. At the same time, the remarks made to Tito and to the Labour leaders confirm the authenticity of the remarks as recorded by Ulbricht.

63. Djilas, *Gespräche*, pp. 195ff.

64. Anton Ackermann, "Gibt es einen besonderen deutschen Weg zum Sozialismus?", in *Einheit*, issue 1 (February 1946), pp. 22–32. On the origins of the theory, see Dietrich Staritz, "Ein 'besonderer deutscher Weg' zum Sozialismus?", in *Aus Politik und Zeitgeschichte*, B 51–52/82 (25 December 1982), pp. 15–31.

65. Passed by the Unification Party Conference on 22 April 1946, quoted here from Weber, *DDR-Dokumente*, p. 70.

66. Walter Ulbricht, "Die Gegenwartsforderungen der Sozialistischen Einheitspartei Deutschlands", in *Einheit*, issue 2 (March 1946), pp. 18ff.

67. Important documents on the origins of the United Front in Manfred Koch, "Der Demokratische Block", in Hermann Weber (ed.), *Parteiensysteme zwischen Demokratie und Volksdemokratie* (Cologne, 1982), pp. 281–337.

68. FRUS Potsdam, vol. II, pp. 775–8.

69. Soviet suggestion of 30 July 1945 for supplementing the programme, ibid., p. 824; definitive text, ibid., p. 1451. For details on this matter, Elisabeth Kraus, *Ministerien für ganz Deutschland? Der Alliierte Kontrollrat und die Frage gesamtdeutscher Zentralverwaltungen* (Munich, 1990), pp. 38–46.

70. See FRUS Potsdam, vol. II, p. 474.

71. Quoted from *Tägliche Rundschau*, 4 August 1945.

72. Gregory Klimow, *Berliner Kreml* (Cologne, 1952), p. 172.

73. Telegram of the Political Division of the Allied Control Commission/British Element from 3 September 1945, quoted from Kraus, *Ministerien*, p. 56.

74. Grotewohl's memorandum for the Central Committee, AdsD, NL Gniffke, quoted from Hermann Weber, *Geschichte der DDR* (Munich, 1985), p. 100.

75. Report of the Economic Information Section of the British Occupation Authority from 9 May 1946, quoted from Kraus, *Ministerien*, pp. 56ff.

Notes to Chapter 2: First Setbacks

1. Party Executive for Western Westphalia to Kurt Schumacher, 22 September 1945, quoted from Klaus Sühl, "Kurt Schumacher und die Westzonen-SPD im Vereinigungsprozeß", in Dietrich Staritz and Hermann Weber (eds), *Einheitsfront – Einheitspartei. Kommunisten und Sozialdemokraten in Ost- und Westeuropa 1944–1948* (Cologne, 1989), pp. 108–28, here p. 118.
2. Most recently on this, Elisabeth Kraus, *Ministerien für ganz Deutschland? Der Alliierte Kontrollrat und die Frage gesamtdeutscher Zentralverwaltungen* (Munich, 1990), pp. 46–51 and 61–86.
3. Cf. the overview in W. von Buttlar, *Ziele und Zielkonflikte der sowjetischen Deutschlandpolitik, 1945–1947* (Stuttgart, 1980), pp. 58–62.
4. According to the account of S. I. Tulpanov, "Die Rolle der Sowjetischen Militäradministration im demokratischen Deutschland", in *50 Jahre Triumph des Marxismus-Leninismus*, ed. by Party School "Karl Marx" of the Central Committee of the SED (Berlin, 1967), p. 48.
5. Erich Gniffke, *Jahre mit Ulbricht* (Cologne, 1966; 2nd edn 1990), p. 233.
6. Report of the Social Democratic Central Committee Secretary S.F., in Beatrix W. Bouvier and Horst-Peter Schultz (eds), "*. . . die SPD aber aufgehört hat, zu existieren". Sozialdemokraten unter sowjetischer Besatzung* (Bonn, 1991), pp. 63ff.
7. Reported by Wolfgang Leonhard, "Es muß demokratisch aussehen", in *Die Zeit*, 7 May 1965.
8. Gniffke, *Jahre mit Ulbricht*, pp. 184, 223, 298.
9. According to the formulation in the founding proclamation of the SPD, 15 June 1945, *Berliner Zeitung*, 21 June 1945.
10. Cf. Pieck's notes on a conversation with Gorbachev and Zhukov on 11 July 1945, ZPA NL 36/734, ff. 116–18; and Grotewohl's report at the Leipzig district meeting of the SPD, 26 August 1945, ZPA NL 90/125.
11. Most recently on this, the accounts in Michael Klonovsky and Jan von Flocken, *Stalins Lager in Deutschland, 1945–1950* (Berlin/Frankfurt am Main, 1991).
12. Wolfgang Leonhard, *Die Revolution entläßt ihre Kinder* (Cologne, 1955, 1979), pp. 358ff.
13. Gniffke, *Jahre mit Ulbricht*, pp. 39ff, 59ff, 75ff, 88, 91, 121; Leonhard, *Revolution*, p. 375.
14. According to Gniffke, *Jahre mit Ulbricht*, p. 40.
15. ZPA NL 90/125, utilized for the first time by Lucio Caracciolo, "Der Untergang der Sozialdemokratie in der sowjetischen Besatzungszone. Otto Grotewohl und die 'Einheit der Arbeiterklasse' 1945/46", in *Vierteljahrshefte für Zeitgeschichte*, 36 (1988), pp. 280–318, here pp. 289–94.
16. Otto Grotewohl, *Woher – Wohin? Rede des Vorsitzenden des ZA der SPD am 14. September 1945 in Berlin* (Berlin, 1945).
17. According to the report in the Berlin SPD newspaper *Das Volk*, 18 September 1945.
18. Report from S.F., at the time secretary to the executive of the SPD Central Committee (see note 6), p. 88.
19. *Deutsche Volkszeitung*, 20 September 1945, reprinted numerous times, e.g. in *Wilhelm Pieck, Reden und Aufsätze* (Berlin, 1948), pp. 82ff.

20. Wolfgang Leonhard's account in "Einheit oder Freiheit? Zum 40. Jahrestag der Gründung der SED" (minutes of a meeting of the Friedrich-Ebert-Stiftung, 6–8 September 1985; n.p., n.d.), p. 79.
21. Gniffke, *Jahre mit Ulbricht*, p. 67.
22. ZPA NL 36/629, ff. 62–6.
23. Gniffke, *Jahre mit Ulbricht*, p. 43.
24. ZPA NL 36/734, ff. 129–36.
25. Ibid., f. 130.
26. Anton Ackermann, "Der neue Weg zur Einheit", in *Vereint sind wir alles: Erinnerungen an die Gründung der SED* (Berlin, 1966), p. 84.
27. Cf. Leonhard, "Einheit oder Freiheit", pp. 79ff; Leonhard, *Revolution*, pp. 375ff – text of Grotewohl's speech, the publication of which was not permitted and consequently is also not to be found in the collected speeches of Grotewohl, in ZPA NL 90/125. Now published in *Beiträge zur Geschichte der Arbeiterbewegung*, 2/1992, pp. 173–80.
28. Walter Ulbricht, *Zur Geschichte der deutschen Arbeiterbewegung. Aus Reden und Aufsätzen*, vol. II: *1933–1946, 2. Zusatzband* (Berlin, 1968) p. 356; cf. also von Buttlar, *Ziele*, pp. 143ff.
29. Anton Ackermann, "Gibt es einen besonderen deutschen Weg zum Sozialismus?" in *Einheit*, issue 1 (February 1946), pp. 22–32.
30. Ibid.
31. ZPA NL 36/734, ff. 143ff, 146.
32. Gniffke, *Jahre mit Ulbricht*, pp. 90ff.
33. Ibid., p. 84.
34. Cf. Leonhard's compilation, "Einheit oder Freiheit", p. 24.
35. Cf. the corresponding analysis of the Ackermann article in Chapter 1.
36. Reports of different Western sources in Berlin based on confidential conversations with Grotewohl and Dahrendorf, examined by Caracciolo, *Untergang*, p. 311; the offer to remove Ulbricht, regarded by Grotewohl as "baffling", reported as early as in Gniffke, *Jahre mit Ulbricht*, p. 137.
37. He did not inform his Central Committee colleagues about the conversation and thus contributed to the spread of mutual uncertainty.
38. Steel to Foreign Office, 7 February 1946, PRO FO 371/55586, C 1480/131/18, quoted from Rolf Steininger (ed.), *Die Ruhrfrage 1945/46 und die Entstehung des Landes Nordrhein-Westfalen* (Düsseldorf, 1988), p. 486.
39. From a speech manuscript by Ollenhauer quoted by Karl Wilhelm Fricke, *Opposition und Widerstand in der DDR: Ein politischer Report* (Cologne, 1984), p. 34.
40. Report from M.H. (see note 6), p. 130.
41. Conversation of 22 December 1945 (see note 31).
42. Cf. Gavriel D. Ra'anan, *International Policy Formation in the USSR. Factional "Debates" during the Zhdanovschina* (Hamden, CT, 1983), pp. 27 and 179.
43. ZPA NL 36/734, ff. 147–52, 155–7, quotes from f. 148.
44. According to the transcription of a discussion with Bokov on 1 February 1946, ibid., ff. 160–3.
45. Sergei Tulpanov, *Deutschland nach dem Kriege (1945–1949). Erinnerungen eines Offiziers der Sowjetarmee* (Berlin, 1986), pp. 82ff.
46. ZPA NL 36/631, ff. 33ff and 49; date of the meeting from Fjodor J. Bokov,

Frühjahr des Sieges und der Befreiung (Berlin, 1979), pp. 445ff.

47. Ulbricht's report of 6 February 1946 (see note 46); on the context of the programmatic determinations, see Chapter 1.

48. "You need not worry: We have no such intention." Pieck at the Unification Party meeting in Greater Berlin, 14 April 1946. *Einstimmig beschlossen: SED Groß-Berlin. Die Bildung der SED in der Hauptstadt Deutschlands* (Berlin, n.d., 1946), p. 35.

49. Cf. Siegfried Suckut, "Die CDU der sowjetisch besetzten Zone und die Gründung der SED. Parteiinterne Wertungen und Reaktionen", in Staritz and Weber, *Einheitsfront*, pp. 167–90.

50. *Tägliche Rundschau*, 16 April 1946.

51. Protocol note by Waldemar Koch of the discussion on 5 September 1945, published in Ekkehart Krippendorff, "Die Gründung der Liberal-Demokratischen Partei in der Sowjetischen Besatzungszone 1945", in *Vierteljahrshefte für Zeitgeschichte*, 8 (1960), pp. 303–5.

52. Cf. Ekkehart Krippendorff, *Die Liberal-Demokratische Partei Deutschlands in der Sowjetischen Besatzungszone, 1945/48* (Düsseldorf, n.d., 1961), p. 40.

53. Peter Hermes, *Die Christlich-Demokratische Union und die Bodenreform in der Sowjetischen Besatzungszone Deutschlands im Jahre 1945* (Saarbrücken, 1963), pp. 24ff; Siegfried Suckut, "Der Konflikt um die Bodenreformpolitik in der Ost-CDU 1945", in *Deutschland Archiv*, 15 (1982), pp. 1080–95; the session of 19 December in Gniffke, *Jahre mit Ulbricht*, p. 75.

54. The figure given by Heinz Heitzer, *DDR. Geschichtlicher Überblick* (Berlin, 1979), p. 54.

55. At the economics conference in Jena; Walter Ulbricht, *Demokratischer Wirtschaftsaufbau* (Berlin, n.d., 1946), pp. 18ff.

56. Meeting with Ulbricht on 2 February 1946 (see note 46).

57. Robertson to Street, 28 March 1946, quoted from Kraus, *Ministerien*, pp. 162ff; for earlier complaints, ibid., pp. 94, 96 and 114, also Dietrich Staritz, "Parteien für ganz Deutschland? Zu den Kontroversen über ein Parteiengesetz im Alliierten Kontrollrat 1946/47", in *Vierteljahrshefte für Zeitgeschichte*, 32 (1984), pp. 240–68, here p. 250.

58. Murphy (Clay's state advisor) to Matthews, 2 April 1946, excerpts quoted in Jean Edward Smith, "The View from UFSET: General Clay's and Washington's Interpretation of Soviet Intentions in Germany, 1945–1948", in Hans A. Schmitt (ed.), *U.S. Occupation in Europe after World War II* (Lawrence, KS, 1978), pp. 64–85; pp. 68ff. cited here.

59. Cf. Kraus, *Ministerien*, pp. 92–113.

60. Discussion with Tulpanov, Semyonov, Sobelov, and Voskravsinskii, 22 October 1945, ZPA NL 36/734, ff. 140–2.

61. Cf. Kraus, *Ministerien*, pp. 127–9.

62. Quoted from Murphy's report to the US ambassador in Paris, Jefferson Caffery, from 11 April 1946. This passage was missing from the published text of the speech; cf. Kraus, *Ministerien*, p. 59.

63. Roberts (who had been verbally informed by Kennan of his espionage coup) to Harvey, 2 May 1946, quoted from Reiner Pommerin, "Die Zwangsvereinigung von KPD und SPD zur SED. Eine britische Analyse

vom April 1946", in *Vierteljahrshefte für Zeitgeschichte*, 36 (1988), pp. 319–38; p. 323 cited here.

64. ZPA NL 36/734, ff. 190–3.
65. Memorandum of 27 September 1946, quoted from *Diplomatic History*, 15 (1991), p. 537; see Chapter 1, note 42.
66. FRUS 1946, vol. II, pp. 146ff. (talks between Byrnes and Molotov, 28 April 1946) and 167ff. (session of 29 April 1946).
67. Ibid., pp. 842ff. (declaration of 9 July 1946) and pp. 869ff. (declaration from 10 July 1946); these declarations were published in the Soviet press shortly after the end of the conference, German translations of which are in W. M. Molotov, *Fragen der Außenpolitik: Reden und Erklärungen April 1945–Juni 1948* (Moscow, 1949), pp. 59–67.
68. Discussion on 26 July 1946, see note 64.
69. Cf. Staritz, "Parteien", pp. 251–3.
70. On the subsequent negotiations, ibid., pp. 257–61.
71. FRUS 1946, vol. II, p. 876 (session of 10 July 1946); on the previous interventions, ibid., pp. 146ff. (talks between Byrnes and Molotov, 28 April 1946) and pp. 434ff. (session of 16 May 1946).
72. Discussion on 26 July 1946, see note 64.
73. FRUS 1946, vol. II, p. 935 (session of 12 July 1946); Bidault's partial concession, ibid., pp. 909ff.
74. Murphy's report of 25 May 1946, FRUS 1946, vol. V, pp. 559ff.
75. For details on this, Kraus, *Ministerien*, pp. 129, 231–50.
76. FRUS 1946, vol. II, p. 911.
77. Cf. the conference analyses in Hermann Graml, *Die Allierten und die Teilung Deutschlands. Konflikte und Entscheidungen 1941–1948* (Frankfurt am Main, 1985), pp. 176–8; and Kraus, *Ministerien*, pp. 205–7.
78. Ibid., pp. 218–20; see also Murphy's session report of 30 July 1946, FRUS 1946, vol. V, pp. 585ff.
79. This is true of the discussion in Karlshorst on 26 July and of Novikov's memorandum of 27 September 1946; see notes 64 and 65.
80. Cf. the collection of relevant statements in von Buttlar, *Ziele*, pp. 182–7.
81. On this, cf. most recently Jörg Fisch, *Reparationen nach dem Zweiten Weltkrieg* (Munich, 1992), pp. 104ff.
82. Details of the struggle in John H. Backer, *Die deutschen Jahre des Generals Clay* (Munich, 1983), pp. 116–21; Friedrich Jerchow, *Deutschland in der Weltwirtschaft, 1944–1947* (Düsseldorf, 1978), pp. 181–209; Alec Cairncross, *The Price of War: British Policy on German Reparations, 1941–1949* (Oxford, 1986), pp. 100–46.
83. For a closer examination of the political context of reparations, see Fisch, *Reparationen*, pp. 285–94.
84. See the report in Vladimir Rudolph, "The Administrative Organization of Soviet Control, 1945–1948", in Robert Slusser (ed.), *Soviet Economic Policy in Postwar Germany: A Collection of Papers by Former Soviet Officials* (New York, 1953) pp. 18–86.
85. Ulbricht's report of 6 February 1946 (see note 64); the announcement made for the first time during a discussion on 23 January 1946 (see note 43).
86. Ra'anan, *International Policy Formation*, pp. 23, 30, and 89.
87. Declaration of 10 July 1946 (see note 67).

88. Comments on this in Rudolph, *Administrative Organization*, pp. 51ff.
89. Ibid., p. 53.
90. Ibid., p. 55.

Notes to Chapter 3: From Paris to London

1. Erich W. Gniffke, *Jahre mit Ulbricht* (Cologne, 1966; 2nd edn, 1990), p. 192.
2. Ibid.
3. Interview with S.F., 21 March 1974, in Beatrix W. Bouvier and Horst-Peter Schultz (eds), "... *die SPD aber aufgehört hat, zu existieren": Sozialdemokraten unter Sowjetischer* (Bonn, 1991), pp. 63–5.
4. Gniffke, *Jahre mit Ulbricht*, pp. 181ff.
5. Ibid., p. 192.
6. According to figures cited in Hermann Weber, *Geschichte der DDR* (Munich, 1985), p. 133.
7. Cf. Dietrich Staritz, *Die Gründung der DDR* (Munich, 1984), pp. 103–8.
8. *Sozialpolitische Richtlinien der Sozialistischen Einheitspartei Deutschlands, nach dem Beschluß des Zentralsekretariats vom 30. Dezember 1946* (Berlin, 1947), p. 10; cf. Siegfried Suckut, *Die Betriebsrätebewegung in der Sowjetisch Besetzten Zone Deutschlands (1945–1948)* (Frankfurt am Main, 1982), pp. 451–4.
9. According to the *Deutsche Volkszeitung* of 28 August 1945; corresponding statements by Ulbricht to party functionaries as early as the end of June/beginning of July 1945, in Walter Ulbricht, *Zur Geschichte der deutschen Arbeiterbewegung. Aus Reden und Aufsätzen.* vol. II: *1933–1946, I. Zusatzband* (Berlin, 1966), pp. 245 and 428ff.
10. *Neues Deutschland*, 14 September (Fechner) and 21 September (Party Executive) 1946; on the internal debates, Wolfgang Leonhard, *Die Revolution entläßt ihre Kinder* (Cologne, 1955, 1979), pp. 397ff., and Gniffke, *Jahre mit Ulbricht*, pp. 206ff.
11. Cf. Badstrübner, *Friedenssicherung*, pp. 194.
12. Cf. Gniffke, *Jahre mit Ulbricht*, pp. 206–8.
13. Details on this in Manfred Koch, Werner Müller, Dietrich Staritz, and Siegfried Suckut, "Versuch und Scheitern gesamtdeutscher Parteibildungen 1945–1948", in *Die beiden deutschen Staaten im Ost-West-Verhältnis* (Cologne, 1982), pp. 90–107.
14. Gniffke, *Jahre mit Ulbricht*, pp. 208 and 210ff.
15. Cf. Leonhard, *Revolution*, pp. 403–5.
16. Cf. Ulbricht to Bokov, 10 August 1946, ZPA NL 188/1190, ff. 88 – a simultaneous suggestion first to go public with a declaration of the "Formation of a unified German government of the Bloc of Anti-Fascist Democratic Parties" (ibid., ff. 84–7), was obviously not approved by the occupation forces.
17. Session of 14 November 1946, ZPA IV 2/1/6, ff. 5.
18. Cf. Rudolph Nadolny, *Mein Beitrag* (Wiesbaden, 1955), pp. 178ff; and Gniffke, *Jahre mit Ulbricht*, p. 209.
19. Text in *Dokumente der Sozialistischen Einheitspartei Deutschlands*, vol. I: *Beschlüsse und Erklärungen des Zentralsekretariats und des Parteivorstandes* (Berlin, 1952), p. 115.

20. ZPA IV/2/1/5.
21. Gniffke, *Jahre mit Ulbricht*, pp. 234ff.
22. ZPA IV/1/2.
23. ZPA NL 36/734, ff. 244–7.
24. Cf. the reports of the American military government in FRUS 1946, V, pp. 611ff, 622–5, 792ff; and John H. Backer, *Die deutschen Jahre des Generals Clay* (Munich, 1983), p. 179.
25. Cf. FRUS 1946, vol. II, p. 1482.
26. ZPA NL 36/734, ff. 244–50.
27. Cf. the corresponding fears in a communication of the executive member Erich Lübbe to the Central Secretariat of the SED, 15 February 1947, published in Hermann Weber (ed.), *Parteiensysteme zwischen Demokratie und Volksdemokratie* (Cologne, 1982), p. 74.
28. ZPA NL 36/694, ff. 3–7. Grotewohl and Fechner, incidentally, now travelled to the Soviet capital as equals alongside Pieck and Ulbricht, with Fred Oelßner as interpreter.
29. On 11 July 1947, Tulpanov retrospectively criticized "Vaciliation in [the] Party Executive due to admission of the SPD into the Eastern Zone": ZPA NL 36/734, ff. 299–305.
30. Quoted from *Europa-Archiv*, 2 (1947), p. 678.
31. Gniffke, *Jahre mit Ulbricht*, p. 229.
32. Cf. discussions at the Party Executive meeting of May 1947, ZPA IV 2/1/10.
33. State Chairman Heinrich Hoffmann in the secretariat session of the Thuringian State Executive on 30 April 1947 on a discussion with Pieck, Grotewohl, and Ulbricht on the previous day; published by Günter Braun, " 'Regierungsangelegenheiten' in Thüringen im Spannungsfeld von sowjetischer Deutschlandpolitik und SED-Kalkülen 1947", in *Beiträge zur Geschichte der Arbeiterbewegung*, 34 (1992), pp. 67–91; p. 79 cited here.
34. Cf. the protocol of the secretariat session of 30 April 1947, in which this was announced, ibid., pp. 78–91.
35. *Dokumente der Sozialistischen Einheitspartei*, vol. 1, pp. 162ff.
36. Meeting with Marshal Sokolovskii, 21 January 1947, ZPA NL 36/734, ff. 282–4.
37. Meeting of 31 January 1947, ZPA NL 36/694.
38. Ibid.
39. Franz Dahlem, "Zur Frage der Ostgrenze", *Neues Deutschland*, 2 April 1947; see also Leonhard, *Revolution*, p. 406. If as Gniffke relates (p. 251), on the basis of a report by Grotewohl, Stalin actually did add his determination to the matter, saying that the SED "as a German party" could "certainly take a different view than we or the Poles" in the agitation over this question, this had in any event no further effect on the attitude of the SED leadership.
40. Meeting of 31 January 1947, see note 28.
41. According to Grotewohl's report as noted down by Gniffke during the same meeting; Gniffke, *Jahre mit Ulbricht*, p. 250.
42. See note 28.
43. Stalin, according to Grotewohl, see note 37.
44. Pieck's notes, see note 28.
45. Meeting of 25 October 1946, ZPA NL 36/734, ff. 218–29.

46. Meeting of 31 January 1947, see note 28.
47. *Pravda*, 23 January 1947; American version in *Look*, 4 February 1947; German in Joseph W. Stalin, *Werke*, Vol. 15: *May 1945–October 1952* (Dortmund, 1976), pp. 55–9.
48. Walter Bedell Smith, *My Three Years in Moscow* (Philadelphia, 1950), pp. 211–15.
49. Stalin, *Werke*, vol. 15, pp. 62ff.
50. V. M. Molotov, *Fragen der Außenpolitik. Reden und Erklärungen April 1944–Juni 1948* (Moscow, 1949), pp. 387–451.
51. *Europa-Archiv*, 2 (1947), pp. 709ff; see also FRUS 1947, vol. II, pp. 304ff.
52. Cf. among others, Martina Kessel, *Westeuropa und die deutsche Teilung. Englische und französische Deutschlandpolitik auf den Außenminister-konferenzen von 1945 bis 1947* (Munich, 1989), pp. 188 and 201–3.
53. *Europa-Archiv*, 2 (1947), pp. 714–28; Kessel, *Westeuropa*, pp. 241ff and 246.
54. Cf. Elisabeth Kraus, *Ministerien für ganz Deutschland? Der alliierte Kontrollrat und die Frage gesamtdeutscher Zentralverwaltungen* (Munich, 1990), p. 308.
55. *Europa-Archiv*, 2 (1947), pp. 696–9, 709ff, 716–18; Kessel, *Westeuropa*, p. 243
56. FRUS 1947, vol. II, pp. 278ff and 298ff.
57. Kessel, *Westeuropa*, pp. 222–35; also on the following quotation.
58. Peterson to Sargent, 26 March 1947, ibid., p. 227.
59. Cf. Backer, *Clay*, pp. 181, 206–8.
60. Molotov, *Fragen der Außenpolitik*, pp. 479–84.
61. Kraus, *Ministerien*, p. 314.
62. FRUS 1947, vol. II, pp. 337–44.
63. ZPA IV 2/1/10, f. 12.
64. *Europa-Archiv*, 2 (1947), p. 716.
65. OMGUS communiqué to the press, 3 May 1947, quoted in Staritz, *Parteien für ganz Deutschland*, p. 264.
66. Sergej Tulpanov, *Deutschland nach dem Kriege (1945–1949). Erinnerungen eines Offiziers der Sowjetarmee* (Berlin, 1986), p. 297.
67. Leonhard, *Revolution*, p. 408.
68. Hübener's note of 3 June 1947, published in Rolf Steininger, "Dieser Vorfall bedeutet die Spaltung Deutschlands. Neue Dokumente zur Münchener Ministerpräsidentenkonferenz im Juni 1947", in *Geschichte im Westen*, 7 (1992), pp. 213–30, here p. 228. Cf. also Hübener's meeting with Wilhelm Külz on the evening of 2 June, notes taken by Wilhelm Külz, *Ein Liberaler zwischen Ost und West. Aufzeichnungen 1947–1948* (Munich, 1989), pp. 85ff.
69. Gniffke, *Jahre mit Ulbricht*, pp. 236–41.
70. Ibid., p. 241.
71. Cf. ibid., p. 242, and the minutes of the night-time preliminary conference in Rolf Steininger, "Zur Geschichte der Münchener Ministerpräsidentenkonferenz 1947", in *Vierteljahrshefte für Zeitgeschichte*, 23 (1975), pp. 375–453.
72. ZPA NL 36/734, ff. 299–305.

73. Ibid.
74. ZPA IV 2/1/11.
75. *Um ein antifaschistisch-demokratisches Deutschland. Dokumente aus den Jahren 1945–1949* (Berlin, 1958), p. 474ff.
76. Alexander O. Tschubarjan, "Auf dem Weg nach Europa – aus Moskauer Sicht", in Wolfgang J. Mommsen (ed.), *Der lange Weg nach Europa* (Berlin, 1992), pp. 267–302, here p. 288.
77. Memorandum of 5 July 1947, PRO Cab 129/19; cf. Wilfried Loth, *Die Teilung der Welt: Geschichte des Kalten Krieges, 1941–1955* (Munich, 1980), p. 181ff.
78. Molotov's reaction to Stalin's telegram according to Bevin, quoted in Bedell Smith, *My Three Years in Moscow*, p. 198; likewise attested to by Dean Acheson, *Present at the Creation* (New York, 1970), p. 234; the closing declaration in Molotov, *Fragen der Außenpolitik*, pp. 657–9.
79. Gyptner to Pieck, 26 July 1947, ZPA NL 36/734, f. 307.
80. Examination of the local party meetings, ibid., ff. 308–10; the following quotations also from them.
81. Report on the party conferences, 16 and 17 August 1947, ZPA NL 36/734, ff. 316–23.
82. Letter draft at the end of August/beginning of September 1947, ZPA NL 36/734, ff. 332–5.
83. ZPA IV 2/1/12, f. 171.
84. See note 82.
85. Their names are handwritten at the top of the first page.
86. Undated speech manuscript in which the "upcoming Second Party Conference" is referred to, ZPA NL 36/734, ff. 347–62.
87. Conversation of 18 August 1947, BA NL Kaiser, no. 85.
88. See note 86.
89. See note 82.
90. According to Tulpanov on 11 July 1947, see note 29.
91. *Die Welt*, 6 December 1947.
92. *Protokoll der Verhandlungen des II. Parteitages der Sozialistischen Einheitspartei Deutschlands, 20. bis 24. September 1947 in der Deutschen Staatsoper zu Berlin* (Berlin, 1947), p. 537; see also an elucidating radio interview of Grotewohl's in *Neues Deutschland*, 7 November 1947.
93. Otto Grotewohl, *Im Kampf um Deutschland. Reden und Aufsätze* (Berlin, 1948), vol. II, p. 245.
94. Ibid., p. 243.
95. A communication to Wilhelm Pieck of 25 November 1947, published in *Neue Zeit*, 27 November 1947.
96. Cf. Werner Conze, *Jakob Kaiser: Politiker zwischen Ost und West 1945–1949* (Stuttgart, 1969), pp. 182–4.
97. BA NL Kaiser, no. 46.
98. Nuschke's report in the editorial conference of *Neue Zeit*, 22 December 1947, quote from Conze, *Jakob Kaiser*, p. 279.
99. Cf. Klaus Bender, *Deutschland einig Vaterland? Die Volkskongressbewegung für deutsche Einheit und einen gerechten Frieden in der Deutschlandpolitik der Sozialistischen Einheitspartei Deutschlands* (Frankfurt am Main, 1992), pp. 130–47.

100. FRUS 1947, vol. II., pp. 764ff.
101. Marshall to Lovett, 11 December 1947, FRUS 1947, vol. II, pp. 764ff.
102. According to the British Under-secretary of State Orme Sargent on 12 December 1947, PRO FO 371/64631/C 16156, quoted from Kessel, *Westeuropa*, p. 293.
103. *Die Londoner Tagung des Außenministerrates* (Berlin, n.d.; 1948), p. 126.
104. ZPA IV 2/1/19, f. 29.
105. Djilas, *Gespräche*, p. 195.

Notes to Chapter 4: The Cominform Line

1. Report of 11 July 1947, ZPA NL 36/734, ff. 299–305.
2. Johannes R. Becher, *Wir, Volk der Deutschen. Rede auf der I. Bundeskonferenz des Kulturbundes zur demokratischen Erneuerung Deutschlands* (Berlin, 1947), p. 80.
3. Tulpanov, Report of 11 July 1947, see note 1.
4. Report on local party meetings in preparation for the Second Party Conference, late July 1947, ZPA NL 36/734, ff. 308–10.
5. Wolfgang Leonhard, *Die Revolution entläßt ihre Kinder* (Cologne, 1955, 1979), p. 414.
6. Report on local party meetings, see note 4.
7. Report on district party conferences of 16 and 17 August 1947, ZPA NL 36/734, ff. 316–23.
8. Ibid.
9. Erich W. Gniffke, *Jahre mit Ulbricht* (Cologne, 1966; 2nd edn, 1990), p. 256.
10. "Zur Politik unserer Partei. Diskussionsgrundlage zur Vorbereitung des 2. Parteitages", in *Einheit*, 8 (August 1947), pp. 711ff.
11. Cf. his contribution to the Party Executive meeting of 22 and 23 January 1947, ZPA IV 2/1/7.
12. *Protokoll der Verhandlungen des II. Parteitages*, pp. 252ff.
13. Ibid., p. 536.
14. ZPA IV 2/1/15.
15. Cf. Werner Conze, *Jakob Kaiser: Politiker zwischen Ost und West, 1945–1949* (Stuttgart, 1969), pp. 197–205.
16. Report of 11 July 1947, ZPA NL 36/734, ff. 299–305.
17. Conversation of 18 August 1947, BA NL Kaiser, no. 85.
18. Wilhelm Külz, *Ein Liberaler zwischen Ost und West. Aufzeichnungen, 1947–1948* (Munich, 1989), p. 128.
19. Grotewohl's account to Gniffke and Lemmer of 26 December 1947, quoted from Gniffke, *Jahre mit Ulbricht*, p. 273.
20. Ibid., p. 264.
21. According to the formulation of the communiqué in *Neues Deutschland*, 7 October 1947, from the translation in the French party newspaper *L'Humanité*.
22. Gniffke, *Jahre mit Ulbricht*, pp. 264ff.
23. Ibid., pp. 271–5.
24. Text in *Diplomatic History*, 15 (1991), pp. 527–37, quote from p. 537. On its origin, see the commentary from Viktor L. Mal'kov, ibid., pp. 554–8.

25. *Pravda*, 8 February 1946.
26. *Pravda*, 7 November 1946.
27. Gniffke, *Jahre mit Ulbricht*, p. 250.
28. Cf. Werner G. Hahn, *Postwar Soviet Politics: The Fall of Zhdanov and the Defeat of Moderation, 1946–53* (Ithaca/London, 1982), pp. 85ff.
29. E. Varga, "Sotsializm i kapitalizm za tridtsat'let", in *Mirovoe khoziaistvo i mirovaia politika*, 10 (1947), pp. 4ff; see Chapter 1, note 60.
30. Interview with Alexander Werth on 24 September 1946, interview with Hugh Baillie on 28 October 1946; interview with Elliot Roosevelt on 21 December 1946, interview with Harold Stassen on 9 April 1947; Stalin, *Werke*, vol. 15, pp. 45–59 and 62–77.
31. See above, Chapter 3.
32. Gniffke, *Jahre mit Ulbricht*, pp. 250ff.
33. *New York Times*, 4 May 1947. Only the paraphrased version is found in Stalin, *Werke*, vol. 15, pp. 62–77.
34. Cf. Gavriel Ra'anan, *International Policy Formation in the USSR Factional Debates during the Zhdanovschina* (Hamden, CT, 1983), pp. 125–9.
35. *Pravda*, 27 May 1947.
36. The Zhdanov text was first published in *Pravda*, 22 October 1947; now completed by an English version in *The Cominform. Minutes of the Three Conferences 1947/1948/1949* (Milan, 1994), pp. 216–51; the Malenkov report in *Sa procnyj mir, sa narodnuju demokraciju!*, 1 December 1947; now in *The Cominform*, pp. 64–95.
37. Dimitri Wolkogonow, *Stalin. Triumph und Tragödie* (Düsseldorf, 1989), p. 718; and his *Stalin* (Moscow, 1992), vol. 2, p. 499.
38. Jan Foitzik, "Die Bildung des Kominform-Büros 1947 im Lichte neuer Quellen", *Zeitschrift für Geschichtswissenschaft*, 40 (1992), pp. 1109–26; pp. 1120ff cited here.
39. Cf. Jan Foitzik, "Fragen der sowjetischen Außenpolitik nach dem zweiten Weltkrieg", *Zeitschrift für Geschichtswissenschaft* 41 (1993), pp. 329–35, who makes this version his own.
40. Eugenio Reale, *Avec Jacques Duclos au banc des accusés* (Paris, 1958), p. 14.
41. Quotes from the translation of the Malenkov text in Foitzik, "Fragen", pp. 332–5.
42. *The Cominform*, pp. 250–1.
43. The latter published in *Pravda*, 5 October 1947, with English translation in *The Cominform*, pp. 378–83.
44. Cf. Hahn, *Postwar Soviet Politics*, pp. 87–91; and Ra'anan, *Policy Formation*, pp. 68–72.
45. Foitzik, "Fragen", p. 333.
46. *The Cominform*, pp. 250–1.
47. Ibid.
48. Archive of the Soviet Foreign Ministry, Molotov papers, quoted in Mal'kov, *Diplomatic History*, 15 (1991), pp. 554–8.
49. *The Times*, 24 October 1947.
50. *The Cominform*, pp. 242–7.
51. Ibid., pp. 246–7.
52. According to the formulation in the "declaration", ibid., pp. 380–1.

53. In a report of 30 September 1947 to their Central Committee, published in Vladimir Dedijer, *Novi prilozi za biografiju Josipa Broza Tita* (Belgrade, 1984), p. 275.
54. According to the Zhdanov text, *The Cominform*, pp. 226–7.
55. Ibid., pp. 382–3.
56. Report of 30 September 1947, see note 53. Cf. also Reale, *Avec Jacques Duclos*, pp. 176 and 178.
57. *The Cominform*, pp. 230–1.
58. Foitzik, "Fragen", p. 333.
59. *The Cominform*, pp. 230–1.
60. Ibid., pp. 226–7.
61. Ibid., pp. 224–5 and 88–9 respectively.
62. Ibid., pp. 230–1.
63. Külz, *Ein Liberaler*, p. 106 (19 September 1947).
64. Ibid., p. 128 (28 November 1947).
65. As formulated at the eleventh meeting of the Party Executive in late May 1947, ZPA IV 2/1/10, ff. 155ff.
66. Djilas, Gespräche, p. 195.
67. ZPA IV 2/1/10, f. 12.
68. *Dokumente der Sozialistischen Einheitspartei Deutschlands*, vol. 1, p. 265.
69. Külz, *Ein Liberaler*, p. 137; cf. Gniffke, *Jahre mit Ulbricht*, pp. 277ff.
70. *Dokumente zur Deutschlandpolitik der Sowjetunion*, vol. 1, p. 182; Lucius D. Clay, *Decision in Germany* (Garden City, NY: 1950), pp. 355–7.
71. Bevin informed his colleagues in the Brussels Pact of this on 19 July; according to the French protocol quoted by Cyrill Buffet, *Mourir pour Berlin: La France et l'Allemagne, 1945–1949* (Paris, 1991), p. 190.
72. ZPA NL 36/695, ff. 2–29.
73. ZPA IV 2/1/21, f. 23.
74. ZPA NL 36/739, f. 49 R.
75. *Tägliche Rundschau*, 24 June 1948.
76. Report of 8 July 1948 by Saint-Hardouin to Bidault, quoted from Buffet, *Mourir pour Berlin*, p. 185.
77. Note of 14 July 1948, FRUS 1948, vol. II, p. 964.
78. Ibid., p. 997.
79. American protocol of the meeting, ibid., pp. 999–1006; p. 999 cited here.
80. Soviet protocol, excerpts published in *Moskowskije Nowosti*, 18 May 1988.
81. Ibid.
82. American protocol, FRUS 1948, vol. II, p. 1003.
83. Soviet protocol.
84. FRUS 1948, vol. II, p. 1006.
85. Walter Bedell Smith, *My Three Years in Moscow* (Philadelphia, 1950), p. 256.
86. Buffet, *Mourir pour Berlin*, p. 174.
87. Rolf Steininger, "Wie die Teilung Deutschlands verhindert werden sollte – Der Robertson-Plan aus dem Jahre 1948", *Militärgeschichtliche Mitteilungen*, 33 (1983), pp. 49–89.
88. FRUS 1948, vol. II, pp. 1288–96.
89. Clay, *Decision in Germany*, p. 376; Harry Truman, *Years of Trial and Hope* (Garden City, NY; 1956), p. 126.

90. In conversation with Bevin and Schuman, FRUS 1948, vol. II, p. 1178.
91. Undated note by Pieck, ZPA NL 36/735, ff. 141–3.
92. Pieck's note of 13 September 1948, ibid., ff. 145–9.
93. Ibid.

Notes to Chapter 5: Zigzag to the Eastern State

1. ZPA IV 2/13/110, ff. 36–9, published by Günther Glaser, "Sicherheits-
   und militärpolitisches Konzept der SED in der SBZ von 1948", *Beiträge
   zur Geschichte der Arbeiterbewegung*, 34 (1992), pp. 56–74, here p. 66.
2. Ibid., p. 65.
3. Erich W. Gniffke, *Jahre mit Ulbricht* (Cologne, 1966; 2nd edn, 1990),
   p. 368; see also pp. 233, 255, 274–6, 311, 351.
4. According to the formulation before the members of the SED Central
   Secretariat in the summer of 1946, reported by Gniffke, *Jahre mit Ulbricht*,
   p. 205.
5. Ibid., p. 223.
6. *Um ein antifaschistisch-demokratisches Deutschland. Dokumente aus den
   Jahren, 1945–1949* (Berlin, 1968), pp. 496–8.
7. Gniffke, *Jahre mit Ulbricht*, p. 310.
8. Wolfgang Leonhard, *Die Revolution entläßt ihre Kinder* (Cologne, 1955,
   1979), p. 429.
9. Speech manuscript, on which Pieck added the note "8 May 1948 Tulpanov",
   ZPA NL 36/735, ff. 54–79; f. 57 cited here.
10. Gniffke, *Jahre mit Ulbricht*, p. 275.
11. Walter Ulbricht, *Zur Geschichte der deutschen Arbeiterbewegung*, vol.
    III: *1946–50, Zusatzband* (Berlin, 1971), p. 428.
12. Leonhard, *Revolution*, p. 427.
13. *Um ein antifaschistisch-demokratisches Deutschland*, pp. 585ff.
14. Meeting of Tulpanov, Nasarov, Grotewohl, Pieck and Dahlem on 14 May
    1948, ZPA NL 36/735, ff. 84–90.
15. Cf. his explanations in the Party Executive on 11 and 12 February 1948,
    Ulbricht, *Zur Geschichte*, p. 452.
16. See note 9.
17. Leonhard, *Revolution*, p. 427.
18. According to a lecture to the party instructors in mid-April, ibid., p. 428.
19. Gniffke, *Jahre mit Ulbricht*, p. 223.
20. Ibid., p. 298.
21. Cf. Chapter 4, note 72.
22. Gniffke, *Jahre mit Ulbricht*, p. 185.
23. ZPA IV 2/1/23, ff. 60–74.
24. Ibid., ff. 74ff.
25. Party Executive on 20 March 1948, ZPA IV 2/1/21, f. 24.
26. Conversation of 18 March 1948 with Gniffke, in Gniffke, *Jahre mit
    Ulbricht*, p. 298.
27. Ibid., pp. 312ff.
28. According to Gniffke, ibid., p. 318.
29. *Neues Deutschland*, 1 July 1948.
30. Ibid.

31. *Dokumente der Sozialistischen Einheitspartei Deutschlands* (Berlin, 1951), vol. II, pp. 81ff.; cf. Gniffke, *Jahre mit Ulbricht*, pp. 324ff.
32. Cf. their separate meeting in late May at the house of Max Fechner, ibid., pp. 307ff.
33. ZPA IV 2/13/110, ff. 158–61.
34. Resolution of the Conference at Werder, quoted from Gniffke, *Jahre mit Ulbricht*, pp. 329ff.
35. *Dokumente der SED*, pp. 83–8.
36. Ibid., p. 103.
37. *Deutschlands Stimme*, 8 August 1948, p. 5.
38. Meeting of 16 August 1948, ZPA NL 36/735, ff. 114–16.
39. ZPA IV 2/1/26; see also Gniffke, *Jahre mit Ulbricht*, pp. 340ff.
40. Abbreviation of All-Union (vsyesoyusuaya) Communist Party.
41. Anton Ackermann, "Über den einzig möglichen Weg zum Sozialismus", *Neues Deutschland*, 24 September 1948.
42. Gniffke, *Jahre mit Ulbricht*, p. 355. ,
43. Meeting of 16 August 1948, ZPA NL 36/735, ff. 114–16.
44. ZPA NL 36/735, ff. 158–61.
45. Ibid., ff. 164–72.
46. Ibid., ff. 106–8.
47. Ibid., ff. 109–11.
48. Ibid., ff. 154–7.
49. Ibid., ff. 141–3.
50. As it was phrased in a conversation with Sokolovskii, Semyonov, Kusnezov, Russkich and Tulpanov on 31 October 1948, ibid., ff. 154–7.
51. Meeting with Russkich, Russov, Semyonov and Tulpanov on 16 October 1948, ibid., ff. 150–3.
52. Written answer to prepared questions from Stalin for the meeting of 18 December 1948, ZPA NL 36/695, ff. 48–58.
53. Notes for the meetings in Moscow, ibid., ff. 31–41.
54. Ibid., ff. 42–7.
55. The last quotation from the report of a Soviet participant in the conversation to a high SPD functionary, who confided in the Eastern Bureau of the SPD in 1953; Files of the Eastern Bureau No. 0344I (16 October 1953), quoted from Dietrich Staritz, *Geschichte der DDR 1949–1985* (Frankfurt am Main, 1985), p. 22. In Pieck's notes, there is only the remark "struggle too open (cf. Teutons)".
56. T. V. Volokitina: "Razrabotka kommunisticeskimi i rabocimi partiami stran central'noj i úgovostocnoij evropy programm postroenia osnov socialisma", in *Stroitel'stvo osnov socializma v stranach central'noj i úgo-vostocnoj evropy* (Moscow, 1989), pp. 101–37, quotation p. 108.
57. In the notes for his report in the Central Secretariat on 27 December 1948, ZPA NL 36/695, ff. 75–8; the following quotations, ibid.
58. At the Party Congress of the Bulgarian Communists on 19 December 1948; German text in *Neues Deutschland*, 5 January 1949.
59. *Neues Deutschland*, 30 December 1948.
60. According to his report at the Party Executive session of 29 and 30 June 1948, Neues Deutschland, 1 July 1948; also an article in *Einheit* of November 1948, pp. 998ff.

61. Cf. Pieck's explanations to Sokolovskii on 30 October 1948 and to Stalin on 18 December 1948, see notes 50 and 53 respectively.
62. *Protokoll der I. Parteikonferenz der Sozialistischen Einheitspartei Deutschlands, 25. bis 28. Januar 1949* (Berlin, 1949), p. 356.
63. ZPA IV 2/1/1.01/107, f. 9.
64. Resolution of the First Party Conference, ibid., pp. 514–31.
65. ZPA IV 2/1/13, ff. 7ff.
66. According to the report in *Neues Deutschland*, 18 February 1949.
67. Notes for the meetings in Moscow, ZPA NL 36/695, ff. 31–41.
68. ZPA IV 2/1/32.
69. *Deutschlands Stimme*, 27 March 1949.
70. *Tägliche Rundschau*, 5 October 1949.
71. He informed the newly established Politburo in depth about the organization of the CPSU once again: Meeting of 28 January 1949, ZPA NL 36/735, ff. 173–6.
72. *Protokoll der I. Parteikonferenz*, pp. 334ff.
73. Meeting of 5 June 1948, ZPA NL 36/735, ff. 99–105.
74. According to the explanation of the "situation in the zone" in conversation with Sokolovskii on 30 October 1948, see note 50.
75. According to Adenauer, Schumacher and Karl Arnold in a conversation with Bevin in May 1949, FRUS 1949, vol. II, p. 871.
76. Wilhelm Pieck, "Lehren der Parteikonferenz", *Einheit*, 4 (1949), pp. 193ff.
77. Cf. the reconstruction of the Jessup–Malik conversations in Cyrill Buffet, *Mourir pour Berlin. La France et l'Allemagne 1945–1949* (Paris, 1991), pp. 251–5.
78. According to a report by Grotewohl in the Politburo, 23 May 1949, ZPA NL 36/695, ff. 91ff. and 102.
79. Meeting of 10 June 1948, ZPA NL 36/735, ff. 106–8.
80. ZPA NL 36/695, ff. 79–85 and 93–9.
81. Closing communiqué in *Um ein antifaschistisch-demokratisches Deutschland*, pp. 756–8.
82. Meeting of 19 July 1949 ("in my office"), ZPA NL 36/735, ff. 204–13.
83. ZPA NL 36/695, ff. 88–90 and 101.
84. *Deutschlands Stimme*, 3 June 1949.
85. Meeting of 18 May 1949, according to notes of 23 May 1949 by Pieck, see note 78.
86. According to Pieck's notes in late July as to the course of discussion since early May, ZPA NL 36/695, ff. 86ff. and 100.
87. See note 82. Pieck's notes on the course of discussion (see note 86) also refer to the necessity of having to justify themselves to the SMA.
88. Resolution of the Party Executive of 24 August 1949, *Dokumente der SED*, vol. II, p. 294.
89. Accordingly in a conversation with Tulpanov on 28 June 1949, ZPA NL 36/735, ff. 184–7.
90. Notes for a meeting with Molotov, ZPA NL 36/695, ff. 79–85 and 93–9.
91. Notes of 23 May 1949, ZPA NL 36/695, ff. 88–90 and 101.
92. Pieck regarded that as completely useless: "Paris Conference no reason for this haste," according to ibid.
93. See note 82.

94. Siegfried Suckut (ed.), *Blockpolitik in der SBZ/DDR 1945–1949. Die Sitzungsprotokolle des Zentralen Einheitsfront-Ausschusses* (Cologne, 1986), p. 435.
95. ZPA NL 90/643, f. 94.
96. Archive of the Soviet Foreign Ministry 82/36/182/4, ff. 83–6, reported in Jochen Laufer, "Die SED und die Wahlen (1948–1950). Untersuchungen zu den politischen Entscheidungsprozessen", in Elke Scherstjanoi (ed.), *"Provisorium für längstens ein Jahr." Die Gründung der DDR* (Berlin, 1993), pp. 101–24; p. 106 cited here.
97. ZPA NL 36/767, f. 103.
98. ZPA NL 36/768, ff. 1 and 766, ff. 134ff.
99. Pieck's notes "To the introduction of the discussion", ZPA NL 36/695, ff. 108–16. Pieck did not present these arguments himself because he was confined to bed from 18 to 26 September. The exact date of the meeting is for that reason not known.
100. Ibid., f. 103.
101. The Politburo's proposals to the Party Executive (of the SED) for the formation of a provisional government of the German Democratic Republic (presented to the Party Executive on 4 October 1949), ZPA NL 36/735, ff. 339–42.
102. *Tägliche Rundschau*, 8 October 1949.
103. ZPA IV 2/1/38, f. 76.

Notes to Chapter 6: Between Two Goals

1. *Neues Deutschland*, 14 October 1949.
2. *Dokumente zur Deutschlandpolitik der Sowjetunion* (Berlin, 1957), vol. 1, pp. 237ff.
3. G. M. Malenkov, "Tovarshch Stalin – Vozhd' progressivnogo chelovechestva", *Pravda*, 21 December 1949.
4. Quoted in Alexei M. Filitov, "Soviet Policy in Germany in 1950–1955", paper delivered to the conference "New Evidence on the History of the Cold War", Moscow, January 1993.
5. Situation report over the bourgeois parties, 7 June 1949, presented to the SED Party Executive by the Department of Mass Organizations, ZPA NL 36/720.
6. Cf. Siegfried Suckut, "Innenpolitische Aspekte der DDR-Gründung. Konzeptionelle Differenzen, Legitimations- und Akzeptanzprobleme", in Elke Scherstjanoi (ed.), *"Provisorium für längstens ein Jahr." Die Gründung der DDR* (Berlin, 1993), pp. 84–101.
7. Meeting with Semyonov, 24 June 1948, ZPA NL 36/735, ff. 109–11.
8. ZPA NL 36/695, ff. 42–7.
9. Archive of the Soviet Foreign Ministry 82/36/182/3, ff. 29–33, reported by Jochen Laufer, "Die SED und die Wahlen (1948–1950). Untersuchungen zu den politischen Entscheidungsprozessen", in Scherstjanoi (ed.), *"Provisorium"*, pp. 101–24, here p. 105.
10. Ibid., 82/36/182/4, ff. 83–6, reported by Laufer, "Die SED", p. 106.
11. Pieck's notes for a meeting with Stalin, ZPA NL 36/695, ff. 108–16.
12. The Politburo's proposals to the Party Executive, ZPA NL 36/735, ff. 339–42.

13. See note 11.
14. File note on "conversations carried on by WP. regarding formation of a government", ZPA NL 36/715, ff. 62ff.
15. According to Otto Nuschke writing to the CDU district chairmen on 9 October 1949, quoted from Siegfried Suckut (ed.), *Blockpolitik in der SBZ/DDR 1945–1949. Die Sitzungsprotokolle des zentralen Einheitsfront-Ausschusses* (Cologne, 1986), p. 522.
16. Protocol of the CDU Head Executive session of 5 October 1949, BAK NL Kaiser 8.
17. Session protocol quoted in Siegfried Suckut, "Die Entscheidung zur Gründung der DDR", *Vierteljahrshefte für Zeitgeschichte*, 39 (1991), pp. 125–75, here pp. 131–3.
18. Ibid., pp. 134 and 144.
19. Meeting with Tshuikov, 23 January 1950, ZPA NL 36/736, ff. 35–41.
20. Meeting with Tshuikov, 7 March 1950, ZPA NL 36/736, ff. 65–8.
21. Communication in the meeting of 23 January 1950, ZPA NL 36/736, ff. 35–41.
22. At least according to Pieck's notes of the conversation, ZPA NL 36/722, ff. 247–9. In a "Brief Report on the Meetings of the Chairmen of the 5 Parties . . ." of 13 April 1950 (ZPA NL 36/719, ff. 183–5) it is the case that Kastner did not yet want to have himself committed on the issue.
23. Session of 6 July 1950, BAP Z 3/10, quoted in Suckut, "Entscheidung", pp. 136ff.
24. "Guidelines for preparing proposals . . ." and "Guidelines for the work and extension of the party organization in the governmental apparatus . . .", Protocol No. 57 of the session of the Small Secretariat, 17 October 1949, ff. 26–8 and 23–4, investigated by Suckut, "Innenpolitische Aspekte", pp. 91ff.
25. Cf. Jochen Laufer, "Das Ministerium für Staatssicherheit und die Wahlfälschungen bei den ersten Wahlen in der DDR", *Aus Politik und Zeitgeschichte*, B 5/91 (25 January 1991), pp. 17–30.
26. ZPA IV/2/1/37, published in Suckut, "Entscheidung", pp. 146–69, here p. 161.
27. Undated note of Pieck's (November 1949), ZPA NL 36/695, ff. 104–7.
28. ZPA NL 36/736, ff. 56–9.
29. Notes for a meeting of 4 May 1950, ZPA NL 36/696, ff. 2–11.
30. Notes by Pieck, November 1949, ZPA NL 36/695, ff. 104–7.
31. *Neues Deutschland*, 23 July 1950.
32. Semyonov's report, 24 January 1950, ZPA NL 36/736, ff. 42–9.
33. Meeting with Pieck and Grotewohl, 7 March 1950, ZPA NL 36/736, ff. 65–8.
34. On the purpose of the trip from 2 to 6 May 1950, see Tshuikov's communications, ibid.
35. Notes for a meeting of 4 May 1950, ZPA NL 36/695, ff. 2–11.
36. Internal resolution of the Politburo of the SED, 2 June 1950, ZPA NL 36/556, f. 174. Pieck did not make a record of the meeting this time clearly because he had health problems again.
37. Ibid.
38. *Dokumente der SED* (Berlin, 1952), vol. III, pp. 90ff.
39. Party Executive, 2 and 3 June 1950, ZPA IV 2/1/41, f. 212.

40. ZPA NL 36/736, ff. 175–7.
41. According to the formulation in *Neues Deutschland*, 21 July 1950.
42. Statement of 13 March 1951, ZPA IV 2/1/47, f. 9.
43. Text in, among others, *Neues Deutschland*, 22 October 1950.
44. On 28 November 1950, Ulbricht gave to Grotewohl "the letter which has been agreed upon today" with the observation that "it is possible that our friends will suggest more changes". ZPA NL 182/378.
45. *Neues Deutschland*, 16 November 1950.
46. Published in *Neues Deutschland*, 5 December 1950.
47. *Neues Deutschland*, 9 March 1950.
48. *Neues Deutschland*, 5 August 1950.
49. Central Committee Meeting of 26 and 27 October 1950, ZPA IV 2/1/45, ff. 247, 44, and 175.
50. Cf. *Europa-Archiv*, 5 (1950), p. 2931.
51. *Neues Deutschland*, 31 January 1951.
52. See note 49.
53. ZPA NL 36/736, ff. 226–9.
54. Both accounts stemming from a conversation carried on in public in the spring of 1970 over Stalin's attempt to shunt Togliatti off into the post of a Cominform General Secretary, documented in *Osteuropa*, 20 (1970), pp. A 703–318; on the context, Helmut König, "Der Konflikt zwischen Stalin und Togliatti um die Jahreswende 1950/51", ibid., pp. 699–706.
55. *Khrushchev Remembers. The Glasnost Tapes* (Boston, Mass., 1990), pp. 100ff.; similarly in ibid., p. 69.
56. Karel Kaplan, *Dans les archives du Comité central* (Paris, 1978), p. 163.
57. ZPA NL 36/736, ff. 233–6.
58. J. Stalin, *Werke* (Dortmund, 1976), vol. 15, pp. 134ff.
59. *Neues Deutschland*, 5 May 1951.
60. According to a declaration in *Neues Deutschland*, 16 June 1951.
61. Meeting of 4 April 1951, ZPA NL 36/736, ff. 233–6.
62. ZPA NL 36/736, ff. 246–8. It is perhaps no accident that Ulbricht was not in attendance at this more sober stock-taking.
63. Meeting in Karlshorst of 30 July 1951, ZPA NL 36/736, ff. 268–71.
64. After further collection efforts, the "Main Committee for the Public Opinion Poll" reported in April 1952 that "about six million" West Germans had participated in the vote. *Neues Deutschland*, 10 April 1952.
65. See note 63.
66. This stems from a communication by the director of the Third European Department of the Soviet Foreign Ministry, M. Gribanov, to Foreign Minister Wyschinski on 15 August 1951, investigated by Gerhard Wettig: "Die Deutschland-Note vom 10. März 1952 auf der Basis der diplomatischen Akten des russischen Außenministeriums", *Deutschland-Archiv*, 26 (1993), pp. 786–805, here pp. 792ff; information about the decision process up to the point when Stalin approved it, ibid., p. 796.
67. *Europa-Archiv*, 6 (1951), p. 4398.
68. Ibid., p. 4404.
69. *Neues Deutschland*, 11 October 1951.
70. Meeting of 1 November 1951, ZPA NL 36/736, ff. 283–6.
71. *Neues Deutschland*, 4 November 1951.

72. So explicitly in Gribanov to Wyschinski, 15 August 1951, see note 66.

73. See note 70.

74. Lemmer's communication to the Berlin representative of the US High Commission, 29 October 1951, investigated by Hermann Graml, "Die Legende von der verpaßten Gelegenheit", *Vierteljahrshefte für Zeitgeschichte*, 29 (1981), pp. 307–41. Cf. Hans-Peter Schwarz, *Adenauer. Der Aufstieg 1875–1952* (Stuttgart, 1986), pp. 882.

75. See note 70.

76. Draft in *Neues Deutschland*, 3 January 1952.

77. Cf. Wettig, "Die Deutschland-Note", pp. 796ff.

78. Text of the note of 10 March 1952 in, among others, FRUS 1952–1954, vol. VII(1), pp. 169–72.

79. Daniil Melnikov, "Illusionen oder eine verpaßte Chance? Zur sowjetischen Deutschlandpolitik 1945–1952", *Osteuropa*, 40 (1990), pp. 593–601, here p. 599.

80. Reported in Wettig, "Die Deutschland-Note", pp. 793–5.

81. ZPA NL 36/736, ff. 298–300.

82. Text in, among others, FRUS 1952–1954, vol. VII(1), pp. 199–202.

83. Cf. Martin Jänicke, *Der dritte Weg. Die antistalinistische Opposition gegen Ulbricht seit 1953* (Cologne, 1964), p. 228.

84. Quoted from Wettig, "Die Deutschland-Note", pp. 798ff.

85. See below, pp. 140f.

86. Wettig, "Die Deutschland-Note", p. 800.

87. "Plan of the meeting of 1 April 1952", ZPA NL 36/696, ff. 12–15.

88. According to the account of the Italian ambassador in Moscow, Mario di Stefano, who was visited by Nenni directly after his conversation with Stalin; investigated by Rolf Steininger, *Eine Chance zur Wiedervereinigung? Die Stalin-Note vom 10. März 1952* (Bonn, 1985), p. 282. Doubts as to the authenticity of the statement stem from a report by George F. Kennan over a subsequent conversation with di Stefano in which it is missing (published in Hermann-Josef Rupieper, "Zu den sowjetischen Deutschlandnoten 1952. Das Gespräch Stalin–Nenni", *Vierteljahrshefte für Zeitgeschichte*, 33 (1985), pp. 547–57). These doubts are dispelled by an interview which Nenni gave a few weeks later to the British Labour MP Richard Crossman: according to the interview, "Nenni had gotten the firm impression that the first Russian note had been a serious offer." Published in the *New Statesman* and *Nation*, 20 September 1952. The date of the meeting comes from Pietro Nenni, *Tempo di guerra fredda. Diari 1923–1956* (Milan, 1981), p. 534.

89. See note 79.

90. According to Kennan, on the report of di Stefano, 25 July 1952 (see note 88); confirmed by Harrison E. Salisbury, *Moscow Journal* (Chicago, 1962), pp. 272ff; in an interview with Nenni in the *New York Times*, 16 March 1963; as in his diary, out of which the time of the conversations with Grotewohl and Pieck is taken: Nenni, *Tempo*, p. 531.

91. ZPA J IV 2/202/4; together with further corresponding accounts quoted in Michael Lemke, "Die DDR und die deutsche Frage 1949–1955", in Wilfried Loth (ed.), *Die deutsche Frage in der Nachkriegszeit* (Berlin,

1994), pp. 136–71, here p. 164. Cf. also a corresponding document in the holdings of the Ministry for State Security, published in *Neue Zeit*, 23 April 1993.

92. *Neues Deutschland*, 10 June 1960.
93. ZPA J IV 2/2/204.
94. Plan of the meeting of 1 April 1952, ZPA NL 36/696, ff. 12–15.
95. See note 74.
96. See note 29.
97. See note 91.
98. *Neue Welt*, issue 8 (1952), p. 4.
99. Notes of the Secretariat of the Central Committee of the SED over thoughts of Ulbricht's, January 1952, ZPA NL 182/870, f. 39.
100. Conference of the SED county secretaries, 21 and 22 November 1951, *Neue Welt*, issue 1 (1952), p. 6.
101. According to the formulations in the commentary of *Neues Deutschland* to the Soviet note of 12 March 1952.
102. Report of Dertinger's co-worker Gerold Rummler after his flight in the middle of April 1952, on the basis of a conversation with the foreign minister in connection with a visit by Pushkin, HICOG-Berlin to Secretary of State, 26 April 1952, published in Rupieper, "Zu den sowjetischen Deutschlandnoten" (see note 88), pp. 556ff.
103. Plan of the meeting of 1 April 1952, ZPA NL 36/696, ff. 12–15.
104. ZPA NL 36/696, ff. 26–9.
105. *Neues Deutschland*, 28 March 1952.
106. According to *Neues Deutschland*, 17 April 1952.
107. See note 88. First quote from the report by di Stefano, second quote from the report by Crossman.
108. ZPA NL 36/654, ff. 1–6.
109. ZPA NL 36/696, ff. 12–15 and 26–9.
110. De Stefano's report, see note 88.
111. ZPA NL 36/696, ff. 12–15 and 26–9.
112. Notes in preparation for the Second Party Conference, n.d., ZPA NL 36/696, ff. 32–7.
113. Plan for further preparations for the Second Party Congress, 11 April 1952, ZPA NL 90/699, ff. 11–19.
114. Meeting with Tshuikov, 7 May 1952, ZPA NL 36/736, ff. 312–14.
115. Resolution of the Eighth Meeting of the Central Committee on 22 February 1952, Protocol volume, pp. 10ff.
116. ZPA J IV 2/3/294.
117. ZPA J IV 2/2/217.
118. ZPA J IV 2/2/218.
119. Ibid., ff. 36ff, published in Dietrich Staritz, "Die SED, Stalin und der 'Aufbau des Sozialismus'", *Deutschland-Archiv*, 24 (1991), pp. 686–700, here pp. 698ff.
120. ZPA NL 36/696, ff. 26–9.
121. In the framework of the sketch "Economic Problems of Socialism", quoted from Stalin, *Werke*, vol. 15, pp. 285ff.
122. Di Stefano's report, see note 88.
123. Stalin, *Werke*, vol. 15, p. 167.

124. According to the figure in a resolution of the Presidium of the Soviet Council of Ministers of 27 May 1953, ZPA NL 90/699, ff. 27–33; cf. below, Chapter 7, note 27.
125. ZPA IV 2/1/55, ff. 1–10.
126. *Protokoll der Verhandlungen der II. Parteikonferenz der Sozialistischen Einheitspartei Deutschlands. 9.–12. Juli 1952* (Berlin, 1952), p. 58.
127. Ibid., pp. 7ff.
128. *Tägliche Rundschau*, 7 October 1952.
129. Files of the Eastern Office of the SPD, No. 0347, reported by Dietrich Staritz, *Geschichte der DDR 1949–1985* (Frankfurt am Main), 1985, pp. 75ff.
130. Kennan's report, see note 88.
131. Di Stefano's report (first and third quote) as well as Crossman's report (second quote), see note 88.
132. *Protokoll der Verhandlungen der II. Parteikonferenz*, p. 490; *Dokumente der SED* (Berlin, 1954), vol. 4, p. 190.
133. Meeting of 20 October 1952, ZPA NL 36/736, ff. 327–9.
134. According to his explanation in the Politburo, 6 June 1953, ZPA J IV 2/2/287, ff. 31.
135. Stalin, *Werke*, vol. 15, pp. 189ff.

Notes to Chapter 7: Ulbricht's Revolution

1. *Neues Deutschland*, 10 July 1952.
2. ZPA NL 36/696, ff. 27–9.
3. *Protokoll*, p. 160.
4. *Neues Deutschland*, 14 January 1953.
5. Cf. Helmut Müller-Enbergs, *Der Fall Rudolf Herrnstadt. Tauwetterpolitik vor dem 17. Juni* (Berlin, 1991), p. 164.
6. Heinz Brandt, "Die sowjetische Deutschlandpolitik im Frühsommer 1953 aus der Sicht fortschrittlicher Kräfte der SED", *Osteuropa*, 15 (1965), pp. 369–77, here p. 371.
7. Heinz Lippmann, "Der 17. Juni im Zentralkomitee der SED", *Aus Politik und Zeitgeschichte*, 13 June 1956, p. 374; Rolf Stöckigt, "Ein forcierter stalinistischer Kurs führte 1953 in die Krise", *Berliner Zeitung*, 8 March 1990.
8. ZPA NL 36/736, ff. 342–8.
9. ZPA IV 2/1/247, published in Otto Grotewohl, *Im Kampf um die einige Deutsche Demokratische Republik* (Berlin, 1959), vol. 3, p. 362.
10. As a result, Bruno Leuschner, the director of the Commission for Economic Planning, was very disturbed; see the account of his co-worker Fritz Schenk, *Im Vorzimmer der Diktatur. Zwölf Jahre Pankow* (Cologne and Berlin, 1962), pp. 182ff.
11. According to Arnulf Baring, *Der 17. Juni 1953* (Cologne and Berlin, 1965), p. 37.
12. Schenk, *Im Vorzimmer*, p. 185.
13. *Dokumente der Sozialistischen Einheitspartei Deutschlands* (Berlin, 1954), vol. IV, pp. 410ff; *Gesetzblatt der DDR*, 1953, p. 781.
14. Walter Ulbricht, "Karl Marx – der größte Sohn der deutschen Nation", *Neues Deutschland*, 7 May 1953.

15. If one accepts Erich Honecker's account, this was a preventative measure in order to avert possible pressure away from Ulbricht himself: "As in Hungary and in the Czechoslovakian Socialist Republic, it was about the Slansky trial. In practical terms, it was thus about the person of Walter Ulbricht. There was a danger that, like the other general secretaries, Walter Ulbricht too was to be pulled into this trial. Luckily, we prevented that." Reinhold Andert and Wolfgang Herzberg, *Der Sturz. Erich Honecker im Kreuzverhör* (Berlin, 1990), p. 231.

16. Cf. James Richter, "Reexamining Soviet Policy towards Germany during the Beria Interregnum", CWIHP Working Paper No. 3 (Fall 1992).

17. Pavel Sudoplatov, quoted in Lew Besymenski, "1953-Beria will die DDR beseitigen", *Die Zeit*, 15 October 1993, pp. 81–3.

18. The two answers of the Information Committee followed on 21 May and 5 June 1953 respectively; reported by Vladislav M. Zubok, "Soviet Intelligence and the Cold War: The 'Small' Committee for Information", CWIHP Working Paper No. 4 (December 1992). See also Valentin Falin, *Politische Erinnerungen* (Munich, 1993), pp. 314ff.

19. See note 17.

20. Khrushchev before the Central Committee Plenum of the CPSU on 31 January 1955; Molotov in a conversation with the writer Felix Tshuyev after 1969: *Sto sorok besed s Molotowym: Iz dnewnika F. Tschujewa* (Moscow, 1991), pp. 332–6.

21. This stems from James Richter's examination of the files (see note 16) and Pavel Sudoplatov's account (see note 17).

22. According to Andrei Gromyko, *Memories* (London, 1989), p. 315.

23. *Der Fall Berija. Protokoll einer Abrechnung. Das Plenum des ZK der KPdSU Juli 1953, Stenographischer Bericht* (Berlin, 1993), pp. 78 and 66 respectively. In light of the prehistory and the account of Pavel Sudoplatov (note 17), Molotov's and Khrushchev's explanations are in this regard thoroughly credible.

24. An initial translation of the text of the resolution, clearly made in Moscow, is to be found in Nachlaß Grotewohl, ZPA NL 90/699, ff. 27–33, published in *Beiträge zur Geschichte der Arbeiterbewegung* 32 (1990), pp. 651–4. A stylistically-revised version, presumably prepared by Fred Oelßner (Herrnstadt quotes from it on 3 June 1953), was published without citing the source by Peter Przybylski, *Tatort Politbüro. Die Akte Honecker* (Berlin, 1991), pp. 241–8. Cf. critical remarks on the sources in Elke Scherstjanoi, "'Wollen wir den Sozialismus?' Dokumente aus der Sitzung des Politbüros des ZK der SED am 6. Juni 1953", *Beiträge zur Geschichte der Arbeiterbewegung*, 33 (1991), pp. 658–80.

25. *Fall Berija*, pp. 66, 77, 79, 257ff; Gromyko, *Memories*, p. 316.

26. Bulganin reports of a meeting with Beria on the day after the Presidium session (*Fall Berija*, p. 101). In the 1970s, Molotov mentions the appointment of a commission which then after further informal conversations never met again at all (*Sto sorok*, p. 334).

27. According to his report to the Central Committee Plenum, which is credible in so far that Presidium colleagues were present; *Fall Berija*, p. 79.

28. According to the formulation by Bulganin, *Fall Berija*, p. 101; similarly in Gromyko, *Memories*, p. 316. In his memoirs of the 1970s, Molotov makes Beria's proposed resolution into a proposal of his own and claims

that with the assistance of Khrushchev, he was successful in preventing deletion of the word "forcing" as Beria wanted.

29. In the publication of the *Beiträge zur Geschichte der Arbeiterbewegung* (see note 24) it reads incorrectly "defence" (p. 654).
30. *Sto sorok*, see note 20, p. 332.
31. ZPA NL 90/699, ff. 33ff.
32. Thus Oelßner's report of the SED Politburo session of 6 June 1953, according to Herrnstadt's memoir of 1956: Rudolf Herrnstadt, *Das Herrnstadt-Dokument. Das Politbüro der SED und die Geschichte des 17. Juni 1953* (Reinbek, 1990), pp. 58ff. Grotewohl noted as Beria's statement: "You can take the document with you again" and a reason for this through Kaganovich: "Our document is change, yours is reform"; ZPA NL 90/699. Khrushchev, who took part in the meetings, reported in July to the Central Committee Plenum that "Beria shouted at comrade Ulbricht and other German comrades in such a way that it was really embarrassing"; *Fall Berija*, p. 67.
33. ZPA NL 90/699.
34. *Herrnstadt-Dokument*, p. 59.
35. Handwritten note by Grotewohl, Anlage zum Protokol 33/35, ZPA NL 90/699.
36. *Tägliche Rundschau*, 13 June 1953.
37. To Lew Besymenski, see note 17.
38. ZPA NL 90/699.
39. Cf. the notes by Grotewohl, ibid. The quotes are from Nachlaß Oelßner (ZPA NL 215/111) and Herrnstadt's notes (*Herrnstadt-Dokument*, p. 64).
40. Grotewohl's notes, ZPA NL 90/699. According to Heinz Brandt, Semyonov declared maliciously, "We would like to advise comrade Ulbricht to celebrate his sixtieth birthday as comrade Lenin celebrated his fiftieth," meaning in a small circle; Heinz Brandt, *Ein Traum, der nicht entführbar ist. Mein Weg zwischen Ost und West* (Munich, 1967), pp. 214ff.
41. According to information in *SBZ-Archiv*, 4 (1953), p. 200.
42. ZPA NL 90/699.
43. *Herrnstadt-Dokument*, p. 65.
44. Resolution protocol in ZPA J IV 2/2/287.
45. *Herrnstadt-Dokument*, pp. 78ff.
46. Hermann Zolling and Heinz Höhne, *Pullach intern. General Gehlen und die Geschichte des Bundesnachrichtendienstes* (Hamburg, 1971), p. 134.
47. According to *Der Spiegel*, 7, no. 26 (1953), p. 7.
48. Cf. Hermann Osten, "Die Deutschlandpolitik der Sowjetunion in den Jahren 1952/53", *Osteuropa*, 14 (1964), pp. 1–13, here p. 6ff.
49. Quoted from the version in ZPA IV 2/4/391. According to Herrnstadt's explanation at the Central Committee meeting of 24 to 26 July 1953 (ZPA IV/2/1/247) this is probably already the editorially reworked version, which he prepared as instructed for the next gathering of the Politburo. On this, see below, at note 75.
50. Heinz Lippmann, *Honecker. Porträt eines Nachfolgers* (Cologne, 1971), p. 161.
51. Cf. the Politburo's communiqué formulated by Herrnstadt in *Neues Deutschland*, 11 June 1953.
52. *Herrnstadt-Dokument*, p. 83. According to Molotov's later account, "Beria

[was] the first who called out 'Act immediately, ruthlesslessly, without delay!'" (see note 17).

53. On the scope of the unrest and the arrests, see Arnim Mitter, "Die Ereignisse im Juni und Juli 1953 in der DDR", *Aus Politik und Zeitgeschichte*, B 5/91 (25 January 1991), pp. 31–41; Mitter and Stefan Wolle, *Untergang auf Raten. Unbekannte Kapitel der DDR-Geschichte* (Munich, 1993).

54. Sudoplatov's account (see note 17). Cf. also Falin, *Erinnerungen*, p. 316.

55. *Neues Deutschland*, 18 and 19 June 1953.

56. ZPA IV 2/1/246.

57. Copy made by Else Zaisser of notes for a speech by Wilhelm Zaisser in ZPA J IV 2/202/4, published in Wilfriede Otto, "Dokumente zur Auseinandersetzung in der SED 1953", *Beiträge zur Geschichte der Arbeiterbewegung*, 32 (1990), pp. 655–72, here 669ff.

58. *Herrnstadt-Dokument*, p. 105; on Zaisser's motions, see also the explanations by Zaisser and Herrnstadt at the Central Committee meeting of 24 to 26 July 1953, ZPA IV 2/1/247.

59. *Herrnstadt-Dokument*, p. 105.

60. ZPA IV 2/4/391, published in Otto, "Dokumente zur Auseinandersetzung", pp. 658ff.

61. As he was informed by Grotewohl, Ulbricht, and Oelßner after their meetings with the CPSU leadership on 4 June; Przybylski, *Tatort Politbüro*, p. 240.

62. *Neues Deutschland*, 28 June and 3 July 1953.

63. *Khrushchev Remembers. The Glasnost Tapes* (Boston, 1990), p. 165; on Stalin's behaviour toward Politburo members in general, ibid., pp. 72ff.

64. Cf. his explanations, ibid., pp. 99 and 162; fitting with these, his accusation of treason against Beria's address, *Fall Berija*, p. 66.

65. Beria in the Presidium session of 27 May, according to Molotov, *Sto sorok*, p. 334.

66. According to the formulation in the resolution of the Central Committee Plenum of the CPSU of 7 July 1953, "On Beria's criminal activity hostile to party and state", *Fall Berija*, p. 335.

67. Ibid., p. 36.

68. Ibid., p. 80.

69. Ibid., p. 323.

70. Zaisser's report to the Central Committee meeting, 24 to 26 July 1953, ZPA IV 2/1/247.

71. Demonstrated by a statement of Miroshnitshenko's towards the close of the meeting, see below, note 74.

72. Herrnstadt afterwards presumed that Ulbricht had been successful in getting backing from Semyonov (*Herrnstadt-Dokument*, p. 113). Stated so clearly, that may not be accurate given the combination of caution and democratic orientation which otherwise characterized Semyonov.

73. Zaisser's report to the Central Committee meeting, 24 to 26 July 1953, ZPA IV 2/1/247.

74. *Herrnstadt-Dokument*, pp. 114ff.

75. Ibid., p. 122.

76. *Herrnstadt-Dokument*, p. 124; diverse witnesses at the Central Committee session of 24 to 26 July 1953, ZPA IV 2/1/247.

77. *Herrnstadt-Dokument*, p. 128.

78. Ibid., pp. 133ff; account by Else Zaisser (see note 57), p. 671.
79. Quoted from Müller-Enbergs, *Fall Herrnstadt*, p. 249. Ibid., pp. 249–58, full quotes from Oelßner's records of the session in ZPA NL 215/111.
80. Ibid., p. 253.
81. *Neues Deutschland*, 30 June 1953; report on his arrest, ibid., 15 July 1953.
82. Protocol in ZPA IV 2/1/247 fully reported by Müller-Enbergs, *Fall Herrnstadt*, pp. 262–309.
83. *Herrnstadt-Dokument*, pp. 157, 181 and 274.
84. Ibid., p. 163.
85. *Dokumente der Sozialistischen Einheitspartei Deutschlands* (Berlin, 1954), vol. IV, p. 467.
86. Ibid., pp. 453ff.
87. *Neues Deutschland*, 22 June 1953.
88. Mitter, *Ereignisse*, p. 40.
89. According to Joachim Schultz, *Der Funktionär in der Einheitspartei* (Stuttgart and Düsseldorf, 1956), p. 251.
90. Examples in Mitter, *Ereignisse*.
91. FRUS 1952–1954, vol. VII(1), pp. 617–24.
92. Partial protocol of the proceedings in ZPA NL 90/471, quote from f. 106.
93. Communiqué and protocol in *Europa-Archiv*, 8 (1953), pp. 5973ff.
94. Meeting with Eden on the evening of 2 February 1954, documented in a report by Dulles of 3 February 1954, published in Hermann-Josef Rupieper, "Die Berliner Außenministerkonferenz von 1954", *Vierteljahrshefte für Zeitgeschichte*, 34 (1986), pp. 427–53, here p. 449.
95. Meeting with Dulles on the evening of 5 February 1954, American protocol, ibid., p. 450.
96. Meeting with Eden on the evening of 27 January 1954, according to Dulles's report of 28 January 1954, ibid., p. 448.
97. Meeting with Dulles, 5 February 1954 (see note 95), p. 452.
98. It thereby gives the lie once again to Molotov's later claim that in 1953 he had only the "correct" path of the GDR to socialism in mind; cf. note 28.
99. *Europa-Archiv*, 9 (1954), p. 7209.
100. At the opening of the Moscow Security Conference on 29 November 1954, quoted from *Neues Deutschland*, 1 December 1954.
101. *Europa-Archiv*, 9 (1954), p. 7257.
102. *Europa-Archiv*, 10 (1955), pp. 7345ff.
103. See on this Hans Wassmund, *Kontinuität im Wandel. Bestimmungsfaktoren sowjetischer Deutschlandpolitik in der Nach-Stalin-Zeit* (Cologne and Vienna, 1974), pp. 67–97.
104. PRO Cabinet Papers (55) 99. 27.7.1955, CAB 129/76, reported in Rolf Steininger, "Deutsche Frage und Berliner Konferenz 1954", in Wolfgang Venohr (ed.), *Ein Deutschland wird es sein* (Erlangen, 1990), pp. 37–88, here p. 87.
105. *Europa-Archiv*, 10 (1955), p. 8061.
106. Ibid., p. 8121.
107. Ibid., p. 8313.

Notes to the Conclusion: How the GDR Came to Be

1. Stalin termed it "bourgeois-democratic" for the first time in a meeting with the KPD leaders on 4 June 1945, ZPA NL 36/629, ff. 62–6.
2. *Khrushchev Remembers. The Glasnost Tapes* (Boston, MA, 1990), pp. 69ff.
3. See Wolfgang Leonhard, *Spurensuche. Vierzig Jahre nach Die Revolution entläßt ihre Kinder* (Cologne, 1992), p. 162.
4. Erich Gniffke, *Jahre mit Ulbricht* (Cologne, 1966; 2nd edn 1990), p. 351.
5. See Chapter 2, note 1.

Notes to the Epilogue to the English Edition

1. Especially Heinrich August Winkler, "Im Zickzackkurs zum Sozialismus", *Die Zeit*, 17 June 1994; Peter Zolling, "Mut ist oft sehr dumm", *Der Spiegel*, 20 June 1994; Henning Köhler, "Stalin: ein deutscher Demokrat", *Frankfurter Allgemeine Zeitung*, 2 July 1994.
2. For a discussion of the criticism, see Wilfried Loth, "Stalin, die deutsche Frage und die DDR. Eine Antwort an meine Kritiker", *Deutschland-Archiv*, 28 (1995), pp. 290–8.
3. Alexei M. Filitov, "Problems of Post-War Construction in Soviet Foreign Policy Conceptions during World War II", in Francesca Gori and Silvio Pons (eds.), *The Soviet Union and Europe in the Cold War, 1943–53* (London, 1996), pp. 3–22, here pp. 10f.
4. Alexei M. Filitov, "Die UdSSR und das Potsdamer Abkommen: ein langer und leidvoller Weg", paper at the Conference "Vor 50 Jahren: Die Potsdamer Konferenz", 22 to 26 May 1995 in Otzenhausen, Germany. Further details on the origins of the division of the zones are offered in Jochen Laufer, "Die UdSSR und die Zoneneinteilung Deutschlands 1943/44", *Zeitschrift für Geschichtswissenschaft*, 43 (1995), pp. 309–31.
5. Alexei M. Filitov, "Die sowjetische Deutschlandplanung zwischen Parteiräson, Staatsinteresse und taktischem Kalkül", in Hans-Erich Volkmann (ed.), *Ende des Dritten Reiches – Ende des Zweiten Weltkriegs. Eine perspektivische Rückschau* (Munich, 1995), pp. 117–39, here p. 130.
6. Alexei M. Filitov, "The Soviet Union on Germany", paper at the Conference "The Political Structures of Central Europe, 1945–1947", 24 and 25 November 1995 in Vienna.
7. Filitov, "Problems", p. 13.
8. Peter Erler, Horst Laude, Manfred Wilke (eds), *"Nach Hitler kommen wir." Dokumente zur Programmatik der Moskauer KPD-Führung 1944/45 für Nachkriegsdeutschland* (Berlin, 1994), here p. 169.
9. Investigated by Wolfgang Zank, "Als Stalin Demokratie befahl", *Die Zeit*, 16 June 1995.
10. See above, pp. 10 and 13f.
11. Wladimir S. Semjonow, *Von Stalin bis Gorbatschow. Ein halbes Jahrhundert in diplomatischer Mission 1939–1991* (Berlin, 1995), quotes from pp. 217, 260, 200ff.
12. Ibid., pp. 248 and 265.
13. Ibid., pp. 261ff.
14. Ibid., pp. 262 and 273ff.

15. Norman M. Naimark, *The Russians in Germany: A History of the Soviet Zone of Occupation, 1945–1949* (Cambridge, MA, and London, 1995), pp. 335ff. and 341–5.
16. For an initial overview of specific findings on occupation practice, see also Norman M. Naimark, "Die Sowjetische Militäradministration in Deutschland und die Frage des Stalinismus", *Zeitschrift für Geschichtswissenschaft*, 43 (1995), pp. 293–307.
17. Meeting with the author on 1 December 1994.
18. Georg Dertinger, *Erinnerungen und Gedanken, erzählt in einem Freundeskreis November 1967 in Leipzig*, manuscript, p. 23. I wish to thank Mrs Dertinger very much for the opportunity to peruse the manuscript and also for a fascinating conversation.
19. Archive of the President of the Russian Federation, file 45, dept 1, vol. 303, part 179. I thank my colleague Michail M. Narinski for providing this document.
20. See above, pp. 140ff.
21. See note 17. On the interpretation, see also Wilfried Loth, "Spaltung wider Willen. Die sowjetische Deutschlandpolitik nach dem Zweiten Weltkrieg", *Tel Aviver Jahrbuch für deutsche Geschichte*, 24 (1995), pp. 3–17.
22. Memorandum "On Further Soviet Measures on the German Question", approx. 28 April 1953. Archives of the Foreign Ministry of the Russian Federation, file 82, dept 41, vol. 271, part 18, pp. 14–47, provided by Vladislav M. Zubok.
23. Voytech Mastny, *The Cold War and Soviet Insecurity: The Stalin Years* (New York and Oxford, 1996), p. 177.
24. On the last-mentioned issue, see also my essay "Die Deutschen und die deutsche Frage. Überlegungen zur Dekomposition der deutschen Nation", in Wilfried Loth (ed.), *Die deutsche Frage in der Nachkriegszeit* (Berlin, 1994), pp. 214–28.

Bibliography

ARCHIVES

*Stiftung Archiv der Parteien und Massenorganisationen der DDR im Bundes-
archiv: Zentrales Parteiarchiv der SED*

Nachlaß 36	Wilhelm Pieck
Nachlaß 90	Otto Grotewohl
Nachlaß 182	Walter Ulbricht
Nachlaß 215	Fred Oelßner
IV 2/1/1ff	Protokolle des Parteivorstands und des Zentralkomitees
J IV 2/2–84ff	Protokolle des Politbüros

Bundesarchiv Koblenz

Nachlaß Jakob Kaiser

Public Record Office London

FO	Foreign Office
CAB	Cabinet Papers

PRINTED SOURCES

Andert, Reinhold and Herzberg, Wolfgang, *Der Sturz. Erich Honecker im Kreuzverhör* (Berlin, 1990).

Badstübner, Rolf, "'Beratungen' bei J. W. Stalin. Neue Dokumente", in *Utopie kreativ*, 7 (March 1991), pp. 99–116.

Badstübner, Rolf and Loth, Wilfried, *Wilhelm Pieck. Aufzeichnungen zur Deutschlandpolitik, 1945–1953* (Berlin, 1994).

Berlin, *Quellen und Dokumente 1945–1951* (Berlin, 1964).

Bokow, Fjodor J., *Frühjahr des Sieges und der Befreiung* (Berlin, 1979).

Bouvier, Beatrix W. and Schulz, Horst-Peter (eds), "... *die SPD aber aufgehört hat, zu existieren". Sozialdemokraten unter sowjetischer Besatzung* (Bonn, 1991).

Brandt, Heinz, "Die sowjetische Deutschlandpolitik im Frühsommer 1953 aus der Sicht fortschrittlicher Kräfte in der SED", in *Osteuropa*, 15 (1965), pp. 369–77.

Brandt, Heinz, *Ein Traum, der nicht entführbar ist. Mein Weg zwischen Ost und West* (Munich, 1967; 2nd edn, Berlin, 1977).

Braun, Günter, "'Regierungsangelegenheiten' in Thüringen im Spannungsfeld von sowjetischer Deutschlandpolitik und SED-Kalkülen 1947. Die Sekretariatssitzung des SED-Landesvorstands Thüringen vom 30. April 1947", in *Beiträge zur Geschichte der Arbeiterbewegung*, 34 (1992), pp. 67–91.

Clay, Lucius D., *Decisions in Germany* (Garden City, 1950).

Djilas, Milovan, *Gespräche mit Stalin* (Frankfurt am Main, 1962).

Dokumente der Sozialistischen Einheitspartei Deutschlands, vols I–IV (Berlin, 1952–4).

Dokumente zur Deutschlandpolitik der Sowjetunion. Herausgegeben vom Deutschen Institut für Zeitgeschichte, vol. 1 (Berlin, 1957).

Falin, Valentin, *Politische Erinnerungen* (Munich, 1993).

Der Fall Berija. Protokoll einer Abrechnung. Das Plenum des ZK der KPdSU Juli 1953. Stenographischer Bericht (Berlin, 1993).

Foitzik, Jan, "Fragen der Sowjetischen Außenpolitik nach dem Zweiten Weltkrieg", in *Zeitschrift für Geschichtswissenschaft*, 41 (1993), pp. 329–35.

Foreign Relations of the United States. Diplomatic Papers, 1945– (Washington, 1955–).

Glaser, Günther, "Sicherheits- und militärpolitisches Konzept der SED in der SBZ von 1948", in *Beiträge zur Geschichte der Arbeiterbewegung*, 34 (1992), pp. 56–74.

Gniffke, Erich W., *Jahre mit Ulbricht* (Cologne, 1966; 2nd edn, 1990).

Gromyko, Andrej, *Memories* (London, 1989).

Grotewohl, Otto, *Im Kampf um Deutschland. Reden und Aufsätze*, vol. II (Berlin, 1948).

Grotewohl, Otto, *Im Kampf um die einige Deutsche Demokratische Republik*, vol. III (Berlin, 1959).

Herrnstadt, Rudolf, *Das Herrnstadt-Dokument. Das Politbüro der SED und die Geschichte des 17. Juni 1953* (Reinbek, 1990).

Jäckel, Eberhard (ed.), *Die deutsche Frage 1952–1956. Notenwechsel und Konferenzdokumente der vier Mächte* (Frankfurt and Berlin, 1957).

Kaplan, Karel, *Dans les archives du Comité central* (Paris, 1978).

Keiderling, Gerhard (ed.), *"Gruppe Ulbricht" in Berlin. April bis Juni 1945* (Berlin, 1992).

Klimow, Gregory, *Berliner Kreml* (Cologne, 1952).

Khrushchev Remembers: The Glasnost Tapes (Boston, 1990).

Külz, Wilhelm, *Ein Liberaler zwischen Ost und West: Aufzeichnungen, 1947–1948* (Munich, 1989).

Leonhard, Wolfgang, *Die Revolution entläßt ihre Kinder* (Cologne, 1955; paperback edition, Munich, 1979).

Leonhard, Wolfgang, *Spurensuche. 40 Jahre nach Die Revolution entläßt ihre Kinder* (Cologne, 1992).

Lippmann, Heinz, *Honecker. Porträt eines Nachfolgers* (Cologne, 1971).

Melnikow, Daniil, "Illusionen oder verpaßte Chance? Zur sowjetischen Deutschlandpolitik 1945–1952", in *Osteuropa*, 40 (1990), pp. 593–601.

Molotov, Wjatscheslaw M., *Fragen der Außenpolitik. Reden und Erklärungen April 1944 – Juni 1948* (Moskow, 1949).

Nadolny, Rudolph, *Mein Beitrag* (Wiesbaden, 1955).

Nenni, Pietro, *Tempo di guerra fredda. Diari 1923–1956* (Milan, 1981).

Otto, Wilfriede, "Dokumente zur Auseinandersetzung in der SED 1953", in *Beiträge zur Geschichte der Arbeiterbewegung*, 32 (1990), pp. 655–72.

Otto, Wilfriede, "Sowjetische Deutschlandnote 1952. Stalin und die DDR. Bisher unveröffentliche handschriftliche Notizen Wilhelm Piecks", in *Beiträge zur Geschichte der Arbeiterbewegung*, 33 (1991), pp. 374–89.

Pieck, Wilhelm, *Reden und Aufsätze* (Berlin, 1948).

Pieck, Wilhelm, *Reden und Aufsätze*, 4 vols (Berlin, 1954–6).

Pommerin, Reiner, "Die Zwangsvereinigung von KPD und SPD zur SED. Eine britische Analyse vom April 1946", in *Vierteljahrshefte für Zeitgeschichte*, 36 (1988), pp. 318–38.

Procacci, Giuliano (ed.), *The Cominform. Minutes of the Three Conferences 1947/1948/1949* (Milan, 1994).

Protokoll der 1. Parteikonferenz der Sozialistischen Einheitspartei Deutschlands, 25. bis 28. Januar 1949 (Berlin, 1949).

Protokoll der Verhandlungen der II. Parteikonferenz der Sozialistischen Einheitspartei Deutschlands, 9.–12. Juli 1952 (Berlin, 1952).

Protokoll der Verhandlungen des II. Parteitages der Sozialistischen Einheitspartei Deutschlands, 20. bis 24. September 1947 (Berlin, 1947).

Reale, Eugenio, *Avec Jacques Duclos au banc des accusés* (Paris, 1958).

Rudolph, Vladimir, "The Administrative Organization of Soviet Control, 1945–1948", in Robert Slusser (ed.), *Soviet Economic Policy in Postwar Germany. A Collection of Papers by Former Soviet Officials* (New York, 1953), pp. 18–86.

Rupieper, Hermann-Josef, "Zu den sowjetischen Deutschlandnoten 1952. Das Gespräch Stalin–Nenni", in *Vierteljahrshefte für Zeitgeschichte*, 33 (1985), pp. 547–57.

Rupieper, Hermann-Josef, "Die Berliner Außenministerkonferenz von 1954", in *Vierteljahrshefte für Zeitgeschichte*, 34 (1986), pp. 427–53.

Salisbury, Harrison E., *Moscow Journal* (Chicago, 1962).

Scherstjanoi, Elke, "'Wollen wir den Sozialismus?' Dokumente aus der Sitzung des Politbüros des ZK der SED am 6. Juni 1953", in *Beiträge zur Geschichte der Arbeiterbewegung*, 33 (1991), pp. 658–80.

Schenk, Fritz, *Im Vorzimmer der Diktatur. Zwölf Jahre Pankow* (Cologne, and Berlin, 1962).

Schollwer, Wolfgang, *Potsdamer Tagebuch 1948–50* (Munich, 1988).

Smith, Walter Bedell, *My Three Years in Moscow* (Philadelphia, 1952).

Stalin, Joseph W., *Über den großen Vaterländischen Krieg der Sowjetunion* (Moskow, 1946).

Stalin, Joseph W., *Werke*, vol. 15: *Mai 1945 – Oktober 1952* (Dortmund, 1976).

Steininger, Rolf, *Eine Chance zur Wiedervereinigung? Die Stalin-Note vom 10. März 1952. Darstellung und Dokumentation auf der Grundlage unveröffentlichter britischer und amerikanischer Akten* (Bonn, 1985).

Steininger, Rolf, "Dieser Vorfall bedeutet die Spaltung Deutschlands. Neue Dokumente zur Münchener Ministerpräsidentenkonferenz im Juni 1947", in *Geschichte im Westen*, 7 (1992), pp. 213–30.

Stöckigt, Rolf, "Ein Dokument von großer historischer Bedeutung vom Mai 1953", in *Beiträge zur Geschichte der Arbeiterbewegung*, 32 (1990), pp. 648–54.

Suckut, Siegfried (ed.), *Blockpolitik in der SBZ/DDR 1945–1949. Die Sitzungsprotokolle des Zentralen Einheitsfront-Ausschusses* (Cologne, 1986).

Suckut, Siegfried, "Die Entscheidung zur Gründung der DDR", in *Vierteljahrshefte für Zeitgeschichte*, 39 (1991), pp. 125–75.

Truman, Harry S., *Years of Trial and Hope* (Garden City, NY, 1956).

Tschujew, Felix, *Sto sorok besed s Molotowym: Iz dnewnika F. Tschujewa* (Moscow, 1991).
Tulpanov, Sergej, *Deutschland nach dem Kriege (1945-1949). Erinnerungen eines Offiziers der Sowjetarmee* (Berlin, 1986).
Ulbricht, Walter, *Zur Geschichte der deutschen Arbeiterbewegung. Aus Reden und Aufsätzen, vols II/III: 1933-1950* (Berlin, 1963).
Ulbricht, Walter, *Zur Geschichte der deutschen Arbeiterbewegung. Aus Reden und Aufsätzen, vol. II: 1933-1946,* 1st updated edition (Berlin, 1966).
Ulbricht, Walter, *Zur Geschichte der deutschen Arbeiterbewegung. Aus Reden und Aufsätzen, vol. II: 1933-1946,* 2nd updated edition (Berlin, 1968).
Ulbricht, Walter, *Zur Geschichte der deutschen Arbeiterbewegung. Aus Reden und Aufsätzen, vol. III: 1946-1950,* updated edition (Berlin, 1971).
Varga, Eugen, *Veränderungen in der kapitalistischen Wirtschaft im Gefolge des zweiten Weltkrieges* (Moscow, 1946; translation by Manfred Kerner, Berlin, 1975).
Voznesenskii, Nikolai, *The Economy of the USSR during World War II* (Washington, 1948).
Weber, Hermann (ed.), *Parteiensystem zwischen Demokratie und Volksdemokratie. Dokumente und Materialien zum Funktionswandel der Parteien und Massenorganisationen in der SBZ/DDR 1945-1950* (Cologne, 1982).
Weber, Hermann (ed.), *DDR. Dokumente zur Geschichte der Deutschen Demokratischen Republik 1945-1985* (Munich, 1986; 3rd edn, 1987).

BOOKS AND ARTICLES

Backer, John H., *Die deutschen Jahre des Generals Clay: Der Weg zur Bundesrepublik, 1945-1969* (Munich, 1983).
Badstübner, Rolf and Heitzer, Heinz (eds), *Die DDR in der Übergangsperiode. Studien zur Vorgeschichte und Geschichte der DDR 1945 bis 1961* (Berlin, 1979).
Badstübner, Rolf et al. (Autorenkollektiv), *Deutsche Geschichte,* vol. 9, *Die antifaschistisch-demokratische Umwälzung. Der Kampf gegen die Spaltung Deutschlands und die Entstehung der DDR von 1945 bis 1949* (Berlin, 1989).
Badstübner, Rolf, *Friedenssicherung und deutsche Frage. Vom Untergang des "Reiches" bis zur deutschen Zweistaatlichkeit (1943 bis 1949)* (Berlin, 1990).
Badstübner, Rolf, "Zum Problem der historischen Alternativen im ersten Nachkriegsjahrzehnt. Neue Quellen zur Deutschlandpolitik von KPdSU und SED", in *Beiträge zur Geschichte der Arbeiterbewegung,* 33 (1991), pp. 579-92.
Baring, Arnulf, *Der 17. Juni 1953* (Cologne and Berlin, 1965; 2nd edn, Stuttgart, 1983).
Belezki, Viktor N., *Die Politik der Sowjetunion in den deutschen Angelegenheiten in der Nachkriegszeit 1945-1976* (Berlin, 1977).
Bender, Klaus, *Deutschland, einig Vaterland? Die Volkskongreßbewegung für deutsche Einheit und einen gerechten Frieden in der Deutschlandpolitik der Sozialistischen Einheitspartei Deutschlands* (Frankfurt am Main, 1992).
Benser, Günter, *Die KPD im Jahr der Befreiung. Vorbereitung und Aufbau*

der legalen kommunistischen Massenpartei (Jahreswende 1944/45 bis Herbst 1945) (Berlin, 1985).

Benser, Günter, "Quellenveröffentlichungen ja, doch so präzis wie möglich", in *Utopie Kreativ*, 11 (July 1991), pp. 101–7.

Besymenski, Lew, "1953 – Berija will die DDR beseitigen", in *Die Zeit*, 15.10.1993, pp. 81–3.

Bleek, Wilhelm, "Einheitspartei und nationale Frage 1945–1955", in *Der X. Parteitag der SED, Deutschland-Archiv*, special edition (1981), pp. 87–99.

Bonwetsch, Bernd, "Deutschlandpolitische Alternativen der Sowjetunion, 1949–1955", in *Deutsche Studien*, 24 (1986), pp. 320–40.

Broszat, Martin and Weber, Hermann (eds), *SBZ-Handbuch* (Munich, 1990).

Buffet, Cyrill, *Mourir pour Berlin. La France et l'Allemagne 1945–1949* (Paris, 1991).

Bullock, Alan, *Hitler und Stalin. Parallele Leben* (Berlin, 1991).

Buttlar, Walrab von, *Ziele und Zielkonflikte der sowjetischen Deutschlandpolitik 1945–1947* (Stuttgart, 1980).

Cairncross, Alec, *The Price of War. British Policy on German Reparations 1941–1949* (Oxford, 1986).

Caracciolo, Lucio, "Der Untergang der Sozialdemokratie in der sowjetischen Besatzungszone. Otto Grotewohl und die 'Einheit der Arbeiterklasse' 1945/46", in *Vierteljahrshefte für Zeitgeschichte*, 36 (1988), pp. 280–318.

Conquest, Robert, *Stalin. Der totale Wille zur Macht* (Munich and Leipzig, 1991).

Conze, Werner, *Jakob Kaiser. Politiker zwischen Ost und West 1945–1949* (Stuttgart, 1969).

Dedijer, Vladimir, *Novi prilozi za biografiju Josipa Broza Tita* (Belgrade, 1984).

Diedrich, Torsten, "Der 17. Juni 1953 in der DDR. Zu militärhistorischen Aspekten bei Ursachen und Verlauf der Unruhen", in *Militärgeschichtliche Mitteilungen*, 51 (1992), pp. 357–84.

Duhnke, Horst, *Die KPD von 1933 bis 1945* (Cologne, 1972).

Fisch, Jörg, *Reparationen nach dem Zweiten Weltkrieg* (Munich, 1992).

Fischer, Alexander, *Sowjetische Deutschlandpolitik im Zweiten Weltkrieg 1941–1945* (Stuttgart, 1975).

Fischer, Alexander, "Die Sowjetunion und die 'deutsche Frage' 1945–1949", in *Die Deutschlandfrage und die Anfänge des Ost-West-Konflikts 1945–1949* (Berlin, 1984), pp. 41–57.

Flechtheim, Ossip K., *Die KPD in der Weimarer Republik* (Frankfurt am Main, 1969).

Foitzik, Jan, "Die Sowjetische Militäradministration in Deutschland", in Martin Broszat and Hermann Weber (eds), *SBZ-Handbuch* (Munich, 1990), pp. 9–69.

Foitzik, Jan, "Die Bildung des Kominform-Büros 1947 im Lichte neuer Quellen", in *Zeitschrift für Geschichtswissenschaft*, 40 (1992), pp. 1109–26.

Fricke, Karl Wilhelm, *Opposition und Widerstand in der DDR. Ein politischer Report* (Cologne, 1984).

Geschichte der Sozialistischen Einheitspartei Deutschlands. Abriß (Berlin, 1978).

Geyer, Dietrich, "Deutschland als Problem der sowjetischen Europapolitik am Ende des Zweiten Weltkriegs", in Josef Foschepoth (ed.), *Kalter Krieg und Deutsche Frage. Deutschland im Widerstreit der Mächte 1945–1952* (Göttingen and Zürich, 1985), pp. 50–65.

Graml, Hermann, "Die Legende von der verpaßten Gelegenheit", in *Vierteljahrshefte für Zeitgeschichte*, 29 (1981), pp. 307–41.

Graml, Hermann, *Die Alliierten und die Teilung Deutschlands. Konflikte und Entscheidungen 1941–1948* (Frankfurt am Main, 1984).

Hahn, Werner G., *Postwar Soviet Politics. The fall of Zhdanov and the defeat of moderation, 1946–1953* (Ithaca and London, 1982).

Heitzer, Heinz, *DDR. Geschichtlicher Überblick* (Berlin, 1979).

Heitzer, Heinz, "Entscheidungen im Vorfeld der 2. Parteikonferenz der SED (Februar bis Juli 1952)", in *Beiträge zur Geschichte der Arbeiterbewegung*, 34 (1992), pp. 18–32.

Hermes, Peter, *Die Christlich-Demokratische Union und die Bodenreform in der Sowjetischen Besatzungszone Deutschlands im Jahre 1946* (Saarbrücken, 1963).

Hough, Jerry F., "Debates about the Postwar World", in Susan J. Linz (ed.), *The Impact of World War II on the Soviet Union* (Totowa, NJ, 1985), pp. 253–81.

Jänicke, Martin, *Der dritte Weg. Die antistalinistische Opposition gegen Ulbricht seit 1953* (Cologne, 1964).

Kaplan, Karel, *Der kurze Marsch. Kommunistische Machtübernahme in der Tschechoslowakei 1945–1948* (Munich and Vienna, 1981).

Kessel, Martina, *Westeuropa und die deutsche Teilung. Englische und französische Deutschlandpolitik auf den Außenministerkonferenzen von 1945 bis 1947* (Munich, 1989).

Klonovsky, Michael and von Flocken, Jan, *Stalins Lager in Deutschland 1945–1950* (Berlin and Frankfurt, 1991).

Koch, Manfred, Müller, Werner, and Staritz, Dietrich and Suckut, Siegfried, "Versuch und Scheitern gesamtdeutscher Parteibildungen 1945–1948", in *Die beiden deutschen Staaten im Ost-West-Verhältnis* (Cologne, 1982), pp. 90–107.

König, Helmut, "Der Konflikt zwischen Stalin und Togliatti um die Jahreswende 1950/51", in *Osteuropa*, 20 (1970), pp. 699–706.

Kraus, Elisabeth, *Ministerien für ganz Deutschland? Der Alliierte Kontrollrat und die Frage gesamtdeutscher Zentralverwaltungen* (Munich, 1990).

Laufer, Jochen, "Das Ministerium für Staatssicherheit und die Wahlfälschungen bei den ersten Jahren in der DDR", in *Aus Politik und Zeitgeschichte*, B 5/91 (25.1.1991), pp. 17–30.

Laufer, Jochen, "Die SED und die Wahlen (1948–1950). Untersuchungen zu den politischen Entscheidungsprozessen", in Elke Scherstjanoi (ed.), *"Provisorium für längstens ein Jahr". Die Gründung der DDR* (Berlin, 1993), pp. 101–24.

Lemke, Michael, "'Doppelte Alleinvertretung'. Die nationalen Wiedervereinigungskonzepte der beiden deutschen Regierungen und die Grundzüge ihrer politischen Realisierung in der DDR (1949–1952/53)", in *Zeitschrift für Geschichtswissenschaft*, 40 (1992), pp. 531–43.

Lemke, Michael, "Die DDR und die deutsche Frage 1949–1955", in Wilfried Loth (ed.), *Die deutsche Frage in der Nachkriegszeit* (Berlin, 1994), pp. 136–71.

Linz, Susan J., "Measuring the Carryover Cost of World War II to the Soviet People: 1945–1953", in *Explorations in Economic History*, 20 (1983), pp. 375–86.

Linz, Susan J. (ed.), *The Impact of World War II on the Soviet Union* (Totowa, NJ, 1985).

Loth, Wilfried, "Frankreichs Kommunisten und der Beginn des Kalten Krieges", in *Vierteljahrshefte für Zeitgeschichte*, 26 (1978), pp. 9–65.

Loth, Wilfried, *Die Teilung der Welt. Geschichte des Kalten Krieges 1941–1955* (Munich, 1980; 8th edn, 1990).

Loth, Wilfried, *Ost-West-Konflikt und deutsche Frage. Historische Ortsbestimmungen* (Munich, 1989).

Loth, Wilfried, "Die Historiker und die Deutsche Frage. Ein Rückblick nach dem Ende des Kalten Krieges", in *Historisches Jahrbuch*, 112 (1992), pp. 366–82.

Loth, Wilfried, "Das ungeliebte Kind. Stalin und die Gründung der DDR", in Elke Scherstjanoi (ed.), *"Provisorium für längstens ein Jahr". Die Gründung der DDR* (Berlin, 1993), pp. 31–8.

Loth, Wilfried, "Ziele sowjetischer Deutschlandpolitik nach dem Zweiten Weltkrieg", in Klaus Schönhoven and Dietrich Staritz (eds), *Sozialismus und Kommunismus im Wandel. Hermann Weber zum 65. Geburtstag* (Cologne, 1993), pp. 303–23.

Loth, Wilfried (ed.), *Die deutsche Frage in der Nachkriegszeit* (Berlin, 1994).

Mastny, Vojtech, *Moskaus Weg zum Kalten Krieg* (Munich and Vienna, 1981).

McCagg, William O., Jr, *Stalin Embattled 1943–1948* (Detroit, 1978).

Meiners, Jochen, *Die doppelte Deutschlandpolitik. Zur nationalen Politik der SED im Spiegel ihres Zentralorgans "Neues Deutschland" 1945 bis 1952* (Frankfurt am Main, 1987).

Meissner, Boris, *Rußland, die Westmächte und Deutschland. Die sowjetische Deutschlandpolitik 1943–1953* (Hamburg, 1953; 2nd edn, 1954).

Mitter, Armin, "Die Ereignisse im Juni und Juli 1953 in der DDR", in *Aus Politik und Zeitgeschichte*, B 5/91 (25.1.1991), pp. 31–41.

Mitter, Armin and Wolle, Stefan, *Untergang auf Raten. Unbekannte Kapitel der DDR-Geschichte* (Munich, 1993).

Müller, Werner, *Die KPD und die "Einheit der Arbeiterklasse"* (Frankfurt am Main, 1979).

Müller-Enbergs, Helmut, *Der Fall Rudolf Herrnstadt. Tauwetterpolitik vor dem 17. Juni* (Berlin, 1991).

Osten, Hermann, "Die Deutschlandpolitik der Sowjetunion in den Jahren 1952/53", in *Osteuropa*, 14 (1964), pp. 1–13.

Przybylski, Peter, *Tatort Politbüro. Die Akte Honecker* (Berlin, 1991).

Raack, R. C., "Stalin Plans his Post-War Germany", in *Journal of Contemporary History*, 28 (1993), pp. 53–73.

Ra'anan, Gavriel D., *International Policy Formation in the USSR. Factional "Debates" during the Zhdanovschina* (Hamden, CT, 1983).

Resis, Albert, *Stalin, the Politburo, and the Onset of the Cold War* (Pittsburgh, 1988).

Richter, Michael, *Die Ost-CDU 1948–1952* (Düsseldorf, 1990).

Rollet, Henri, "Un nouveau serpent de mer. La note soviétique du 10 mars 1952 et la visite de Pietro Nenni à Staline", in *Revue d'histoire diplomatique*, 102 (1988), pp. 297–317.

Schröder, Lothar, "Zwischen Wirklichkeit und Klischee. Bedrohungsvorstellungen in der DDR-Führung in den 50er Jahren", in *Beiträge zur Geschichte der Arbeiterbewegung*, 34 (1992), pp. 3–13.

Scherstjanoi, Elke (ed.), *"Provisorium für längstens ein Jahr"*. *Die Gründung der DDR* (Berlin, 1993).

Schwarz, Hans-Peter, *Vom Reich zur Bundesrepublik*. *Deutschland im Widerstreit der außenpolitischen Konzeptionen in den Jahren der Besatzungsherrschaft 1945–1949* (Berlin and Neuwied, 1966; 2nd edn, Stuttgart, 1980).

Schwarz, Hans-Peter, *Adenauer*. *Der Aufstieg 1975–1952* (Stuttgart, 1986).

Smith, Jean Edward, "The View from UFSET, General Clay's and Washington's Interpretation of Soviet Intentions in Germany, 1945–1948", in Hans A. Schmitt (ed.), *U.S. Occupation in Europe after World War II* (Lawrence, 1978), pp. 64–85.

Staritz, Dietrich, *Sozialismus in einem halben Land. Zur Problematik und Politik der SED in der Phase der antifaschistisch-demokratichen Umwälzung in der DDR* (Berlin, 1976).

Staritz, Dietrich, "Ein 'besonderer deutscher Weg' zum Sozialismus?" in *Aus Politik und Zeitgeschichte*, B 51–52/82 (25.12.1982), pp. 15–31.

Staritz, Dietrich, "Parteien für ganz Deutschland? Zu den Kontroversen über ein Parteiengesetz im Alliierten Kontrollrat 1946/47", in *Vierteljahrshefte für Zeitgeschichte*, 32 (1984), pp. 240–68.

Staritz, Dietrich, *Die Gründung der DDR. Von der sowjetischen Besatzungsherrschaft zum sozialistischen Staat* (Munich, 1984; 2n edn, 1987).

Staritz, Dietrich, *Geschichte der DDR 1949–1985* (Frankfurt am Main, 1985).

Staritz, Dietrich, "Zwischen Ostintegration und nationaler Verpflichtung. Zur Ost- und Deutschlandpolitik der SED 1948–1952", in Ludolf Herbst (ed.), *Westdeutschland 1945–1955. Unterwerfung, Kontrolle, Integration* (Munich, 1986), pp. 278–89.

Staritz, Dietrich and Weber, Hermann (eds), *Einheitsfront – Einheitspartei. Kommunisten und Sozialdemokraten in Ost- und Westeuropa 1944–1948* (Cologne, 1989).

Staritz, Dietrich, "Die SED, Stalin und die Gründung der DDR", in *Aus Politik und Zeitgeschichte*, B 5/91 (25.1.1991), pp. 3–16.

Staritz, Dietrich, "Die SED, Stalin und der 'Aufbau des Sozialismus' in der DDR", in *Deutschland-Archiv*, 24 (1991), pp. 686–700.

Staritz, Dietrich, "The SED, Stalin, and the German Question, Interests and Decision-Making in the Light of New Sources", in *German History*, 10 (1992), pp. 274–89.

Staritz, Dietrich, "Einheits- und Machtkalküle der SED (1946–1948)", in Elke Scherstjanoi (ed.), *"Provisorium für längstens ein Jahr"*. *Die Gründung der DDR* (Berlin, 1993), pp. 15–31.

Steininger, Rolf, *Deutsche Geschichte 1945–1961* (Frankfurt am Main, 1983).

Steininger, Rolf, "Wie die Teilung Deutschlands verhindert werden sollte. Der Robertson-Plan aus dem Jahre 1948", in *Militärgeschichtliche Mitteilungen*, 33 (1983), pp. 49–89.

Steininger, Rolf, "Deutsche Frage und Berliner Konferenz 1954", in Wolfgang Venohr (ed.), *Ein Deutschland wird es sein* (Erlangen, 1990), pp. 37–88.

Stößel, Frank Thomas, *Positionen und Strömungen in der KPD/SED 1945–1954* (Cologne, 1985).

Strunk, Peter, "Die Sowjetische Militäradministration in Deutschland (SMAD)", in Hans Lemberg (ed.), *Sowjetisches Modell und nationale Prägung* (Marburg, 1991), pp. 143–76.

Suckut, Siegfried, *Die Betriebsrätebewegung in der Sowjetisch besetzten Zone Deutschlands (1945–1948)* (Frankfurt am Main, 1982).

Suckut, Siegfried, "Der Konflikt um die Bodenreformpolitik in der Ost-CDU 1945", in *Deutschland-Archiv*, 15 (1983), pp. 1080ff.

Suckut, Siegfried, "Die CDU in der sowjetisch besetzten Zone und die Gründung der SED. Parteiinterne Wertungen und Reaktionen", in Dietrich Staritz and Hermann Weber (eds), *Einheitsfront – Einheitspartei* (Cologne, 1989), pp. 167–90.

Suckut, Siegfried, "Innenpolitische Aspekte der DDR-Gründung. Konzeptionelle Differenzen, Legitimations- und Akzeptanzprobleme", in Elke Scherstjanoi (ed.), *"Provisorium für längstens ein Jahr"*. *Die Gründung der DDR* (Berlin, 1993), pp. 84–101.

Sühl, Klaus, "Kurt Schumacher und die Westzonen-SPD im Vereinigungsprozeß", in Dietrich Staritz and Hermann Weber (eds), *Einheitsfront – Einheitspartei* (Cologne, 1989), pp. 108–28.

Tikos, Laszlo, *E. Vargas Tätigkeit als Wirtschaftsanalytiker und Publizist* (Tübingen, 1965).

Tschubarjan, Alexander O., "Auf dem Weg nach Europa aus Moskauer Sicht", in Wolfgang J. Mommsen (ed.), *Der lange Weg nach Europa* (Berlin, 1992), pp. 267–302.

Voßke, Heinz and Nitzsche, Gerhard, *Wilhelm Pieck. Biographischer Abriß* (Berlin, 1975; 3rd edn, 1979).

Voßke, Heinz, *Otto Grotewohl. Biographischer Abriß* (Berlin, 1979).

Voßke, Heinz, *Walter Ulbricht. Biographischer Abriß* (Berlin, 1983).

Wassmund, Hans, *Kontinuität im Wandel. Bestimmungsfaktoren sowjetischer Deutschlandpolitik in der Nach-Stalin-Zeit* (Cologne and Vienna, 1974).

Weber, Hermann, *Geschichte der DDR* (Munich, 1985; 3rd edn, 1989).

Wendler, Jürgen, *Die Deutschlandpolitik der SED 1952–1958. Publizistisches Erscheinungsbild und Hintergründe der Wiedervereinigungsrhetorik* (Cologne, 1991).

Wettig, Gerhard, "Zum Stand der Forschung über Berijas Deutschland-Politik im Frühjahr 1953", in *Deutschland-Archiv*, 26 (1993), pp. 674–82.

Wettig, Gerhard, "Die Deutschland-Note vom 10. März 1952 auf der Basis der diplomatischen Akten des russischen Außenministeriums", in *Deutschland-Archiv*, 26 (1993), pp. 786–805.

Wolkogonow, Dimitri, *Stalin. Triumph und Tragödie* (Düsseldorf, 1989).

Wolkogonow, Dimitri, *Stalin*, Vol. 2 (Moscow, 1992).

Zolling, Hermann and Höhne, Heinz, *Pullach intern. General Gehlen und die Geschichte des Bundesnachrichtendienstes* (Hamburg, 1971).

Name Index

229

Subject Index